THE

EVERYTHING

LEADERSHIP
BOOK

The 20 core
concepts every
leader must know

Bob Adams

Adams Media Corporation
Holbrook, Massachusetts

An Everything® Series Book.
Everything® is a registered trademark of Adams Media Corporation.

Published by Adams Media Corporation
260 Center Street, Holbrook, MA 02343
www.adamsmedia.com

ISBN: 1-58062-513-4
Printed in the United States of America.

J I H G F E D C B A

Library of Congress Cataloging-in-Publication Data
Adams, Bob.
The everything leadership book / by Bob Adams.
p.   cm.
Includes bibliographical references and index.
ISBN 1-58062-513-4
1. Leadership–Handbooks, manuals, etc. I. Title.

HD57.7 .A3   2001
658.4'092–dc21   2001022400

Illustrations by Barry Littmann

This book is available at quantity discounts for bulk purchases.
For information, call 1-800-872-5627.

Visit the entire Everything® series at everything.com

Contents

Chapter 1
Knowing the Rules / 1

Communication 2
Motivation 3
Teamwork 5
Organization and Time Management 6
Resolving Conflict and Solving Problems 7
Accepting Change 7
Hiring the Right Person for the Job 8
Evaluating Employees 8
Dealing with Problem Employees 9
Employee Recognition and Retention 9
Leadership Is an Expression of You 10
Self-Discipline Is a Big Part of Success 11
Learning from Mistakes 11
Volunteerism as a Form of Leadership 12
Even If You Are Not in Charge, You Can Still
    Be a Leader 12
Understanding the New Workforce 12
Keep Yourself Educated 14
You Can Lead 14

Chapter 2
Information Exchange: The Art of Communication / 15

Getting the Point Across 16
Personality of a Listener 16
Communicating on All Levels 18
Fostering Positive Interactions 20
Meetings—Can't Live with 'Em, Can't Live Without 'Em .. 21
More Ideas to Promote Communication 23
The Dos and Don'ts of Communication 25
Consistent Application 26

Chapter 3
Motivation: Get Them Moving and Get Results! / 29

Scared into Submission: Fear as a Motivator 30
What's in It for Me? 30
Recipe for Motivational Success 31
Don't Forget to Keep Yourself Motivated! 39

Chapter 4
The Importance of Coaching / 41

What Does It Mean? 42
Coaching Benefits Individuals 44
Coaching Benefits Organizations 44
Coaching Basics 44
The Coaching Process 45
Successful Coaching Session One 47
Successful Coaching Session Two 49
Another Use for Coaching 51

Chapter 5
There s Plenty to Go Around: Passing on Power / 53

What's the Buzz about Empowerment? 54
Utilize the Potential of Others 55
The Relationship Between Empowerment
    and Delegation 56
Life Skills Can Transfer to the Workplace 58
Practice Trust 59
Two Leadership Mantras 60
Power Failure: Downsizing and Layoffs 61
Strategies to Help the Process 63
Common Difficulties with the Empowerment
    Approach 65

Chapter 6
Go Team! / 67

The Home Team Advantage 68
Leader-Directed Versus Self-Directed Teams 70
Watch Out for Team Destroyers! 75

Chapter 7
Getting Organized and Managing Time / 77

You've Heard It All Before 79
Organizing Your Work Space 80
Multitasking 85
Capitalize on Your Commute 86
Maintenance—The Toughest Job You'll Ever Love! ... 90
Successful Time Management 91
Stop Bothering Me! 92
Interruptions 95

Chapter 8
Keeping the Peace: Resolving Conflict and Solving Problems / 99

Divide and Conquer 100
Unnecessary Conflict 100
Resolvable Conflict 101
10 Steps to Victory 101
The Dos and Don'ts of Conflict Resolution 103
Problem-Solving Approach 104
Examples of Successful Conflict Resolutions 104
Make It Go Away! 107

Chapter 9
Coming to Grips with Change / 109

Stage One: Understanding Change 110
Stage Two: Becoming Aware of Change 111
Building Walls 112
Real World Problems 114
Stage Three: Accepting Change 119

Chapter 10
The Classified Information on Hiring / 121

Assess Your Needs and Start Recruiting 122
Sorting Those Resumes 124
The Interview Process 128
One Step at a Time 129
Sample Interview Questions 133
Make 'Em an Offer They Can't Refuse 135
Employee Orientation 136

Chapter 11
Evaluating Employees / 139

Performance Evaluation Objectives 141
Preparing for the Process 141
Writing a Review 145
The Elements of Successful and
    Not-So-Successful Evaluations 148
Let's Answer Some Common Questions about
    the Evaluation Process 149

Chapter 12
Dealing with Difficult Employees / 153

Back to Basics 155
The Problems You Will Face 159
Some Common Problems and Some
    Plausible Solutions 165
Leadership Worksheet 168
Firing a Problem Employee 172
Let Them Down Gently 173

Chapter 13
Retention and Recognition / 177

What's All the Fuss about Retaining Employees? 178
What Is Turnover Anyway? 179
Uncover the Root of the Problem 182
Environment Means Everything 186
Define the Culture 192
The Role of Employee Recognition 194

Chapter 14
Express Yourself / 197

It's All about Personality and Self-Confidence 198
Leadership Self-Assessment 199
Personality Traits of Leaders 205
Presentations and Public Speaking 209
Tricks of the Trade 210

Chapter 15
Self-Discipline Brings Success / 213

Self-Discipline Involves Motivating Yourself 214
Working Alone, Telecommuting, and the World
    of the Self-Employed 216
Self-Discipline Means Being Organized 221
Personal Planners Can Help 222
Self-Discipline Can Be Learned 223

CONTENTS

Chapter 16
If at First You Don t Succeed
Learn from Your Mistakes / 225

Dealing with Common Leadership Mistakes 227
Major Blunders from Corporate America 231
What-If Syndrome 235
Famous Takes on Failure 235

Chapter 17
Take the Lead as a Volunteer / 237

Reasons for Volunteering 238
Making the Right Choice 239
Initiative and Commitment 240
100 Volunteer Organizations 241
Recruiting and Training Volunteers 250
How to Retain Volunteers 252
Corporate Volunteerism 253

Chapter 18
Being a Leader Without Being in Charge / 255

Take Initiative 256
Above All, Be Committed 257
Lead Through the Simple and the Mundane 258
Step Right Up and Ask for New Responsibilities 259
Be a Spokesperson for the Group 259
Networking Is Not a Dirty Word 260
Manage Your Projects as Well as Your Time 261
Take Them Under Your Wing—Be a Mentor 261
So Now That I'm a Mentor, What Do I Do? 262
Five Myths about Mentorship 265

Chapter 19
The New Workforce / 267

A Little Bit of History 268
What You Need to Do 271
Values Are Consistent 272
Pay Attention to Retention 273
Why You Could Feel Lost 274
The New Trend to Teamwork 275
Balancing Your Company's Wants and Your
   Employees' Needs 276
Promoting Self-Improvement 277
Respecting Your Elders 277
Diversity in the Workplace 278

Chapter 20
Teaching the Old Dog Some New Tricks / 279

Staying in School 280
Formulate Your Plan 283
Internal Education 284
Utilizing Your Space 286
Scope Out the Competition 287
Create an Intelligence Team 289
Finding Additional Business Tips 290

Appendix A
Leadership Q & A Session / 291

Appendix B
Leadership Web Sites / 297

Appendix C
Glossary of Leadership Theories and Concepts / 301

CHAPTER 1
Knowing the Rules

Are leaders born or are they created out of circumstance and experience? The debate on this topic has gone on as long as the chicken-and-egg one. There are strong arguments for each side. No one answer can be labeled as correct. For our purposes, we will say that the answer is a little bit of both. Some individuals, such as royalty (Queen Elizabeth, Prince Charles, Prince William, etc.), are born and bred to take on leadership roles in later life. Other people develop into leaders over a sustained period of time. This is the type of leader we can all strive to become. Leadership is a thing that anyone can aspire to and achieve if he or she is determined.

To become a great leader, you need to start with the first core concept—know the rules and understand that leadership is a total commitment. All too often, people find themselves in awe of great leaders, wondering, "What do they have that I don't?" What these same individuals fail to realize is that although personality and luck can contribute to a leader's success, those things are not the essence of what makes an exceptional leader. Before deciding that leadership is or is not for you, it is a good idea to take a look at the main concepts that contribute to leadership success. A person who can balance all these concepts can develop into a great leader and role model for others.

All of the following concepts will be discussed in greater detail later on in this book. However, before taking a more in-depth view of the concepts, it is best to get an overall idea of what will be covered. Keep in mind that leadership is most successful when each individual concept plays off the others. Each should compliment the other in order for any to work at all.

Communication

Effective communication skills are integral to any working partnership/team or personal relationship. Therefore, it is safe to say that good communication skills are one of the building blocks of being an effective leader. Ongoing dialogue ensures that there is interaction with others to reach a shared meaning. A leader who can communicate positively and effectively can achieve the highest level of dialogue. As a result, things will get accomplished.

However, communication is a two-way street. When one party is sending a message, the other party needs to receive that message in the way it was intended. As a leader you must also develop a positive listening technique. The people you work with should always feel that they can come to you with ideas, suggestions, and problems and that you will hear what they have to say and actually listen to the message they are projecting.

The downfall of many businesses has been caused by a lack of communication. When sending messages, you have to be able to communicate on all levels to employees, key players, and customers alike. You must also be able to foster positive interactions among coworkers. A leader's communication strategy should always provide support and encouragement as well as reinforce the mission of the company.

If you want people to follow you, they have to know who you are, what you represent, and what you can do, and they have to have an understanding of your vision. Conveying this message is easy . . . just come right out and tell them. Be open about your priorities, dreams, and goals for the future. If you are willing to communicate, others will communicate with you.

You can learn to use your communication skills to cultivate relationships throughout your organization. If you communicate your desire to lead or to try new things, the leadership opportunities will present themselves over and over again.

Words of the Wise

"The challenge of leadership is to be strong, but not rude; be kind, but not weak; be bold, but not bully; be thoughtful, but not lazy; be humble, but not timid; be proud, but not arrogant; have humor, but not without folly."

—*Jim Rohn, American author and businessman*

Motivation

After clearly communicating the desired goal that is to be achieved, the next step will be to motivate people to get the job done. This is no small task. It can be hard enough to motivate yourself, never mind ensuring that other people get down to business. Most leaders do not "manage" people in a way that brings out the best in them. In order to motivate people, traditional as well as creative motivation approaches need to be combined. The idea is to inspire people to go beyond just doing a good job. You will need to explore ways to ignite the creative spark that is lying dormant in people and probably has been for years. So where do you begin?

Ironically enough, the process of motivating others begins with you. First *you* need to change *your* behavior to make sure you are giving creative and constructive feedback to others while at the same time challenging and rewarding them. Communication will be the catalyst for motivation. Leaders who can clearly articulate their expectations will likely have an easier time motivating employees than someone who barks out orders with no rhyme or reason.

Remember, no great leader has ever led alone, and the days of people following based on pure faith are over. In order to garner the support of your group members and keep enthusiasm levels up, you have to offer them work that has value and that provides job satisfaction. If you don't provide that type of environment, you won't get very productive or satisfying results. A mixture of positive reinforcement, the thrill of a challenge, and some coaching will surely put you on the right track.

Coaching

All leaders act as coaches to some extent. In this book, coaching is viewed as a process of facilitation involving questions, active listening, and support. Through this process, the leader (or coach) helps the employee to solve problems on his own and encourages more creative thinking patterns. In this way, coaching can become a communication tool that makes life easier for everyone involved. At its best, coaching can build stronger relationships between employee and employer with a minimal amount of conflict.

In the capacity of coach, think of yourself as a team captain of sorts. People up and down the office hierarchy will be looking to you for answers, strategies, ideas, and positive outcomes. Your vision constitutes the overall goal of your group and the company, and it is your responsibility to nurture it and watch it grow.

By learning to accept that management doesn't always know best, you can use coaching techniques to ensure a more respectful and participatory communication process where everyone wins. Coaching

Words of the Wise

"It is a terrible thing to look over your shoulder when you are trying to lead—and find no one there."

—*Franklin Delano Roosevelt, president of the U.S. from 1933–1945* can build trust, boost morale, and help employees grow and develop professionally. Overall, it can result in higher-quality products and an overall increase in efficiency and productivity.

Employee Empowerment

Empowerment is the transmittal of the idea that employees are valuable contributors to the success of the organization. It allows employees to learn from their mistakes and to effectively work better and smarter. The more you can make employees feel empowered, the more productive they are going to be. Unfortunately, the idea of passing on power to employees is not easy for all leaders to accept. The best type of leader is one who utilizes the potential of other workers. In case you haven't guessed already, I'm talking about delegation here.

Leaders need to closely examine the strengths and weaknesses of their coworkers to determine who can handle what. They must also realize the employees may bring skills to the table that they have acquired outside the office. Leaders encourage, convince, and help people to share their skills and talents. An employee who has the authority to control the circumstances of another person's work life also has the power to share this tool. When authority and responsibility are shared, trust builds. And as trust builds, confidence increases and productivity grows. Knowing the difference between motivating and manipulating is the key here. A company or group that has clearly defined goals and objectives has a greater chance to achieve them than a company that has no idea of what it needs to accomplish.

Teamwork

In today's fast-paced and ever-changing economy, companies have started to place an emphasis on getting more productivity out of smaller work groups. Thus, more businesses are turning toward a more team-oriented environment. Within these teams each member contributes her own diverse skills and talents. Leaders must have the ability to tap the strengths and weaknesses of each individual team member and use those strengths to achieve the overall goal of the group.

Profile

Religious Leaders

Jesus
Buddha
Dalai Lama
Brigham Young
The Pope
Muhammad
Martin Luther
Lao-Tzu
Confucius
Zoroaster
John Huss
George Fox
Mary Baker Eddy
Gandhi
John Calvin

Successful teams share an objective; are committed to the project; have a sufficient amount of time to operate; represent all functional areas of the company; recognize who is best suited to each aspect of the job; are supported by management; and, last but not least, have a designated leader—you!

It is a big task to monitor the efforts of a team. As a leader this job falls on your shoulders. Once again, think of yourself as the team captain. You are the one the team will look to for guidance and information. Your vision will constitute the overall goal of the group, and it will be your responsibility to nurture the growth of that goal while eliciting the participation and dedication of the entire group.

Organization and Time Management

Many leaders find themselves overwhelmed by the amount of work they have to accomplish, and thus time management becomes a major issue. Leaders need to organize themselves and prioritize their responsibilities in order to complete the greatest amount of work in the shortest amount of time.

Your work environment can put a strain on you that has the potential for some pretty severe side effects (headaches, ulcers, divorce, demotion, just to name a few). The best solution for these problems is prevention. Learn to not allow things to pile up. Develop a system that works for you and stick with it. Effective leaders know how to prioritize, develop a game plan, and then implement that plan. These types of leaders also consistently have a positive attitude about life and work in general.

Organization is another area to consider when developing a time management plan. A place for everything and everything in its place is a good rule of thumb. If you decide where to put things and actually put them there, less time will be wasted in searching for them.

Once you have developed the time management and organizational systems, the tough part truly begins . . . maintaining what you have set up. This book will offer advice on planning your time wisely and working flexibility into your schedule. It has been said that a leader should not have a million things to do; instead, he or she should always be looking for another project or a way to advance the

company. In other words, do what you need to do, pass on the other stuff, and then set your sights on nurturing your visions for the future.

Resolving Conflict and Solving Problems

Every workplace will have some conflict, no matter how great the leadership team may be. Leaders need to identify conflict as early as possible and determine what kind of conflict is involved and its underlying causes. The affected persons must then be actively involved in finding solutions.

Conflict occurs on many levels, and if it is addressed effectively, the outcome can benefit individuals and organizations in numerous ways: It can (1) produce stronger, more resilient working relationships, (2) improve creative output, and (3) generate innovative problem-solving solutions.

The problem-solving approach to conflict resolution is the one that works best for most leaders and managers. It seeks input from everyone involved and often results in a creative and lasting resolution. Using this type of approach involves the leader being direct and confronting the issues head-on. For some first-time leaders, a fear of the conflict will get in the way of the resolution. Effective leaders find ways to overcome the fear and develop personal skills and tools to come up with a solution.

Preventing conflicts from arising will become easier as time goes on. This characteristic of good leadership is not something that will happen overnight. It will take time and experience to become a pro. After all, there are people whose jobs focus on solving conflicts and acting as mediators. This involves training and practice to perfect, so don't get upset if you need to polish your skills for a while.

Accepting Change

This is another skill crucial to the survival of any leader. Change occurs whenever there is a shift in the economy, whenever people are hired or fired, and during periods of reconstruction and evaluation. The workforce

Profile

Women in Power

Debbi Fields
founder & president,
Mrs. Fields' Cookies

Carly Fiorina
president & CEO,
Hewlett-Packard Company

Andrea Jung
president & CEO,
Avon Products, Inc.

Shelly Lazarus
Chairperson & CEO,
Ogilvy & Mather

Florine Mark
president & CEO,
Weight Watchers

Amy McIntosh
CEO, Zagats

Martha Stewart
Chairperson & CEO,
Martha Stewart Omnimedia LLC

Meg Whitman,
president & CEO,
eBay Technologies

of today demands clear explanations of why these changes are happening. Those who are in the lead must be able to understand why change is necessary and be able to articulate these reasons to the group.

In the real world, change can invoke feelings of insecurity, uneasiness, and even hostility in workers who are left uninformed and in the dark. A leader's role is to help others through the transition of change with as much empathy and grace as possible. Leaders will encounter all sorts of reactions, from resistance to apathy. Each reaction needs to be dealt with in the most painless manner possible. Who ever said leadership was all fun and games?

Hiring the Right Person for the Job

In your role as leader, you may be asked to hire new employees. Whether this is your first experience with hiring or this is something you have handled in the past, there are all kinds of tips that can help you along the way to hiring the best possible people. Of course, it sounds a lot easier than it actually is. The hiring process requires a well-thought-out strategy, planning, and a good amount of time. People are the human assets of an organization, and they have far more value than any financial assets. Without the right combination of human assets, financial success will not follow.

The objective in hiring is to get the best, most qualified, and most enthusiastic people possible to fill the positions that are available. Leaders need to assess their needs, develop a plan of action, and then begin to sort through applications. Taken one step at a time, the hiring process is manageable and can even be fun. Leaders who recognize the importance of the process will get the best candidates and ultimately the strongest work environment.

Evaluating Employees

Once the support network is in place, it becomes the leader's duty to evaluate the workers and their work. Many leaders and managers alike shudder at the thought of employee evaluations and so they fail to express their concerns about what employees have been doing. As a result, they harm not only themselves and the employee but also the organization at large. Don't let this critical part of leadership be your downfall.

You've heard it before and now you'll hear it again: If you start by developing a strategy that works for you, the process will be less stressful and time consuming overall. Evaluation should not be something that happens once a year, it should be ongoing. As a leader, you need to offer both positive and negative criticisms when they are necessary. You also need to realize that each person needs to be handled with a different approach. Some will need more constant supervision, whereas others may need to be held back because they are overly enthusiastic. Staying on top of what goes on in the group and organization every day will make those more formalized yearly evaluations seem like a walk in the park.

Dealing with Problem Employees

There is simply not an office or company in the world that does not have at least one or two problem employees. The problems can be wide ranging, from lack of skill to sloppiness to outright insubordination. Being prepared for these types of situations will make you a more effective leader.

With a little determination and a lot of hard work and patience, virtually anyone's performance can be turned around. As often as possible, when problems arise, the job of the leader becomes one of encourager and supporter rather than vindictive accuser.

Disagreements between employee and employer have an effect on the whole company. Negative energy and vibes have a funny way of spreading like wildfire. As a leader, it is up to you to take control of these difficult situations. You can be proactive by employing some of the tools and suggestions this book will provide. By taking the lead, you can work to find the best solution with minimal residual effects.

Employee Recognition and Retention

Another important part of handling employees is to make sure they are happy and that they want to continue working for you and the company.

Profile

Joan of Arc
(1412–1431)

Also known as the Maid of Orléans, Joan of Arc played a leading role in French history when she convinced Charles VII to fight off the invading English and seize the throne. Dressed as a man, she led the French troops in the Battle of Orléans. Joan of Arc died as a martyr when she was convicted of heresy and was burned at the stake. She received canonization in 1920.

Often this is the aspect of management that is overlooked, and it ends up causing irreparable damage to the organization.

Good managers and leaders should always be concerned about losing not only employees, but also the information and skills they will take with them. The skills and knowledge employees develop over time are important assets that should not be overlooked.

Employee turnover is a common problem. When the economy is on an upswing, it becomes harder and harder to keep good employees. Employers are at the mercy of those seeking new and more exciting positions—not to mention more money in their paychecks! As a leader it will be your job to make sure that employee satisfaction is at the highest level it can be. This can be achieved in a variety of ways. First and foremost, you want to make sure that each employee is being challenged with the work he or she is doing. Second, you want to be sure that each employee is recognized often for the contributions he or she makes to the company. Monetary rewards are great, but you can be much more creative with your expressions of thanks for a job well done. Some ideas will be explored later in this book; feel free to create your own.

Leadership Is an Expression of You

Leaders are very special people in many ways. Above all, leaders *are* leaders because they are self-confident and committed to making a change in whatever capacity they can. Personality plays a major part in deciding who will be a leader and who will be left on the sidelines.

Think about some of the great leaders of the past century. Who comes to mind? Most likely you came up with names that exude charisma and revolutionary thinking—Mao Zedong, Martin Luther King Jr., Lech Walesa, and Margaret Thatcher. All of these people share some common traits. These leaders were self-confident, were excellent communicators, had strong followers to support them, played up their strengths, believed in themselves and the work they were doing, understood the politics of their causes, were highly visible, learned from their mistakes, and extended their leadership to others.

You can adopt all of these characteristics. Following the examples of true leadership that are outlined in this book is a good way to begin on a path to leadership victory. True leaders emerge when there is a need for change and intolerance for the status quo. Step out and take a stand for something. You have to be willing to go out on a limb every once in a while, or leadership will never be a reality in your life. People are generally attracted to those who move in reasoned, affirmative, innovative, or intrepid directions. It is up to you to make sure others see you in that light.

Self-Discipline Is a Big Part of Success

Self-discipline goes hand in hand with motivation. Whether you work independently in your home office or you manage a group in a corporate office, self-discipline is a necessity. Without it, nothing will ever get accomplished. Effective leaders are able to utilize the same tools they use to motivate others to get themselves into a productive mode.

A leader's time will constantly be jeopardized and manipulated. You must learn to work within the limits that are placed upon you.

This section of the book will show you how to maximize time and energy. It will provide advice on putting off procrastination, making time for privacy, and developing a plan for yourself. After all, how can you manage others if you haven't figured out how to manage yourself?

Learning from Mistakes

Every person who reads this book would like to say that he or she has never made a mistake or had an error in judgment. The fact of the matter is, there is not one single person on this planet who hasn't messed up once or twice along the way. Mistakes, unfortunately, are an inevitable part of life.

Leaders rise above the negativity mistakes can bring by learning from them and moving on. Each mistake has some value. Finding that value is what leaders do. No one is immune to mistakes, so don't spend any time agonizing over them. Instead, channel all that energy into making sure that the same thing does not happen again. Leadership is about the ability to move forward, not about wallowing in the problems of the past.

Volunteerism as a Form of Leadership

Perhaps you have never considered joining a volunteer organization, but participating in an activity where you give something back to the community is an excellent way to gain leadership experience. All types of leadership traits may be utilized when you take part in a charitable or volunteer organization. Above all, you need to demonstrate a strong commitment to the group. Without that from the start, you are setting yourself up for disaster.

With a little self-reflection and some time spent researching, you should be able to find a group that shares a common belief, goal, or concern with you. If you join a group dedicated to a cause you believe in, you will be much more likely to remain passionate about doing the work and taking on additional responsibilities.

Even If You Are Not in Charge, You Can Still Be a Leader

Gone are the days when you have to hold a lofty title in order to be a leader. There are always ways to lead no matter what position you hold in the company. Everyone has the potential—it just needs to be tapped.

The key here is to take the initiative whenever possible and to keep your eyes open for new leadership possibilities. In a group setting, you can take the lead and get the group organized, assigning tasks and checking to make sure everyone is involved.

Mentorship is another way to act on the leadership bug. Take someone under your wing and teach him or her the tools of the trade; show him or her the inner workings of the office. As long as you possess the knowledge and experience to help someone come along, those are all the qualifications you need to fulfill your duties as a mentor.

Understanding the New Workforce

"The New Workforce" is becoming a common catch phrase in business today. But what does it mean? Well, it refers to the fact that the workers of today are more independent, self-reliant, and creative than any

Leadership Lessons on Film

The American President	(1995)	The Lion King	(1994)
Apollo 13	(1995)	Lord of the Flies	(1963)
Born on the Fourth of July	(1989)	The Magnificent Seven	(1960)
Braveheart	(1995)	Matewan	(1987)
Bridge on the River Kwai	(1957)	Mr. Smith Goes to Washington	(1939)
Business As Usual	(1987)	Mutiny on the Bounty	(1935)
Butch Cassidy and the Sundance Kid	(1969)	Newsies	(1992)
Citizen Kane	(1941)	Nine to Five	(1980)
Courage Under Fire	(1996)	Norma Rae	(1979)
Crimson Tide	(1995)	One Flew Over the Cuckoo's Nest	(1975)
Dave	(1993)	The Patriot	(2000)
Dead Poets Society	(1989)	Patton	(1970)
Erin Brockovich	(2000)	Platoon	(1986)
The Firm	(1993)	Remember the Titans	(2000)
Get on the Bus	(1996)	Salt of the Earth	(1953)
Gladiator	(2000)	Saving Private Ryan	(1998)
Glengarry Glen Ross	(1992)	Schindler's List	(1993)
Glory	(1989)	Shane	(1953)
The Godfather	(1972)	The Shawshank Redemption	(1994)
The Grapes of Wrath	(1940)	Stand and Deliver	(1989)
Harlan County, U.S.A.	(1977)	The Ten Commandments	(1956)
High Noon	(1952)	To Kill a Mockingbird	(1962)
Hoosiers	(1986)	Twelve Angry Men	(1957)
In the Name of the Father	(1993)	Twelve O'Clock High	(1949)
The Killing Fields	(1984)	Wall Street	(1987)
Lean on Me	(1989)	Watership Down	(1978)

Marian Anderson
(1902–1993)

Anderson was the first African American singer to break the color barrier at the Metropolitan Opera. Despite being acclaimed in her own country, she was able to obtain major engagements only in Europe, where she became a star. In 1939, the Daughters of the American Revolution (DAR) canceled her contract to sing at Constitution Hall in Washington, DC, when they found out that she was black. There was an outcry from public figures like Eleanor Roosevelt, who resigned from the DAR in protest. Following the controversy, Anderson was catapulted to the top of her profession, where she remained until her retirement.

generation has been before. They have different standards for the workplace and will not settle for anything less than what they feel they deserve, and rightly so. The modern worker is more skilled and educated than the worker of the past, and leaders need to be flexible in order to embrace these changes and move forward into the next millennium.

Luckily this book is here to help you throw out those old notions of what a worker should be. It can guide you through the changes that have occurred over the past few decades and help you implement a plan for success in the future.

Keep Yourself Educated

The easiest way to outplace yourself is to stop learning and acquiring new skills and knowledge about your job or industry. Business and technology are evolving at a breakneck pace, and those who can keep up with them will be the most valued and sought after.

Keeping yourself up to speed does not necessarily mean that you will have to sit in a classroom and listen to lectures. On another level it can involve integrating new software into your business or talking to other people in the industry about how they are incorporating new technology and ideas into their offices. It can also mean getting to know what other members of your organization are involved in and participating in group projects in areas that you have never previously showed interest in. Keep on top of industry and market trends, develop a task force, read trade journals. *Be informed!*

You Can Lead

As stated before, anyone can be a leader. It just takes a little hard work and determination and, of course, this book. By incorporating each of the core leadership concepts into your work, you will be well on your way to becoming an effective leader. Mistakes will be made along the way, but each should be looked at as a learning opportunity and a chance to grow and develop your skills.

No matter what may happen along the way, remember to take initiative wherever possible, be committed to your work, and be self-confident in whatever you do. If you can manage all of that, others will follow you.

CHAPTER 2

Information Exchange: The Art of Communication

Getting the Point Across

Communication is the second core concept. Once you know the rules and understand that leadership is a total commitment, you are ready to begin strengthening your leadership skills. Communication is key to getting off to a good start. Strong leadership cannot be accomplished without communication; this is why it has been deemed the second core concept.

Effective communication occurs when information has been absorbed and understood by the targeted audience. The cycle of communication has three points. First, the sender verbally sends out the message in a clear and straightforward manner. Next, the receivers accept the message and confirm that they comprehend it. Last, the sender needs to verify that the message has been understood and received in the manner it was intended.

Misunderstood communication can be one of the largest problems facing businesses today. Businesses have lots of messages being sent, but not all of the information is received, and not all of the information is understood.

Without a complete communication cycle there is no dialogue, there is only a series of monologues. Dialogue ensures that we are interacting with others to reach a shared meaning. Without the confirmation and verification of a message, all the sender has is a monologue of what was intended to be transmitted. When leaders communicate in a positive, respectful manner, the highest level of dialogue is reached.

Personality of a Listener

Listening is the most important tool available to ensure that you are communicating completely to reach a shared meaning through dialogue. This shared meaning is the essence of communication and must be achieved if you are to be a successful leader. What kind of listener are you?

People listen in many different ways. The way in which you listen determines how much of the message you may be screening.

Up to 70 percent of a message can be screened out due to your style of listening. When you recognize and understand what type of listener you are as well as the style of listening those around you have, you will then be able to modify your listening to capture an even larger percentage of the message.

There are five basic types of listeners:

The Appreciator: Arnold is happy to listen to what his manager has to say about new company strategies. He pays close attention to all the information and thinks about what points he can add to the meeting. He is relaxed and enjoys the interactive atmosphere.
Warning! Appreciators may miss a point if they are not totally engaged.

The Empathizer: Esther listens to all the points her manager makes and tries to identify situations she has experienced that support his points. Esther comes away from the meeting feeling like she has learned something and is in no way judgmental or condescending.
Warning! Empathizers may sometimes miss an important component of the communication if they are too wrapped up in another aspect of the information.

The Comprehender: Christopher wants to capture as much information as possible. Throughout the meeting he tries to organize and make sense of the messages being sent. Christopher also likes to make connections between or among personal experiences and attempts to find and understand the relationships between or among ideas.
Warning! Comprehenders frequently don't catch all the unspoken or subtextual messages being communicated.

The Discerner: Darby carefully takes in all the information her manager is presenting. She wants to get complete and accurate information; and she is driven to determine the

Words of the Wise

"You can have brilliant ideas, but if you can't get them across, your ideas won't get you anywhere."

—*Lee Iacocca*

main message and sift out what she considers important details. Each bit of information is carefully weighed and measured for accuracy, validity, and content.
Warning! Discerners may miss some critical information as all the information is processed.

The Evaluator: Elton wants to know how the information his project leader is presenting fits into the big picture. Every few minutes he questions the speaker's motives and will accept or reject messages based on personal beliefs. Throughout the communication Elton will make decisions based on the information provided.
Warning! Evaluators will miss critical information if it doesn't fit into their belief system.

As you can clearly see, you must incorporate all types of listening styles to really receive a complete message. Think about how you generally listen. At your next opportunity, begin using all forms of listening to get the most comprehensive message from the sender. For the success of your employee and business dealings, good listening is critical.

Communicating on All Levels
Communicating with Employees

This is considered the hardest aspect of communication. The attitude is usually, "We hired them, they do what we want." Other times the people in authority have no idea what they want, or maybe what they want is not in the best interest of the company. In any event, as a leader, you must begin to encourage, support, and embrace communication with, to, and from your employees. In truth, they are the ones who have the best idea of what is really happening. When you listen to employees, you will learn more than you ever imagined (and perhaps more than you care to know). When you listen, and when you show them understanding, they will see that they are valued as a partner of sorts in the business.

Words of the Wise

"Leaders must invoke an alchemy of great vision."

—*Henry Kissinger (1923–), American political scientist*

Your simple act of listening and communicating back to your employees will spark motivation and start your team on the road to thinking more creatively and strategically.

Communicating with Your Key Players

It is critical that other leaders within the organization are communicating the same message to employees as you are. It is with this group that you develop communication strategies and policy statements. When you clearly communicate your vision and ideas and the other key players understand and espouse your message, you are well on your way to success.

Now that the entire team shares a common language, the whole company will be on the same page and working toward the same well-defined goal. It is vital that all employees and customers hear the same words and meaning coming from all the key players.

The dialogue between key players must allow for all views to be presented and shared among all members. Everyone should feel that she has contributed to the decision, and all should agree to support it—even if it is not exactly what a specific team member wanted.

Communicating with Customers

It doesn't matter if your company provides goods or services, either way you will eventually have to deal with customers. This is the ultimate challenge in communication. As a leader, it is your job to set the example for others to learn from. Communicating with customers is merely an extension of good employee communication. The same skills and techniques apply. Companies who communicate with customers by listening end up being the most successful. Customers have very simple needs—they want what they want when they want it.

When a business listens to the customer as part of the communication cycle, it is guaranteed success. When a business listens to what it *thinks* the customer is saying, it is gambling with success. The successful business is able to clearly understand the needs and expectations of the customer and find the best ways to make the customer happy.

Leadership Tip

How do I communicate my vision so that it is our vision?

Of course you are going to be committed and excited about the image you've sculpted for tomorrow because it is *your* idea. The challenge you'll face as a leader is to stimulate that same enthusiasm in those around you. First, carefully introduce the concept. Ask for critical impressions. Receive and welcome suggestions for changes. Recognize and try to minimize apprehension. Talk to your people often and try to articulate how their ideas support or conflict with yours. Over time, the group will be using the same language and similar images and will share your enthusiasm. If you are really persuasive, they may even start to believe that the vision was their idea.

Fostering Positive Interactions

Good communication encourages creative interaction between employees. Your communication strategy should support, encourage, and reinforce the mission and culture of the organization.

There are some very simple steps every member of an organization can do to ensure positive, healthy communication interactions:

- Help others to be right, not wrong.
- Whenever possible, have fun.
- Exhibit enthusiasm in all that you do.
- Figure out ways for new ideas to work, not reasons why they won't.
- Act with initiative.
- Be bold and courageous; take a chance.
- Help others be successful in their endeavors.
- Maintain a positive mental attitude.
- Don't believe gossip; check it out before you repeat what you hear.
- Speak positively about others whenever the opportunity arises.
- If you don't have anything positive to say, don't say anything at all.

It really is very simple to begin demonstrating these basic principles within your organization. Why not try some of these ideas tomorrow at work:

1. All day long, choose to verbally acknowledge only those actions and behaviors that are positive and productive for the company.
2. When speaking to someone be brief. Always use clear statements to capture his attention. Try not to engage in a conversation unless you have something important to say. Don't waste your time or his.

3. Whenever possible, ask open-ended questions that allow the person you are speaking with to talk with you. Once you have asked the question, truly listen to the answer.

4. When someone mentions an idea that may sound a bit off the mark, ask, "Oh, how would that actually work?" rather than "Oh, I don't think that is a viable option for us."

5. When you become engaged in conversation with another person, allow him or her to complete the full thought before responding. Listen to the total idea or statement; don't jump on one word or phrase. Hear the person out and then offer your responses.

6. Whenever possible, rephrase the information you just heard to ensure that you are really communicating. Example: "So you think we should start by implementing a more direct marketing campaign to older women?"

7. Allow yourself to recognize the importance of this topic or information to the speaker. Even if you think it is unimportant, demonstrate to the person that you value and respect her contribution.

If you try these simple yet profound tactics, you will be amazed at the impact they have on your own ability to learn and the impact they will have on your organization. The key to all this is consistent application of these strategies. Practice makes perfect!

Meetings—Can't Live with 'Em, Can't Live Without 'Em

Do you have weekly staff meetings with the same old problem—no one talks except for you? This is a common complaint among leaders and managers. Let's examine some ways to change the outcome of these necessary evils.

Meetings have the potential to be either really fantastic and exciting or coma inducing. A meeting without an agenda is much like a fish out of water—it won't survive for very long. It is

---

Profile

Dr. Martin Luther King Jr.
(1929–1968)

A black Baptist minister and pivotal leader of the Civil Rights Movement, King practiced passive resistance techniques to work for racial equality and bring an end to segregation. As president of the Southern Christian Leadership Conference, King spoke nationally and inspired many to join forces against oppression. In 1963, he led the March on Washington (250,000 civil-rights supporters were in attendance). The event culminated with King's now famous "I Have a Dream" speech. In 1964 he won the Nobel Peace Prize, and on April 4, 1968, he was tragically assassinated in Memphis, Tennessee.

absolutely critical for everyone to know and understand why he or she is attending a meeting and what the outcome is intended to be. Meetings need not drag on for hours on end. They can be effective carried out in a hallway or even with attendees standing up. (The natives are more likely to stay awake this way!) Frequently the best, most efficient meetings are short, direct, and well planned.

The following are some simple guidelines you can use when planning a meeting.

- Clearly identify the objectives of the meeting at the beginning, or even before the group gets together.
- Collect all the necessary data and materials.
- Create a clear, written agenda that you can refer to later.
- Be sure to give everyone who will attend a copy of the agenda before the meeting.
- Give everyone a chance to modify the agenda.
- Double check to make sure all the necessary people have been invited.
- Make sure everyone will be able to make it at the time scheduled.
- Set a clear time for beginning and ending as well as a defined location.
- Remind everyone to come to the meeting with an open mind and respectful attitude toward all other participants.

No matter how large or how small the meeting, no matter how long or short the meeting, the same basic principles must apply if you wish to achieve a high level of productive communication.

Weekly Update Meetings

As a technique to communicate what is happening in various departments or various teams, you may want to institute update meetings. During this type of exchange, each participant gives a brief update of the status of the project, workload, or activity. It allows all to be informed, and it keeps everyone focused on his objectives.

Creating a Visible Communication Device

If your company or department is contained in a single space with all members able to see or hear a message, try something like this: Obtain a gong or large bell and use this device to announce important information for everyone to hear. Breaking news *does not* include the latest person to get voted off or the announcement that Charlene's twins finally slept through the night. However, you will want to announce the signing of a new contract or the completion of a particular project. This way, everyone knows about the success immediately, and you save a bit of paperwork in the process. Also, everyone feels like he or she is part of the loop and doesn't have to depend on idle gossip for information.

Memos and E-mail

Written and electronic messages save both time and energy. However, they can be overused. To ensure quality communication, an organization must define the parameters of these tools and the ways in which they may and may not be used. You *don't* want people spending hours sending personal e-mails. You *do* want e-mail to help departments communicate more easily and efficiently.

Wherever possible, use these as regular and routine ways to communicate and reinforce the mission of your company. Consider including the mission statement for your company on all memos or use powerful motivating statements such as "None of us is as smart as all of us."

More Ideas to Promote Communication

There are countless ways you can build communication in your group or organization. It is important that you use ideas that match your personality and style. Don't adopt an idea that worked for IBM; come up with an idea that will meet your needs.

The following are some ideas that may fit into your leadership style and help eliminate communication blocks.

Words of the Wise

"The leader can never close the gap between himself and the group. If he does, he is no longer what he must be. He must walk a tightrope between the consent he must win and the control he must exert."

—*Vince Lombardi*
(1913–1970),
legendary football coach

Take a Walk

This communication style works best for leaders who are actively engaged in the day-to-day activities of the business. This approach works well when a manager has made a commitment to spend a dedicated amount of time on the floor with the employees or in various employee offices each day. Again, this approach must be compatible with your style; if it is forced, it will not be effective.

In effect, you are able to be yourself walking throughout the organization looking for opportunities to make positive comments and receive feedback. This approach allows you to see everything that is going on, and it also allows you to listen directly to the employees. It is especially effective in an organization with many management layers. The approach permits all employees direct access to you (the leader) and frequently generates high levels of spontaneous, creative synergy while the employees and the boss exchange ideas.

Brainstorming

When faced with a challenging problem or opportunity, brainstorming can be a great way to resolve the issue. The objective of brainstorming is to obtain as many wild and crazy ideas as possible to formulate possible solutions. During brainstorming, people are encouraged to throw out as many ideas as possible without anyone critiquing, analyzing, or discussing the ideas. Once the group gets used to the process, and no one is making fun of the ideas presented, even more ideas will flow. When you begin to use the brainstorming strategy regularly, you will see a larger number of new ideas emerging. One of these may end up being the actual solution; others will trigger the solution.

Suggestion Boxes

Almost every company has tried a suggestion box at one point or another. Invariably, the idea falls flat. The reason is simple: Employees do not trust it. It is difficult to put faith in an inanimate object.

Words of the Wise

". . . a sense of humor can be a great help—particularly a sense of humor about [oneself]. William Howard Taft joked about his own corpulence and people loved it . . . Lincoln eased tense moments with bawdy stories, and often poked fun at himself—and history honors him for this human quality. A sense of humor is part of the art of leadership, of getting along with people, of getting things done."

—*Dwight D. Eisenhower, president of the U.S. from 1953–1961*

In many cases the suggestion box emerges because management is frustrated over how to get things accomplished. Rather than meet directly with employees, company leaders decide to create an anonymous vehicle to collect ideas. Then the ideas enter into the black hole, never to be seen or heard from again. Sure managers and supervisors may read them; but instead of meeting with the people who made the suggestions, the ideas are usually shrugged off for one reason or another.

If you decide to put a suggestion box in your office, make sure it allows exciting creative exchanges for the discussion of all ideas on a regular basis. Even if only one idea emerges victorious from a discussion, the employees who participated know that their input was valued and respected and that they had the opportunity to engage in a highly creative and stimulating interaction.

The Dos and Don'ts of Communication

DO:
- Communicate anything and everything that has a direct impact on the employees.
- Listen carefully and work to clarify views.
- Use nonverbal forms of communication (i.e., e-mails and memos) whenever possible.
- Talk to people at all levels within the organization to make sure you are all on the same page.
- Exhibit enthusiasm and speak positively about others.
- Have brief, regularly scheduled, well-thought-out meetings.

DON'T:
- Have a meeting because you think you should: Be sure the meeting has a purpose.
- Believe or spread gossip and rumors.
- Offer negative feedback: If you don't have anything nice to say, say nothing at all.
- Interrupt others in the midst of communication.
- Send mixed messages.

Profile

Tommy Lasorda
(1927–)

Just as baseball is known as America's favorite pastime, Tommy Lasorda is known as one of baseball's greatest ambassadors. He was at the helm of the Los Angeles Dodgers for 20 years, leading them to two World Series titles (1981 and 1988). He retired during the 1996 season with 1,599 regular-season wins. Tommy Lasorda also led the Dodgers to eight National League West championships and four National League pennants. He was inducted into the Baseball Hall of Fame in 1997. In another defining moment as a coach, manager, and leader, Tommy Lasorda led the U.S. baseball team to a gold medal in the 2000 Summer Olympic Games.

Words of the Wise

"I believe managing is like holding a dove in your hand. If you hold it too tightly you kill it, but if you hold it too loosely, you lose it."

—*Tommy Lasorda (1927–), legendary baseball coach*

Consistent Application

How does your company communicate with employees? Your company should be able to communicate information within the organization to employees in a clear and efficient manner.

Check all of the items below that you and your company use frequently.

- ❏ written memo to employee bulletin board
- ❏ written memo to individual employees
- ❏ messages on payroll checks or inserted into pay envelope
- ❏ voice mail
- ❏ e-mail
- ❏ company newsletter published weekly
- ❏ company newsletter published monthly
- ❏ company newsletter published quarterly
- ❏ weekly meeting of all staff
- ❏ monthly meeting of all staff
- ❏ meetings as requested and necessary

If you were unable to check specific items with certainty, you should seriously consider redefining your communication strategy within your department or company.

Look at your department or company and consider the way your employees work. Which vehicles are best suited for your employees to receive communication, and which ensure that you have shared meaning?

Will the posted messages give you shared meaning and understanding? Will memos sent directly to employees do this? Will it be necessary to have meetings with all employees? How efficient is each of these approaches within your organization?

What must you do to ensure that you have a message not only sent and received but also understood? This is the ultimate challenge of your communication strategy.

The successful communication strategy includes vehicles that have clearly defined systems to deliver the messages, allowing for clarification and verification while confirming receipt of the message by all employees. This type of system must be very efficient, with very few problems.

For example, a newsletter sent out monthly by the Busy Bee Company is attached to all payroll checks. This ensures that all employees receive a newsletter. Within the format of the newsletter is a statement that reads: "If you have any questions about the content of this newsletter, especially in regard to policies and procedures, please call 1-800-BEE-HELP. Leave your question on the machine and we will get back to you within 48 hours."

In another section of the newsletter is the following statement: "Policies and procedures published in this newsletter become effective the first day of the month following the publication date. Please be prepared to comply with any and all policies and procedures published in this newsletter."

This example of the Busy Bee Company newsletter, distributed as described, is capable of transmitting critical business information to all members of the organization in a fashion that places the responsibility on the employees. This newsletter vehicle can also carry traditional soft news and information and is a bona fide communications vehicle for the organization. You can be sure that every employee will read it, knowing that business decisions and operational policies and procedures will be presented, explained, and introduced. The ability of the employees to operate within the policies and procedures of the company will be dependent on their faithful review of the company newsletter.

Leadership Tip

Laugh a Little

Bring humor into the workplace wherever possible. Laughing eases tension and stress and reduces anxiety levels. It also makes for a more personalized work atmosphere.

CHAPTER 3

Motivation: Get Them Moving and Get Results!

Motivation is the third core concept. After you are able to clearly communicate the desired goal that is to be achieved, the next step is to motivate people to get the job done. Achieving desired results and goals is a direct result of motivation. As we all know, some days it can be harder to get moving than others. Whether you work independently or as part of a larger team, it is imperative that each person be able to motivate himself to get the job done and done well. It is equally important that the leader of the group is able to set the work in motion. Communication (discussed in Chapter 2) is the heart and soul of motivating employees. So long as managers provide clear expectations, instructions, information, and time frames, employees will gain a sense of security, respect, power, and control in their jobs. All these factors will in turn create a productive and happy working environment.

Scared into Submission: Fear as a Motivator

Fear can be a powerful motivator. Unfortunately, managers who use fear as a tactic may realize a negative rather than a positive trend in productivity. People usually react to fear by becoming angry and distrustful. They may harbor resentment and begin to exhibit anxiety and stress. In the short term, fear may get the job done, but in the long term the effects can be devastating to a department or company as a whole. Overall, scare tactics fail miserably because people will look to leave a situation where fear is an ever-present part of their daily routine. On the other hand, when people receive praise, encouragement, and recognition, they respond with increased effort and enthusiasm. Motivation comes from caring, *not* scaring.

What's in It for Me?

Ah yes, the age-old question. It's human nature to want to know, "What's in it for me?" Employees are motivated to complete projects only when they perceive the outcome will benefit them in some way. For the most part, a person is looking to fulfill a basic need (i.e., security, acceptance, respect, fun, power, fulfillment, or self-esteem). Managers should not operate under the assumption that employees are solely motivated by monetary rewards, benefits, promotions, and recognition. These *extrinsic motivators* are nice from time to time, but they don't work on an interpersonal level. Often, these kinds of rewards will only produce short-lived results and a brief boost in morale. Although free soda and stock options are nice perks, they will hardly be enough to keep a person striving to do their best for months on end.

To help employees work up to their potential over a prolonged period of time, managers need to move beyond the extrinsic model. The challenge comes in creating a work environment that provides the opportunity for employees to satisfy *all* their needs. This type of atmosphere will establish *intrinsic motivation,* where employees will be motivated by their own inner drives rather than outside factors like money and benefits.

Words of the Wise

"Motivation is the art of getting people to do what you want them to do because they want to do it."

—*Dwight D. Eisenhower, president of the U.S. from 1953–1961*

Recipe for Motivational Success
A Pinch of Positive Reinforcement

Rewarding someone for achieving the desired outcome is positive reinforcement, and it can go a long way in motivating employees. A kind word or outward sign of recognition will be effective only if it is directly tied to a tangible success.

Example: A project in your department has hit a glitch and fallen way behind schedule. Nina has been the only staffer to stay late and do whatever it takes to put the project back on track. She has also managed to do all this without so much as one complaint. Because of her efforts, the project is completed on time and in better shape than expected. How do you handle the situation?

Solution: You want Nina to know that her work has been recognized and is appreciated. It would also be nice and beneficial to set Nina apart as an example for others in the department to follow. There are lots of ways to show Nina your appreciation: give her a paid day off, present her with a gift certificate for a favorite restaurant, or let her choose her next project and give her the responsibility of project leader.

Example: Travis comes to you and says he is having trouble staying on top of deadlines. He just doesn't seem to know what projects to handle first. How do you handle the situation?
Solution: Sit down with Travis and make sure to: (a) agree on priorities, (b) brainstorm possible solutions, and (c) offer information and resources to help get to the bottom of the issue. Maybe Travis has recently been given additional responsibilities and is still trying to work them into his schedule. Simply identifying what tasks should be high priorities might make the workday more productive for him. And letting him know that he is doing a good job and that you appreciate his approaching the problem head-on will go a long way.

Mix in the Thrill of a Challenge

Challenging employees with new situations encourages growth and creativity. Most employees, when given a chance to do something different, benefit from the stimulation and enjoyment of a new challenge. They experience a sense of acceptance, fulfillment, power, and recognition. Suddenly you will notice laughter in the office and brainstorming throughout the day. New ideas and suggestions may start to emerge, and the office will still be abuzz with activity long after five o'clock. Okay, you can't expect miracles, but you can count on a marked improvement.

Example: The quality of Sandra's work has been progressively getting worse. She seems disinterested and bored. How do you handle the situation?
Solution: Instead of replacing Sandra with a new employee, give her new responsibilities and provide her with a change of pace. Give her the opportunity to train new employees.

Words of the Wise

"To succeed . . . you need to find something to hold on to, something to motivate you, something to inspire you."

—*Tony Dorsett,*
1976 Heisman Trophy
Winner

Provide her with an assignment that encourages her to work with members of a different department. Also, let her voice opinions about the productivity within the department and allow her to make suggestions for improvement.

Add a Dash of Creative Problem Solving

When an employee experiences a lack of freedom, choice, and control in the workplace, his response is usually to play the role of victim and blame others. Of course, this is not a fun situation for a manager to deal with. Creative problem solving motivates employees to take responsibility for both the problem and the solution. The manager should *guide* the employee toward a solution but allow the employee to come up with the actual solution on his own.

Example: Broderick just isn't getting enough accomplished during the nine-to-five workday. How do you handle the situation?

Solution: It isn't necessary to make overtime mandatory or to force Broderick into taking work home with him. This will only exacerbate the situation and most likely provoke him into looking for a new job. Instead, encourage Broderick to make a list of his responsibilities and how he goes about completing them during the day. Then, give him time to analyze his system and come up with ways to increase efficiency. You may also suggest he keep a log of the amount of time it takes him to complete each project without interruptions. By giving him the ability to provide input about his job, Broderick will feel empowered to make the changes necessary for increased productivity. He might even begin to enjoy his work again and smile every so often!

Example: Peter is the top salesperson in the department, but he can't seem to get his paperwork finished on time. His procrastination is interfering with the productivity of the entire office. How do you handle the situation?

Joshua Lawrence Chamberlain
(1828–1914)

A general in the Union Army and a hero at Gettysburg, Chamberlain was chosen by Robert E. Lee to receive the formal surrender of the Army of Northern Virginia at Appomattox. Chamberlain held the office of governor of Maine for four terms and helped establish the University of Maine. Joshua Lawrence Chamberlain also served as the president of Bowdoin College (1871–1883).

Solution: Explain how the problem is interfering with the company's productivity, and assign Peter the task of finding at least two solutions to the problem. If he is unable to find agreeable solutions, analyze the task and procedures to discover new strategies for dealing with the problem. Because he finds filling out paperwork monotonous, he probably procrastinates and then the paperwork begins to pile up; soon he is overwhelmed by the amount of work that has accumulated.

One solution could be to make it a daily task of 30 minutes to an hour rather than a weekly task of four hours or more. Another solution could be to pair Peter with another employee who is more efficient at the task so they can share organizational strategies. In this situation, you should also consider Peter's personality. Is he the most productive in people-stimulating situations? Arrange a work environment that accommodates that need.

The Buck Stops Here

One of the most annoying and frustrating situations you can face in a leadership situation is the Pass-the-Buck syndrome. This occurs when an employee refuses to take responsibility for an error or mistake she has made, instead passing the blame on to someone else. You can do your part to eradicate this habit by encouraging employees to be held accountable for their performance through open communication and realistic goal setting. In this type of environment, employees feel safe and know the work they do is meaningful. Also in this environment, risk taking is encouraged, goal setting is ongoing, and both leaders and employees are involved in making decisions and problem solving. In addition, managers nurture the employees by providing feedback, resources, and growth opportunities; by communicating encouragement; and by providing recognition, rewards, and increased responsibility to those with leadership potential. In this way, employees will experience the benefits of taking responsibility for their performance.

Sprinkle with Some Coaching

Coaching encompasses a lot of different areas. In general, when coaching is mentioned in this book it refers to meeting with employees to go over problems/progress, providing support and resources to employees, and providing guidance and encouragement to them. Managers who coach employees enable them to experience that ever-important sense of power and purpose. During the process managers often help employees discover personal strengths and success strategies they can utilize in the future. Keep in mind that clearly defined explanations will also help to elicit effective results.

Example: Manuela has just completed a project that she has been working on for weeks. Unfortunately, she seems to have entirely misunderstood the direction she was supposed to have taken. In effect, it needs to be completely redone. How do you handle the situation?

Solution: Always start on the assumption that *you* were not clear enough in your instructions. Somewhere along the way there was a miscommunication or a misunderstanding that needs to be rectified. Start over and clearly state to Manuela what your expectations are for the project. Give her as much input as possible to help her create a more polished product. Meet at a designated time every week to discuss the ongoing progress of the project. This will prevent future problems from snowballing into major flaws in the finished project. This process will instill confidence in Manuela and a noticeable difference in performance should result.

You Are Now Entering . . . the Comfort Zone

A comfort zone is that safe place where everything is familiar and risk free. Reaching for higher goals means leaving this comfort zone; leaving the comfort zone means taking risks. The fear of change can be paralyzing for leaders and followers alike. Through coaching, a manager can encourage an employee to set goals that will take her out of her comfort zone. If the risks are reasonable

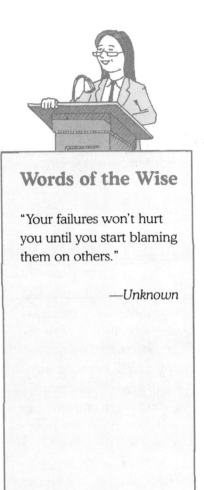

Words of the Wise

"Your failures won't hurt you until you start blaming them on others."

—*Unknown*

and the goals are reachable, everyone in the office will start feeling better about herself and see results.

Garnish with Continuous Training

It can be discouraging for an employee to feel that he lacks a certain skill or skill(s) that he needs to get the job done. By providing continuous training and growth opportunities, managers motivate employees to feel recognized and empowered. With these feelings should also come an improvement in performance. A leader in the workplace recognizes that most employees want to do the work and will succeed with clear guidelines, proper training, and adequate resources.

Example: Philip has been your assistant for two years and his work has always been top notch. You recently asked him to design a new company newsletter and the results are sloppy and unprofessional. How do you handle the situation? **Solution:** Once again, communication is key. Ask Philip about how he put the newsletter together. You may be surprised to find out that he just hasn't had enough time to learn the new page layout program required to create the newsletter. If this is the case, make arrangements to have someone more familiar with the program act as a mentor to Philip. Or, if that is not feasible, bring in an outside trainer to help him acquire the skills he needs.

Overview

This assessment will help you, the leader, to effectively incorporate the key components of a motivating work environment into your department based on the employee feedback you receive. Give this chart to your employees to complete. Once they have completed the short analysis, you'll be aware of specific areas in which you need to implement new strategies. Patterns may emerge indicating weaknesses in your style as well as indications of specific individual needs.

Employee Assessment Tool

	Frequently	Sometimes	Rarely/Never
PART I: COMMUNICATION			
1. Do you feel that you are kept informed and are not "in the dark" about your job?	_____	_____	_____
Are you:			
Aware of priorities?	_____	_____	_____
Clear about expectations?	_____	_____	_____
Sure of responsibilities?	_____	_____	_____
Clear about time frames and deadlines?	_____	_____	_____
2. Do you feel that you receive adequate acknowledgment of and recognition for your contributions?	_____	_____	_____
PART II: COACHING			
1. When you are having difficulty with a task, do you receive:	_____	_____	_____
Support?	_____	_____	_____
Direction?	_____	_____	_____
Feedback?	_____	_____	_____
2. When you are given a new responsibility, do you receive:	_____	_____	_____
Support?	_____	_____	_____
Direction?	_____	_____	_____
Feedback?	_____	_____	_____
3. Are you involved in setting your own performance goals?	_____	_____	_____

(continued on next page)

Employee Assessment Tool

(continued from previous page)

	Frequently	Sometimes	Rarely/Never

PART III: CONTINUOUS TRAINING

1. Do you feel that you have all the necessary skills and competencies to perform your job?   _____ _____ _____

2. When you are given a new task or responsibility, do you receive adequate training?   _____ _____ _____

3. Are you given opportunities to learn, grow, and develop to expand your career options?   _____ _____ _____

PART IV: CREATIVE PROBLEM SOLVING

1. Are you given opportunities to:

   Participate in decision making?   _____ _____ _____
   Provide solutions?   _____ _____ _____

2. Are you involved in determining methods and procedures?   _____ _____ _____

3. Do you experience a sense of power and control in your job?   _____ _____ _____

PART V: CHALLENGE

1. Do you associate feelings of achievement and satisfaction with your job?   _____ _____ _____

2. Do you feel that your skills and talents are being utilized to their fullest?   _____ _____ _____

3. Are you comfortable with your level of responsibility?   _____ _____ _____

Employee Assessment Tool

TOTALS: Frequently _____
Sometimes _____
Never _____

Leadership Tip

A good leader . . .

- Makes an effort to keep employees informed
- Discusses time frames and deadlines
- Meets with employees periodically to discuss progress
- Provides constructive feedback on a regular and ongoing basis
- Encourages employees to participate in setting goals
- Provides training and support where new tasks are involved
- Involves employees in problem solving
- Utilizes the talents and skills of all employees

Scoring

If you scored between 23 and 28 on "Frequently," congratulate yourself; you're doing a great job in creating an environment that fosters motivation in employees. However, there is always room for improvement, so look at the areas where you didn't receive such a high rating.

If you scored between 11 and 22 on "Frequently," you're doing a good job but you need to focus on the questions in which you were marked "Sometimes" or "Rarely/Never," because they point to areas where you need to set goals and make changes in your behavior.

If you scored between 0 and 10 on "Frequently," you definitely need to change your leadership style. First, work on the areas where you received the "Rarely/Never" rating. Then, move on to the areas where you received the "Sometimes" rating and determine how you intend to implement these strategies on a more frequent basis.

Don't Forget to Keep Yourself Motivated!

When *you* become overwhelmed and feel criticized and unappreciated . . . give yourself a boost. Walk your talk. If you want motivated employees, you need to become a role model for motivation.

In addition, becoming more aware of what motivates you will increase your understanding of what motivates other people.

- Focus on your past successes.
- Remember times when you were highly motivated, and look for what pushed you and gave you that internal drive.
- Break down your work into manageable tasks and don't be afraid to delegate.
- Let go.
- Look at criticism to see if there are ways you can improve your performance.
- Face your critics, and ask them for advice and suggestions.
- Appreciate yourself by acknowledging your personal efforts.
- Use your strengths to move forward, and seek to improve in areas where you are weak.
- Put things in perspective.
- Take a vacation day, and do something you enjoy.
- Remember, when you are motivated, your employees will be motivated.

Keep the Fires Burning

Motivating employees is an ongoing process because people are continually growing and changing. As they achieve something they want or value, they then seek to achieve more of the same. If motivation is not kept on your managerial front burner, you'll see the fires in your employees slowly fade and flicker out.

CHAPTER 4

The Importance of Coaching

What Does It Mean?

Well, it might be easier to start off with what it doesn't mean. Coaching does not mean standing on the sidelines and screaming at someone to get his work finished faster. Coaching does not mean giving your coworkers a play-by-play schedule for each work day. Coaching also does not mean throwing in the towel when Alice doesn't understand how to use a new database after one hour of explanation.

Since coaching is the fourth core concept, it is important to fully understand this process. Following along the lines of motivation, coaching will help you to encourage and support your team to achieve the very best results for all parties involved.

Coaching is based on an implicit trust and confidence in the abilities of employees. It is the ability to foster growth and continued success in your team. It is a process of using questions, active listening, and support to assist employees in developing fundamental self-assessment tools that result in increased productivity, skill levels, and overall job satisfaction. Got that? Good, now it's time to put the plan into action.

There is a difference between coaching and managing, and it is important to make that distinction. The main difference between the two lies in the approach management takes in communicating with employees. Management's approach to attaining its objectives is controlling and directing. Coaching attains its objectives through influence and leadership. In many ways, coaching is the polar opposite of managing.

Coaching is a communication tool that can make your life much easier and more rewarding. Coaching can help build good relationships between employer and employee with a minimum of conflict and a reduced level of stress. The overall benefit is definitely worth the initial investment of time.

When Do I Use Coaching Skills?

Coaching can be used in all steps of the management communication process. At the outset, it provides for thorough and comprehensive input from employees and managers, often resulting in more effective solutions, quicker results, more "buy in," higher quality, and higher team spirit and morale. This is especially important today in light of employment security and trust.

Over time, coaching keeps everyone on the team involved and contributing to the project or task success. Mistakes or less effective methods are caught and corrected earlier in the process, resulting in higher-quality results and higher employee or team member self-confidence and self-esteem.

On completion, coaching creates an open environment in which completed projects can be effectively reviewed and critiqued and fosters learning that can be employed in successfully completing the next project.

The Traditional Approach Model

Coaching and managing are part of the same family of management communication tools. However, they represent very different approaches for obtaining a desired result. In the traditional approach model (management by directive), it is generally accepted that the manager possesses the knowledge, information, and decision-making rights. Here, employees exist only to carry out the orders of management. Essentially, employees are not expected to think but only to do as they are told. This was the popular approach for many years. Your parents and grandparents probably experienced work environments very similar to what has been described here. The model has undergone many changes as of late, but the traditional model is still followed in many businesses today.

As a leader you must recognize that coaching moves away from this traditional approach. As the coach you must be willing to give up some of the control you have had because coaching is based on leading and influencing rather than directing. You achieve results through questions and discussion rather than directives; through listening and support rather than controlling. As with everything new, the process may feel strange at first, but in time you'll get the hang of it.

Profile

Robert E. Lee
(1807–1870)

Robert E. Lee was a Confederate general and commander of the Army of Northern Virginia during the U.S. Civil War. His military strategy and leadership are credited as major factors in keeping the Confederate Army alive throughout the four long and treacherous years of the Civil War. After the end of the war, Lee served as the president of Washington College, now known as Washington & Lee University (Lexington, Virginia).

Vince Lombardi
(1913–1970)

One of the nation's greatest football coaches, Vince Lombardi led the Green Bay Packers to five NFL championships and two Super Bowl victories in his nine years of coaching the team.

Coaching Benefits Individuals

In addition to proactive communication, coaching is based on influence and leadership. It is not so much a tool of management as it is a management style. Through the use of coaching, employees are recognized as valuable and contributing members of the company. An employee who has had successful coaching is able to solve most problems on her own when encouraged to do so. The employee will not be successful if you as leader have not supplied her with the appropriate information, tools, and support to take risks.

Coaching Benefits Organizations

Companies that implement a coaching system see benefits and results including:

- A more confident and motivated workforce
- Products of a higher quality
- Employees who can handle a broad range of responsibilities
- An overall increase in efficiency and productivity

Coaching Basics

The following are some thoughts to keep in mind when incorporating the coaching process into your leadership system.

Management does not have all the answers. The coaching relationship should leave room for discussion and suggestion from those being coached. The coach's mantra should be, "The creativity and insight of my workers should never be overlooked." After all, the employees are those closest to the problems and issues at hand. They possess the vital information that is necessary to develop both short- and long-term solutions to problems.

It is critical then, that the coach develops a good technique for probing and questioning the thought process of the employee. Understanding how each person approaches a problem will help you to be a better coach.

Responsibility + Accountability + Encouragement = Power. Only when a person accepts responsibility and is held accountable for his actions will there be personal growth. Ownership is important. Giving a person a project and allowing him to make all the decisions along the way provides a sense of ownership. Since there is no question about accountability, usually this project leader is successful in bringing forth a finished product that is well organized and on target.

A successful coach is a good listener and uses feedback techniques. As an active listener, the coach is able to clear her mind of any distractions and give total attention to the employee. Active listening allows the coach to improve on the ability both to hear what the employee is saying and to understand what the employee is feeling. In other words, it allows the manager to "hear" what is not being said out loud. Leaders must also possess the ability to avoid judging individuals and responses during coaching sessions.

Feedback allows the coach to make better decisions about what to say and how to say it. Language is critical here—even the choice between using "but" rather than "however" can set a framework for the employee to better understand the message you are trying to get across.

Goal setting is a priority. A leader must understand how to set reachable goals for employees with different skill sets and abilities. This means using different techniques and finding which ones work best within the department to help employees develop new and better ways to do a job.

Put yourself in someone else's shoes. Some people need more coaching than others, especially if emotional issues are involved. It is necessary for the person in the leadership position to show empathy, especially during difficult times at the company.

Words of the Wise

"The cornerstone of Vince Lombardi's teaching methods were commitment, sacrifice, and mental toughness, three attributes which continue to be stressed by many of today's successful coaches and by many successful business people as well."

—*Vince Lombardi Jr.*

The Coaching Process

In preparation for the coaching session, establish parameters by specifically defining what the coaching session will cover and how much time will be involved. Be sure to tell the employee of the time, place, and goals of the session. Keep the session to between 30 and 45 minutes. You don't want to overwhelm the person with too much instruction and information, but you want to allow enough time for questions and feedback. Be relaxed and cordial and try to alleviate any stress or anxiety the employee may be feeling. Throwing in some humor might not be a bad idea either! Now, you are ready to begin.

- Set a specific time period and length for the session. This way, you will find it easier to cover all the necessary topics and you will have a better shot at a productive session.
- Define and agree on the goals for the session. In an ideal situation the coach would actually observe the employee working on a particular task and follow-up would be immediate. However, that scenario is not always possible.
- Start by asking a question that gets to the root of how the employee *feels* about the particular task or project to be discussed. Example: "How do you feel about the Anderson project?" or "What do you think about this problem we are having with manufacturing?" Coaching is effective because it recognizes the fact that employees have thoughts and feelings; they are more than just business assets.
- Actively listen throughout the session. Clear your mind of all other agendas, acknowledge your attention with verbal and nonverbal signs, paraphrase as appropriate, and ask for clarification. Using this skill is the key to success. It means that you suspend the all-too-human tendency to apply judgment and carefully listen to what the other person is saying and feeling.
- Offer support or acknowledge understanding of the response. Even if you get a response that does not address the issue at hand, you can still acknowledge that you understand what the other person is saying. Acknowledgment does not mean agreement, yet it indicates involvement in the discussion.

Words of the Wise

"We must open the doors of opportunity. But we must also equip our people to walk through those doors."

—*Lyndon B. Johnson, president of the U.S. from 1963–1969*

- Continually move the discussion in the direction of self-discovery. Your questions should lead the employee toward how to solve the problem without your help or input. Coaching is an interactive process that might even teach the leader a thing or two about herself.
- Repeat the process until the employee reaches the desired outcome. There will be times when the employee just doesn't get it. When you find yourself at this point, don't get frustrated. State a more specific direction and move on from there. You're striving for structured leading, not a guessing game.
- Give recognition where recognition is due. Acknowledge learning gains, creative ideas, and progress toward improvements.
- Agree to the next step and set the groundwork for the next coaching session. Be prepared to follow up on your mutual commitment to progress. If you've set measurable goals for a future date, plan to meet regularly to update the progress toward these goals. Remember that coaching is an *ongoing* commitment, and both you and the employee are responsible for maintaining momentum toward effective coaching results.

Words of the Wise

"Leadership and learning are indispensable to each other."

—John F. Kennedy, president of the U.S. from 1961–1963

Successful Coaching Session One

In this situation, the leader is meeting with an employee who is having difficulty creating monthly reports that accurately reflect data gathered from a questionnaire.

Mr. Chen: Good morning Lewis. I've been reviewing your latest reports and there seems to be a problem with the data you've gathered and the final conclusions in the report. Can you give me your insights on what you think may be happening here?

Lewis: Well, the questionnaire that I get from research is generic. When I confront a special situation, like the Avac

Company report, I can't seem to make the adjustments necessary to reflect Avac's data in the overall report.

Mr. Chen: That can happen. But it's important for you to understand, Lewis, that your report reflects not only external customer buying decisions but also the performance of your entire department. What do you see as the impact on the rest of the department and external customers when reports become skewed?

Lewis: Wow, I have to admit, I had no idea that the skewed data had such a negative effect on the department and the customers. If I don't do these reports properly, we stand to lose business and customer confidence. I don't want this to happen again.

Mr. Chen: I am glad to see that you understand the importance of making these reports more accurate. Let's take a look at how important your job is and how it supports the overall success of our entire department. What are the specific problem areas that seem to be giving you the most trouble?

Lewis: The questions don't seem to fit their specific type of work, and they're measured on different criteria.

Mr. Chen: Based on your experience to date, what changes in the questions do you think would help solve the problem?

Lewis: I think that if we change the reporting format to include a step-by-step interview process, which can be used with special situations, I will be able to draw the proper conclusions and combine them with the generic formats for more accurate final reports.

Mr. Chen: I'm glad you understand the importance of this matter. Let's take a moment to outline a plan to help in implementing this new method. I'll expect progress reports from you on a weekly basis, and by all means, ask as many questions as you need to fully grasp what we are doing.

Why Did This Situation Work?

This situation was a success because Mr. Chen took the time to carefully understand the problem that Lewis was facing. He set up a forum in which he clearly stated the problem to the employee, then listened carefully to try and understand the problem from Lewis's perspective. Based on what he learned, Mr. Chen used his questioning skills to lead Lewis to an understanding of the impact of his actions. Lewis was then able to develop possible solutions to the problem. Mr. Chen followed up with a mutual commitment to monitor progress.

Successful Coaching Session Two

Here Alison is being coached on a new set of responsibilities she will be taking on. Ms. Galvin realizes that because of staff reductions, Alison is being asked to shoulder more of the workload and she is not thrilled about it.

Ms. Galvin: Good morning, Alison. As you know, because some positions were terminated, you are being asked to handle some additional work. I just want to go over with you specifically what needs to be done and get your thoughts as to how we can achieve the new workload objectives.

Alison: I'm sorry, but this just doesn't seem fair to me. How am I supposed to do the work of two people when I am already overextended with my own job?

Ms. Galvin: I understand how you feel Alison, and I empathize with your situation. In regard to being fair, we want everyone to understand that, based on current business and financial conditions, if we had not taken the steps to reduce the number of positions, we could not have protected the jobs that you and other team members still have. It was a tough but also fair decision to cut two jobs for the good of the department. Our challenge now is to design

ways to continue to do the work we need to do at the current employee levels. Let's review the new responsibilities you'll have and figure out ways to get them done.

Alison: There just aren't enough people to handle the work as you have laid it out. There has to be a different way.

Ms. Galvin: Can you offer any suggestions for getting it done?

Alison: Well, looking at my two sets of responsibilities, there seem to be several redundant tasks that could be eliminated. That would save several hours a week.

Ms. Galvin: Sounds great, let's use that as a starting point. What else do you suggest?

Alison: I think maybe we've been following procedures that aren't necessary to meet customer needs. You know, we're doing it because "we've always done it that way." I bet that if you asked others in the department, they would agree with me.

Ms. Galvin: Let's do that. I appreciate your positive approach to this difficult challenge. I wonder if you've taken time to think about the personal gains you'll get out of this, too.

Alison: What do you mean?

Ms. Galvin: You've been doing your current job here for several years and you've done it very well. But maybe it's lost some of its challenge and stimulation. What new skills will you have to use now to master this new challenge?

Alison: Well, even though I am not happy about this change, I never really had a chance to use my creativity in my current job. It could be rewarding to use more creativity from day to day.

Ms. Galvin: Sounds great, Alison. You're already showing new skills and abilities that may even position you for a different job in the future. We should talk once the restructuring is complete.

Why Did This Situation Work?

This is a common situation faced by many leaders and managers who are short on resources and long on workload. In this case, Ms. Gavin recognized that Alison was not happy about the change, so she immediately outlined the specific reasons why the change will have benefits. Next, Ms. Gavin asks Alison for her thoughts, input, and ideas. This helped Alison to feel some ownership in regard to the solution.

Ms. Gavin was also able to demonstrate empathy and fairness, which in turn led to a more open discussion between the two women. Lastly, Alison was prompted to see the additional self-fulfillment opportunities in the new responsibilities. All around, this was another successful session.

Another Use for Coaching

Traditionally coaching is thought of in terms of the manager or leader coaching an employee. Coaching is a communication tool that can be equally successful with:

- Vendors, to create partnerships in the design, construction, or implementation of new and effective solutions
- Customers, to resolve customer-satisfaction issues and build long-term, profitable relationships
- People and situations outside of the workplace (see Chapter 15)

Overall, coaching is a respectful, participatory, and mutual communication process designed to honor different perspectives and the valuable input of many. Coaching should be used regularly throughout all steps of the communication process in order to build trust and morale as employees feel their views and suggestions are being heard.

Words of the Wise

"The best morale exists when you never hear the word mentioned. When you hear a lot of talk about it, it's usually lousy."

—Dwight D. Eisenhower, president of the U.S. from 1953–1961

One Last Point

Don't let your personal perceptions cloud your judgment of the coaching tool. However, be aware that coaching is a commitment that at times may not be easy.

- Coaching does take more time and patience than just shouting out orders and giving directions. Remember, the results for the whole organization will be immeasurable.
- Coaching can appear threatening for leaders who are not secure in their self-image or job skills and may be uncomfortable in letting go of control.
- The "what are they going to need me for now?" syndrome may set in if the leader helps other employees grow and develop.

CHAPTER 5

There's Plenty to Go Around: Passing on Power

What's the Buzz about Empowerment?

Assuming you have had success with the coaching process, it is time to move on to empowerment, the fifth core concept. If you have been able to coach effectively, your employees should be well suited to take on a bit of power themselves. Empowering your employees will help you to stand out as a successful and respected leader.

Like so many others before it, the word "empowerment" is now a favorite of managers nationwide. Although it is much less intimidating than "downsizing" or "restructuring," the word may conjure up images of Sally Field rallying her troops in the movie *Norma Rae*. Rest assured, it need not be taken to that level! What it all boils down to is this: Empowerment is the transmittal of the idea that employees are valuable contributors to the success of an organization. As such, leaders should involve employees in the process of running the business at all levels.

Empowerment allows employees to learn from their mistakes and to effectively work better and smarter. Each situation becomes a learning experience. A well-designed empowerment strategy will lead employees to more success and fewer mistakes. And that should make everyone happy!

Empowerment can work for all employees, but you may feel a need to bring people to the point where they will accept this new level of responsibility. Frequently resistance will emerge because a person or persons lack self-confidence. If that is the case, your job is to help these individuals to develop that self-assurance. This can be a tedious process, so patience and consistency will play major roles throughout.

The more you can make your employees feel empowered, the more productive they are going to be. Unfortunately, empowering employees doesn't always come naturally to leaders, and it will take some self-discipline and practice. You're going to have to work to build trust in other people's abilities, learn to delegate, and instill a sense of passion for the organization and the work with employees.

Utilize the Potential of Others

To be successful as a leader you must try to utilize the potential of each follower. In today's workplace more and more people are being given the responsibility to make day-to-day decisions. This is a change from the workforce of a generation ago. In a sense, today's workers are outpacing their parents in the empowerment department.

To ensure the success of any business or group, you must be ready, willing, and able to recognize the value that each employee brings to the table. Everyone will have different strengths and weaknesses, but each can play a crucial role in the organization.

Here are some reflective questions to help you decide how empowering you are.

Are you creating an environment where:
- People behave as though they own their job and the company?
- People behave in a responsible fashion?
- People see the consequences of what they do?
- People know how they are doing and how much they are valued in the company?
- People are included in determining solutions to problems?
- People have direct input into the way in which the work they do gets done?
- People spend a good deal of time smiling?
- People are asking other people if they need any help?

Now ask yourself:
- Do you find yourself constantly saying, "I should have done that myself"?
- How many people do you have reporting to you directly?
- How many people have you had with you since the company started or for a long time?
- How frequently are people absent from work when it is obvious that they are not really sick?

Profile

William H. Gates
(1955–)

Bill Gates developed the programming language known as BASIC and went on to become the chairman and chief software architect for Microsoft Corporation. Today, Bill Gates is one of the wealthiest men in the world, and his company continues to be on the cutting edge of technology.

- How many people have you directly supervised who still work with you?
- How many people would follow you to another company if you were to leave?

Examine your answers to these questions closely. Do you see any patterns emerging? In the final analysis, it all comes down to you and how you choose to delegate at work. You have the power to make the work environment more positive and enjoyable for everyone.

The Relationship Between Empowerment and Delegation

Many leaders fail to see how empowerment and delegation play off each other. Take a look at the following examples to help illustrate this point.

Situation A: You ask Wyatt to handle all the sales figures for the past few months. You instruct him to update the database and print up new reports based on the numbers received from the accounting department.

Wyatt does the work but is not too enthusiastic about the task. You are left wondering why he seems so lackluster and why he isn't coming up with brilliant ideas to improve sales. To Wyatt, this is a trivial task anyone could handle. In a sense he feels unimportant and unrecognized. The delegated task doesn't imply that you have much trust in his abilities, and, therefore, he doesn't feel empowered.

Situation B: You ask Wyatt to enter the sales figures and he does so accurately yet with a noticeable lack of enthusiasm. You meet with him to go over the numbers and encourage him to develop a marketing plan to help give sales a boost. Now Wyatt feels a sense of increased responsibility as he gets to take the task to the next level. At this point, he has been given ownership of the project and the freedom to exercise his judgment in developing an effective solution.

Fostering Involvement

To move toward happier, more involved working teams, you'll need to keep in mind the following guidelines.

- Create a communication process that is complete, consistent, and clearly understood by all.
- Ensure that all your employees understand what is expected of them within their respective positions.
- Supply the appropriate training, information, and tools so that everyone can accomplish their duties.
- Clearly define and establish measurement tools for the responsibilities of each job.
- Create controls as guidelines allowing for flexibility.
- Constantly give encouragement, support, and clear feedback.
- Promote a sense of responsibility in each worker.
- Create opportunities for people to work together as a team.
- Make it easy for people to give praise to each other. Recognize and acknowledge the hard work of others.
- Listen to your employees all the time.
- Trust your employees.

Words of the Wise

"As we look ahead into the next century, leaders will be those who empower others."

—William Gates (1955–), chairman of Microsoft Corporation

Making sure that Situation B occurs more often than Situation A is going to take some perseverance. Empowerment is not a miracle cure or a quick fix. Everyone involved must work together to make this notion work. As the leader, you will act as the catalyst and driving force to make it work. So, for starters, you must dedicate a significant portion of your time to seeing it through and nurturing the process.

Just because employees don't jump on the bandwagon at first mention of the concept does not mean that they will remain totally unreceptive to it. Give them a chance. Maybe you'll need to bolster their confidence along the way. Start with smaller, individual projects so each person can have the opportunity to experience success before you place him on a team.

Take the time to explain to them what you really want to achieve, how long they have to complete the work, what resources are available, and how they can help you without making it seem like they are not doing their job. You want them to feel comfortable with the process. Let them succeed.

If you take it slow and stay consistently focused on the need to share the responsibility and authority with your employees, you will be able to make this empowerment thing work.

Life Skills Can Transfer to the Workplace

Every so often remember to recognize employees as individuals who function outside of the office. Remove yourself from the work mindset and think about the fact that these people make major decisions in life all the time—without your help. Every adult must decide where to live, decide what car to buy, and handle bills and loan payments. Yet somehow the world keeps spinning and the stock market doesn't crash because of these choices that were made without your approval. Companies for the most part do not recognize the abilities of their people. The existing workforce is constantly making these important decisions, and these life skills are brought to the office and should be integrated into the work environment.

The real question we are faced with is: What happens to this capability when employees get to the workplace? Why does it appear that highly functioning individuals who are capable of balancing budgets at home and making life decisions routinely are not considered competent to make decisions about what kind of copy paper to buy or the correct phone service to use?

Generally companies are unwilling to *trust* employees. Companies are unable to trust that the employee can achieve the objective. In many instances there is an enormous amount of distrust and arrogance on the part of management. What impact does this lack of trust have on the workforce that is driving our economy? Mainly we see a lack of loyalty on the part of the worker. Why should a person stay with a company where she is constantly micromanaged or not encouraged to make any decisions on her own?

Words of the Wise

"Take away my people, but leave my factories, and soon grass will grow on the factory floors. Take away my factories, but leave my people, and soon we will have a new and better factory."

—*Andrew Carnegie (1835–1919), American industrialist and philanthropist*

Practice Trust

To move beyond this limiting approach to leadership, we must first encourage, convince, and help people share the "power" they have. An employee who has the authority to control the circumstances of another person's work life also has the power to share this tool. When authority and responsibility are shared, trust builds. And as trust builds, confidence increases and productivity grows.

Power Defined

Power is the ability to do or act. Power is the ability to control others, to have authority, to sway, to influence. Power is special authority assigned to or exercised by a person or group holding office. Power is a legal ability or authority; also, it is a document giving it.

It can also be said that knowledge is power. When people are enriched with knowledge, they become more powerful by using this knowledge to shape their own destiny. Knowledge also helps people to understand the factors that affect their world. The more they understand their world, the better prepared they are to handle situations that arise in the day-to-day environment of work or home.

If we accept that knowledge is power, then the sharing of knowledge is equal to the sharing of power. With the sharing of power, everyone wins: the employee who now feels the gratification of participating in a job well done, the supervisor who has the assistance in achieving the objective, and the company whose employee production and quality increase dramatically.

Frequently the sharing of power can be viewed between skilled supervisors and employees. This positive interaction can also exist and survive within an organization even without upper management support. But there is a limit. As long as the interactions take place and stay within the parameters of the supervisor's area of responsibility, everything will work out well. Once they go beyond this area, the wall of inflexible management is reached and everything is stopped dead in its tracks. Therefore, management must also understand, believe in, and support the idea that

Eva Perón (Evita)
(1919–1952)

When Juan Perón became the president of Argentina in 1946, Evita became his unofficial copresident. Dedicated to helping the lower classes, Evita instituted education reforms, aided the poor, and helped achieve suffrage for the women of Argentina. Evita also started her own foundation and used the donated funds to establish new schools, hospitals, orphanages, and other social institutions. She is considered by many to be a saint.

employees can and should be trusted and valued for the skills they bring to the workplace.

Two Leadership Mantras

Leaders must continuously promote two basic ideas or mantras:

*If you are not part of the solution,
you are part of the problem.*

None of us is as smart as all of us.

The basic understanding that leadership must maintain is that each individual brings to the company the capacity to be responsible for the work assigned. Employees who have the opportunity to share power and experience trust will successfully work together to figure out ways to increase productivity, reduce turnover, or solve other problems facing an organization.

In many ways, leadership is like parenting.

- Enormous resources are invested to bring the child to a certain level of maturity. Enormous resources are invested to bring an employee to a certain level of knowledge and competency.
- A parent raises a child to be a responsible citizen within a community. A company orients, trains, and encourages an employee to be a highly productive member of the staff.
- A child displays skills and abilities in his developmental growth. An employee demonstrates skills and abilities in the various areas of responsibility.
- A child often learns additional information outside the scope of the traditional classroom or home environment. An employee brings to the job complementary skills that were not formally required in the job description.
- Parents are not always aware of what their child really knows and understands. Companies do not always know the skill level and knowledge of employees.

- Parents seldom bother to discover what their child really knows and uses in her daily life. Companies seldom bother to discover what additional skills and abilities employees have.

This gap in awareness is frequently a critical factor affecting the efficient operation of the home or the workplace. The parents or company are typically happy with the child or employee and don't want to rock the boat. They want everything to remain stable, normal, just the way it is. But we all know how this story ends!

Such a rigid and structured way of thinking will eventually force the child or employee to leave. At home, many children rebel and take extreme actions in response to a restrictive, controlling parental environment. In many companies the employees quit and go to "better companies" where they will be allowed to continue growing and learning to advance within the organization.

The innate desire of people to learn, grow, and successfully conquer challenges will make it impossible for employees to stay with a company that does not offer opportunities for personal growth and development. Companies, like parents, must learn to trust their employees and allow them to become partners in solving larger and more complex business problems.

Power Failure: Downsizing and Layoffs

In any company there is always the chance that economic conditions will lead to downsizing and layoffs. Downsizing must have a financial benefit as well as a personal benefit to the employees who "survive" the process. It is these survivors who will be responsible for reaching the goals and objectives of the downsizing plan.

The survivors of downsizing are much like the participants of the television game show *Survivor*. (Except the game show contestants endured downsizing on a weekly basis.) Each week the survivors emerged from a highly traumatic experience. For days, even months, they had waited for the ax to fall on their neck. They watched friends and fellow tribe members get voted off the island one by one. They saw entire functioning tribal units disintegrate and fall apart. Each week only one was lost and the rest survived until the next grueling tribal council.

As in any trauma, the impact lingered on after each incident. Those left on the island were forced to restructure the work schedule, take on increased responsibilities, deal with a frequently chaotic structure, and, in many cases, develop feelings of personal guilt for alliances formed and trusts broken.

Although not on a deserted island, the "office survivors" are expected to handle the news and changes with ease, while performing at peak efficiency. It is no wonder that recent studies of companies who have downsized have shown that:

- Fewer than 30 percent of these companies met their profit objectives.
- Fewer than 50 percent of these companies met their expense reduction objectives.
- Fewer than 25 percent of these companies increased shareholder return on their investment.

In most companies little or no planning goes into considering the employees who will stay (i.e., survive) after the downsizing. The process of recognizing and respecting employees needs to be nurtured at every turn in the life of the company. Always keep the employees as major considerations in any and all decisions. How will employees help your company to meet the stated objectives?

There are specific steps you can take to ensure that each employee who survives a downsizing is prepared and able to work toward achieving company goals and objectives. In the planning and implementation of a downsizing effort, be sure to include the following steps:

1. Present the future vision and encourage and support employees to work with you to implement this vision.
2. Communicate, communicate, communicate. You can never do too much of that!

3. Keep all employees involved. Be sure that everyone knows that her input is welcomed and respected.

4. Celebrate and reward performances that advance the goals of the company.

When you apply these simple principles to leading a group or running a business, you will reap enormous rewards, especially during critical periods. In some cases you will run across employees who don't have any desire to be empowered. They don't want any additional responsibilities. They don't want to have control over their situation at work. They want things to remain peaceful and stable—no surprises.

Stop to think about this. Although this approach may be acceptable for some jobs, it may not be appropriate where you are. In every job there are basic duties and responsibilities. Employees, by the nature of the job duties they were hired to do, are "empowered" to carry out their assigned tasks. You as a leader need to be sure of who is responsible for making each duty happen. There is no escaping this term "empowerment." It is a double-edged sword, working for both the company and the employee. Have faith in your human assets and in yourself. They will surprise you favorably if you let them.

Strategies to Help the Process
The 80/20 Rule

One way to allow employees to grow, develop, and achieve high levels of productivity is to employ the 80/20 Rule. When you are speaking with an employee, monitor how much you say and how much the other person says. Monitor this for a week or so and track your results. You can easily estimate the time via a simple "I talked 50 percent of the time, the employee talked 50 percent of the time."

In order to achieve a highly functional and productive employee workforce, you should do only 20 percent of the talking. Let the

other person talk 80 percent of the time while you listen. You will be surprised by what you learn about the company simply by listening.

Encourage Passion

A company that has clearly defined goals and objectives has a greater chance to achieve them than a company with poorly defined goals and objectives. When a company finds individuals who share a passion for the product, service, or industry of the company, a dynamic synergy takes place. Synergy is the action whereby separate people, working together, have a greater total effect than the sum of their individual effects.

The employee with a passion for customer service and quality products discovers a company that promotes and supports high levels of customer service and quality. The blending of these two, employee and company, creates a powerful synergy whereby the individual passion is intensified and enriched by the company philosophy, mission statement, operational procedures, and objectives.

The company's vision is translated into real-life, real-time experiences that customers and other employees can hear, see, feel, and experience. The employee with passion helps a company to actualize its vision. A single passionate employee has the capacity to touch the soul of many others.

The story of General Motors's Saturn division illustrates this concept. Saturn started out as an experiment in new design and new styles of management for manufacturing automobiles. The employees who were chosen to work for Saturn were selected because they shared an enthusiasm for a new idea and a new way of working. Part of this new idea was the ability for any employee on the assembly line to stop production on the line if there was a defect or problem found with the process or a specific part. By allowing individual employees to stop the assembly line, Saturn was able to ensure that the problem would be found early on in the manufacturing process, saving thousands of dollars. The exciting aspect of allowing employees to stop the assembly line is the power it puts in their hands. They feel totally committed and connected to the Saturn process. The positive

Words of the Wise

"If this capsule history of our progress teaches us anything, it is that man, in his quest for knowledge and progress, is determined and cannot be deterred. The exploration of space will go ahead, whether we join in it or not, and it is one of the great adventures of all time, and no nation which expects to be the leader of other nations can expect to stay behind in the race for space."

—*John F. Kennedy,*
address at Rice University
on the nation's space program,
September 12, 1962

impact on employees is immeasurable, but the positive impact on the Saturn division is clear—in saved time, reduced quality issues, and fewer recalls and defects.

Common Difficulties with the Empowerment Approach

Giving Too Much Authority to Employees

Always keep in mind the reasons for an initiative. If you are empowering employees to help reduce defects or to improve quality, that should be the scope of the empowerment. The term "empowerment" does not mean employees will have authority to change policy or to impact the company in every area. As part of your program you should define the guidelines and the parameters. All programs and initiatives need boundaries; it is your job as leader to set these initial boundaries.

Running Scared

The concept of empowerment will definitely scare some people. Others will greet it with a sigh of relief. Still others will not know what is happening until they find themselves faced with making a decision at work. Team an employee who is scared by the concept with others who understand and embrace the concept. You may even want to do some initial training to create a comfort level for all involved. The best training, however, will be discussions of real-life situations.

Some of the more experienced employees will need support in rising to the challenge of an empowered workforce. You will need to carefully explain to them the reasons for your taking these actions and the thinking process that was involved. By explaining all the history behind the decision you demonstrate respect and recognition of their commitment. You may need to do a little more hand holding and you may have a longer adjustment period for these employees, but if you are willing to put in the effort, you will teach these old dogs a new trick.

No Looking Back

Once you set in motion the process of empowerment, you cannot turn back. You must continue with your plans. If you don't, your employees will lose faith in you and any future initiatives you try to implement. Additionally, once your employees get a taste of empowerment, they will recognize their own abilities and will want to participate at a higher level of involvement. If you start this, be prepared to continue and reap the benefits of an empowered workforce.

CHAPTER 6

Go Team!

The sixth core concept, teamwork, is imperative in today's world. By empowering your employees, you will get a firm grasp on each individual's strengths and weaknesses. Once this has been accomplished, it is time to pull all this knowledge together to create a team that is proficient and dynamic.

With an increase in global competition, companies are placing an overwhelming emphasis on greater productivity from a smaller number of employees. In doing so, more and more companies are turning to team building as an effective and efficient way to achieve their objectives.

Building a team is a simple concept when you recognize that teams are made up of individuals with diverse skills and talents. Each individual member of the team has a clearly defined skill set that needs to be identified and measured against the skill sets of the other team members. Once the individual team member recognizes what he can best accomplish for the team, achieving the goal or objective becomes not only attainable but eagerly anticipated. Companies that are committed to building a team realize the value of bringing together a select group of employees to improve a particular aspect of the business.

Leaders who direct and influence teams are encouraged to consider the diverse strengths of each participant. The leader is responsible for tapping into the strengths and abilities of each team member and using those strengths to achieve the overall objective. She must also consider the need for balancing personal agendas of each team member in favor of that overall objective.

The Home Team Advantage

Teams offer an organization the opportunity to achieve results in a more efficient manner. Because they are more flexible, teams leverage resources more effectively and can respond more rapidly to constantly changing market circumstances. Teams also allow individual employees to learn from each other, thus increasing their competence and broadening their experience.

Outline of a Successful Team

Objective: All members of the team should share a clearly articulated team objective. A sports team's objective is to win the game. A work team's objective may be to find three ways to cut back on manufacturing costs. But no matter what type of team you are a part of, without direction, the team cannot and will not succeed. It's very easy for a team to spin its wheels and realize the wrong outcome. The team must constantly check its progress against the defined objective.

Commitment: Team members must develop guidelines and procedures that all members commit to, even if some members are uncomfortable with the final mandate. If the team is to achieve its objectives, it must have clearly defined operating guidelines. Even if all members of the team do not agree with all the operating guidelines, they must agree to follow the guidelines until the objective has been reached.

Time: You must have time allotted to create a supportive and responsive structure for allowing the team to operate. The members need sufficient time to create the procedures and strategies that will allow them to work efficiently.

Membership: You should ensure that members represent functional areas of the company that have significant interest in the outcome of the team's work. More importantly, the members must have the authority to bring critical issues back to their departments and have input into decisions that affect these issues.

Skills: Don't forget that the skills and talents of each member must be clearly and accurately identified and assessed. The team needs to know who is the best equipped to deal with the situations as they arise. An informed team has a greater potential for success.

Advocacy: A team must always have a designated leader serving as an advocate, advisor, and supporter. The identification and assignment of this role immediately signals the value of this team to the rest of the organization.

Support: Senior management and other teams within the organization must consistently support and recognize the team's efforts. The company must demonstrate on a regular basis the value and importance of the team's work.

> **Profile**
>
> ### Henry Ford
> **(1863–1947)**
>
> In 1903, Henry Ford and 11 others started the Ford Motor Company in Michigan with a mere $28,000 investment. What started as a tiny operation has grown into one of the world's largest producers of cars and trucks. The company is also a cultural icon in America.

Leader-Directed Versus Self-Directed Teams

Leader-Directed Teams

A team run by a team leader runs very differently from a self-directed team. In the leader-directed scenario the team leader sets the agenda, runs all team meetings, and delegates tasks to other members of the team. The team leader can really be anyone, but in most cases it is a more senior member of the department. Sometimes the leader actually picks team members from different departments based on expertise that will be relevant to a particular problem or issue within the company.

Team leaders can be outstanding or leave the team in the lurch. An effective leader keeps the team focused through brainstorming, establishing priorities, and, most importantly, setting deadlines. Input is taken from all team members and the skills of each member are utilized to their fullest.

As you can see, working in productive teams is imperative to the success of any group. Therefore, let's go over the key points you need to remember if you are directing a team.

1. Have a clear, concise, measurable objective. Your team must know exactly what goals it is shooting for and when it expects to achieve them. A clearly defined objective, describing the actual outcome, is critical for the success of the team. Without this objective, the team will work hard to produce an outcome that may have no value to the organization. Get everyone on the same page.

2. Create a diverse team. Be sure you involve all areas of the organization that will be impacted. A small functional detail may be the key to successfully solving a problem. Although you may think a department cannot afford to be involved in the team, issues within that department might be the one detail the team forgets to address, so the objective is never achieved.

3. Allow sufficient time for the team to develop. Don't rush the process. Allow for time to ensure quality results. You should

budget time appropriately, and, more importantly, ensure that management supports the time needed to get in gear.

4. Assess the skills and talent of the team members. Be sure all members bring unique skills to the table. Don't be concerned about their weaknesses or deficiencies. Look at bringing the best talent in the company together to solve a problem. The team will leverage each of these strengths for the benefit of the organization.

5. Encourage a clear, open, and responsive communication strategy. All team members must know they can contribute freely and be listened to and heard by other members of the team as well as by management. This will build trust. Trust builds confidence and strength. Do everything in your power to ensure that the team has developed a solid communication strategy.

6. Recognize the success of the team in a public manner. Support the efforts of the team and define specific ways to publicly celebrate its success. Teams will generally have deadlines and milestones upon which they measure their progress. Use these defined terms to reinforce the value and success of the team.

Self-Directed Teams

Self-directed teams are composed of members who may come from multiple areas of the organization, including finance, marketing, operations, sales, and administration. These teams are usually made up of a combination of staff and line managers with different skill levels and talents. Self-directed teams are built on the premise that the team will be driven by internal leadership and will not require senior management on daily or even weekly intervals. Self-directed teams rely upon the roles of individuals to keep the team productive. Ideally, team members will play off each other to come to an agreement on strategy.

Encourage this type of team to build leadership and cooperation in all employees. Also, higher-level managers won't be as directly involved and as a result they will have more time to spend on other matters.

Profile

Famous and Infamous Teams

- Lewis & Clark
- The First Continental Congress
- Bonnie & Clyde
- The Dream Team (1996 U.S. Men's Olympic Basketball Team)
- Fred Astaire & Ginger Rogers
- King Arthur & the Knights of the Round Table
- Franklin Delano Roosevelt & Eleanor Roosevelt
- Laurel & Hardy
- Woodward & Bernstein
- O.J. Simpson's Legal Team (F. Lee Bailey, Johnnie Cochran, Robert Shapiro)
- The Wright Brothers
- Currier & Ives
- Rogers & Hammerstein
- Barnum & Bailey
- The Twelve Disciples
- Watson & Crick
- Robin Hood & His Merry Men

Play the Role

There are many roles that individuals assume as part of a self-directed team. Personality will be the major influence in determining who plays what role.

- *Cheerleader*
  Always there to boost morale, the cheerleader has the pep talk to motivate any group. This person will always try to accentuate the positive and eliminate the negative. Not necessarily a bad person to have around, but there may be some personality clashes with other members of the group.
- *Devil's Advocate*
  This person can seem argumentative but really he just wants to get to the heart of the problem and find the best solution. He focuses on the root of a problem and seeks accountability in all situations.
- *Muse*
  The muse brings creative spark to meetings and inspires others to "think outside the box." This person will bring plenty of ideas to the table and will look to others to help decide on how to go about implementing the new plan.
- *Counselor*
  Wisdom comes from experience and this person comes with lots of it. She can bring firsthand knowledge and observations that provide unique insight into solving problems. Everyone's ideas have value to the counselor, who wants to make sure everyone is part of developing the solution.
- *Facilitator*
  This person knows how to get the job done. Organization and delegation are the strengths of the facilitator. This person can also have a tendency to become overbearing and try to take total control of the team.

Each of these roles will provide an important contribution to the group as a whole. The ability of team members to assume different roles at various times during the process will help define the success of the team. This is why it is best to have a diverse set of people on the team. Be sure you include at least one person who demonstrates the traits of a strong facilitator.

The following is a specific example of how a self-directed team works. In this case, the objective of the team is to suggest methods for reducing insurance claims to prevent an increase in premium charges. Consistent with this, the self-directed team should:

Define team goals by identifying the details of the objective. Be sure all aspects of the objective are identified. What has been the workers' compensation history at the company?

- Identify the actual history of claims within the company during the past six months.
- Identify the present premiums and the history of past premiums.
- What sort of claims are you submitting?
- Who is responsible for reporting claims?
- Who is responsible for managing the workers' compensation administration?

Analyze the entire company situation with respect to the objective. The team must determine the facts. Which departments are responsible for the greatest number of claims? Analyze all claims according to department, type of claim, and dollar value. When did you first notice a significant change in claim patterns? What events coincided with the changes in claim patterns?

Identify the necessary resources not available within the team. The team may not have enough resources or the right people to address this specific issue and may need to bring in additional resources. For example: Is a financial analyst required to assist with calculations? Is there someone at the company who understands the specifics of setting workers' compensation insurance premiums? There may also be a need to obtain assistance from a safety expert.

Create guidelines for communication, feedback, and support within the team. The team needs to establish a clear set of guidelines for anyone to use. For the workers' compensation problem, the team should:

- Set up a regular system for reporting claims data to the various departments.

Leadership Tip

What is a Cross-Functional Team?

Cross-functional teams are teams that include representatives from various areas of the organization. In larger organizations, cross-functional teams allow separate divisions of the organization to learn about other functions through personal interactions, thereby preventing the development of poorly designed solutions.

- Set up a mechanism for departments to input suggestions to reduce claims.
- Create a schedule for officially informing the company of progress.
- Create a master list of all available resources for the project, internal and external.

Brainstorm creative solutions to achieve the objective. The team will generate a large number of possible solutions to the problem. All options will be recorded and discussed. A crazy idea may even end up being the one that makes everything come together. When evaluating the workers' compensation problem, the team should take the following steps:

- Institute comprehensive safety measures.
- Upgrade equipment.
- Provide technical training for necessary personnel.
- Provide training to employees processing claims paperwork.
- Aggressively follow up on claims.
- Hire an employee to specifically monitor claims activity.
- Self-insure claims under $100.
- Establish an incentive award for reduced claims in each department.

Prioritize the possible solutions. Once the realistic options have been identified, the team must then measure the value of all the options. Once the most appropriate options have been selected, the team will have the beginning of a plan of action. It should select the ideas that have the greatest opportunity for success.

Set timetables and deadlines. By setting timetables and deadlines, the team begins to establish its work plan and strategy for dealing with the problem. It is easiest to create a timetable based on the date and new premiums established, then work backward to develop a timetable for implementation. Include periodic times for evaluation, feedback, and confirmation that the project is moving along as designed. The plan should be adjusted as necessary based on new information.

Communicate the selected plan of action to the entire organization. When the plan of action and timetable are clear, the team should communicate these to the entire organization so everyone will be able to support the effort. The plan of action and timetable can be relayed through

Words of the Wise

"When placed in command—take charge."

—*Norman Schwarzkopf, general for the American Armed Forces during the Persian Gulf War* regular communication vehicles. The team should also let managers and key players know when it would like feedback and input.

Execute the plan of action through delegation of tasks and responsibilities. Within the plan of action and the timetable, there will be numerous tasks and responsibilities. These duties must be distributed among the team members, taking advantage of the special skills and abilities of each member. The team should follow these steps.

- Divide responsibility evenly among each member.
- Use each person's strengths in dividing responsibility.
- Set due dates and clear levels of expectation so all members know what each is expected to accomplish.
- Identify and reinforce the need to use each other and not to try to do everything alone.

Evaluate the outcome of the plan of action. Through the guidelines already established and the feedback from the company, the success of the team can be measured. The plan can be evaluated as it progresses, modifications can be made as necessary to achieve success, and the final outcome can be measured based on the information originally collected.

Watch Out for Team Destroyers!

Here are some of the problems that can rip the team-building process apart.

- Jealousy rears its ugly head. Be on guard for jealousy whenever a new member is hired into the group. Go out of your way to tell other team members how much their work is appreciated.
- Everyone's a cynic. Some people are just negative by nature. Others might feel your company can't possibly prosper or they just don't like small companies, big companies, or whatever. Be sure you are emphasizing the company's positive achievements to the group as a whole. Don't hesitate to confront any

openly cynical individual and demand that his behavior change at once.

- Self-confidence is not a strong suit. Some people lack self-confidence and view attacks on their opinions as attacks on themselves, responding with statements like, "Are you telling me my fifteen years of experience don't matter?" Stop any discussion like this immediately, and, in a private one-on-one meeting, patiently point out the defensive behavior.

What If the Team Doesn't Succeed in Solving the Problem?

If a team fails to find an appropriate solution to the problem at hand, use the situation as an opportunity to continue learning. Ask the team to analyze why it was unable to achieve the objective. Ask it to evaluate the process so it is not repeated the same way. Redirect the team to move forward with a more clearly defined objective and plan of action.

Conflict Within the Team

Some conflict between members of a team is a good sign. It indicates that the creative process of problem solving is taking place and that members are comfortable challenging each other. A well-developed team will have a communication strategy in place to resolve conflict. This strategy will serve as a model for the organization. Encourage positive, respectful disagreement.

Recognize the Success of Teams

The success of a team can be celebrated in many ways. Teams will generally have deadlines and milestones upon which they measure their progress. Announce the team's success in the company newsletter, at an informal awards ceremony, during a special event, or through any other tangible outlet that allows other company employees to know just how important the team was in the overall success of the company. Make the celebration an extension of your company culture.

Words of the Wise

"The wicked leader is he who the people despise. The good leader is he who the people revere. The great leader is he who the people say, We did it ourselves."

—Lao-Tzu, philosopher

CHAPTER 7

Getting Organized and Managing Time

Time management is the seventh core concept. You may have succeeded in implementing the previous six core concepts, but without proper organization and management of time, your leadership abilities will come to an abrupt halt.

If you are like most people, your work life is a separate entity that has a tendency to crowd its way into the other aspects of your life. You already know by now that you need to create a balance between all the different areas of your life. This is why it is especially important to create and stick to an effective time management system for your work life. If your work life has a tendency to crowd out your personal and home life, it is most likely due to poor management of time. This chapter will offer suggestions for getting this area in order and creating a balance for a happier and more well-rounded life.

You've Heard It All Before

Often when people think of time management, their jobs are the first things that come to mind. After all, that's the place where the most direct pressure is placed on our time. Consider the following statements:

- You are in a constant state of competition with coworkers, peers, and supervisors.
- You feel the need to be busy at all times because that image is equated with success.
- You have deadlines to meet and people to please.
- Meetings, lunch dates, phone calls, and paperwork overload you with their urgency.
- There is a constant stream of people who need your attention right away, and you are bogged down with stress.

Does any of this sound familiar to you? Your work environment can put a strain on you that has the potential to severely affect your home and personal life. If you don't get a grip on the situation, chances are nothing will get accomplished and the work will become more and more overwhelming.

Leadership Tip

Stress Management

Some degree of stress is inevitable in life, but too much negative stress can and will affect all facets of wellness, including body, relationships, self-image, education/work, and emotional well-being. You need to learn how to manage your stress and use it to your advantage.

Though you may not think so right now, applying time management to your workplace will most likely be easier than applying it to any other area of your life. This is because the workplace is a more structured environment. You have assignments, a specific job to do, and particular resources available to you. You work within the confines of your role. Because you have these set limitations, it is easier to find ways of working within them. With your home life you have free reign to do whatever you please without accountability. This leaves several options available to you, making decisions harder to reach. It is much easier to make a decision when there are fewer options to choose from.

With this in mind, applying time management to work should be a piece of cake. The concept becomes less overwhelming and more exciting by the minute. Now, let's get started.

Step One: It's All about Attitude

Being able to manage your time at work will be a direct result of your attitude about your job. In other words, if you take pleasure in the work you do, you will most likely have a better attitude about the time you spend there than someone who drags herself in to face the monotony day after dreary day.

Step Two: Take Inventory of Your Priorities

Make a list of what is important to you about the work and then rank the items in terms of life value. Keep in mind that your priorities may differ from those of the company you work for or those of the industry overall. That's okay—they should reflect your own values, not those of other people.

Step Three: Develop a Game Plan

The game plan is best thought out in terms of goals. Where do you want this job to take you? Where do you see yourself in 5 years, 10 years, nearing retirement? You need to set goals to achieve your vision of the future. Figure out the steps you need to take to get there. Will you need to further your education?

Leadership Tip

Helpful Hints to Managing Stress

- Identify the source. Recognize what is causing your stress and see what you can do to reduce it.
- Realize what you can change. Figure out the best way to reduce stress by either eliminating it completely or avoiding it temporarily.
- Maintain a healthy lifestyle. Exercise three to four times a week. Get more rest. Eat well-balanced nutritious meals. Reduce caffeine/nicotine consumption. Cut down on alcohol and other depressants. Allow for leisure time. Practice a relaxation technique daily and take breaks when you can. Manage your time more effectively. Have fun, laugh, and maintain a positive attitude!

Leadership Tip

Did You Know?

Stress is your body's reaction to the demands placed upon it and can have physical and psychological effects on the human mind and body. Taking extra care to recognize when your body is reacting to a heightened stress level can make a difference in your well-being.

The Physical Effects of Stress Include:

Rapid heart rate
Rapid breathing
Muscle tension
Headaches
Increase in blood pressure
Clammy skin
Dizziness
Rashes
Nausea
Change in sleeping pattern
Fatigue
Back pain

Perhaps you will want to change your status or position in the company, or change companies all together. How are you going to do all that? Set time limits for specific steps and don't be lax.

Step Four: Implement the Plan

Schedule those activities that will help you achieve your goals, but be realistic. Often people will get slightly out of control when it comes to work and career goals. It is possible to push yourself too hard or to take on more than you can handle. Be wary of overloading yourself with additional responsibilities and commitments. Work your priorities into your schedule but do so in a timely manner. Remember to keep that balance between work and play. Just because you have a little extra time on Wednesdays doesn't mean you should fill it with work-related activities.

Step Five: Get Your Things in Order

Organizing your work space will have a significant impact on the quality of the work you do. Having things in the appropriate place and easily accessible will help you to work more efficiently. Arranging your space to fit your needs and comforts will have a tremendous influence on your stress level and self-esteem.

Organization is an important part of time management. Take notice of your daily activities. Are there any hang-ups you come across that could be ended by better structuring? Anything you spend time looking for is a definite yes to this question. What are some others? An organizational system should be tailored to your needs and habits, and what this section offers may not work as well as an idea you already have. Use these suggestions to get started, but personalize the system or it may fail to meet your needs.

Organizing Your Work Space

Work spaces will differ from one person to the next, but the basics of time management and organization withstand all variances. Once you have the foundation set, you will be able to move forward with your own time management tactics. Some may be universal, while others will work for only you.

Whether you work in an abandoned warehouse or a modern high-rise, your work space needs to be organized. This doesn't mean that your desk will be free of all clutter and every speck of dust gone, it means you know where everything is and everything has a place.

There are several ways to go about this task. Of course, if you have a system in mind already, by all means get that geared up to go. Perhaps you can use a system similar to something you have set up in your home. The more familiar the system, the easier it will be to stick with. This is one reason why it is so important to tailor these systems to your individuality. It would be a waste of time to work so hard to incorporate a time management system into your life only to disregard it two weeks down the road. If you don't have the slightest notion of where to begin, keep reading.

The Paper Trail Is Paved with Good Intentions

You may want to start at the root of most time management and organizational issues—paper. By taming this beast at the start, the task at hand will seem a lot less daunting. Paper, as thin as it may be, takes us the greatest amount of space on a desktop. It miraculously accumulates and multiplies at a staggering pace. Worse than termites on a log cabin, paper can bring your office down in a matter of hours. But, you do have the ability to get it under control before permanent damage is done.

If it is at all possible, handle paper only once. As soon as you get it, figure out what needs to be done with it, and move it along. Either take care of it or dispose of it. Some sort of filing system will work wonders to get stray paperwork under control. Most people go with an alphabetically arranged system because it is simple and convenient. However, if you really want to get down and dirty, you can use a color-coding system within your files. As long as everything is clearly labeled and in a location that makes

sense, a filing system can become your best defense against the paper problem.

If there are papers that you are going to need throughout the course of the day, group those papers together. For example, if you have a report to write, bundle all papers with relevant information into one group. Using a specific folder will help keep these papers together and in one place. Be sure to mark the folder clearly for quick access. You can even use rubber bands to bind papers together if you don't have folders readily available. There is no point in having to make several trips to the filing system if you know you are definitely going to be using certain papers during the day.

Paper trays are another great way to organize the clutter. They stack well and don't take up a lot of room. You can specify a certain function for each tray. For example, if you have papers that need to be dealt with immediately, place them in the top tray. For those papers that are important but can wait a few hours, the second tray comes in handy. Perhaps you can use a specific tray for those items that need to be filed away. (Let's face it, even though handling paper only once is the best route to take, it isn't always the most practical.)

But make sure you aren't letting these trays get too full! Keep them under control as best as you can. Use them for accessibility and practicality, not for procrastination and long-term storage.

Take a good look at the state of your current paper piles. Do you already have a system that you just don't keep up with? Maybe you have never even considered a system. This is the time to get it all under control. Once you have the paper problem in your grasp, you will find that the rest of the disorder can be resolved rather easily.

Convenience

The convenience of the items in your office will directly affect your management of time as well as the constancy of your organization. Take a look around. What items do you use the most? Are they within arm's reach or do you have to cross the room just to get to them? The inconvenient placement of items can destroy the productivity of even the most organized person. Because you continuously stop what you are doing and physically get up and walk across the room each time you need a book, you break your concentration over and over again. This will cost you a good chunk of time in the long run. The physical exertion may even start to wear on you. Suddenly, you find yourself becoming lazy and don't return the books to their home after use. You justify it with the knowledge that you will eventually need them again, so what is the purpose of wasting time and energy?

As a result, your desk becomes a heap of clutter. You can't find anything beneath the heavy books. Not all the books will even fit on the desk, so piles begin to accumulate at your feet. Pages get torn and covers bent. You have managed to turn your desk into a vast wasteland of chaos.

Seems like you just can't win. You feel like you are wasting time either way. So what are you going to do? The best idea is to nip the problem in the bud. A little rearranging is called for, but don't panic. If there is a file cabinet or other mobile object close to your desk, you can switch it with the bookcase. Just make sure that what you decide to move isn't going to re-create the problem you had in the first place. Switching one with the other will do you no good if you use the filing cabinet just as often as the bookshelf. This is the time to allow your creative thinking skills to shine through.

Perhaps you don't need every book on the shelf, just those that are reference books. Consider hanging a shelf next to your desk. Place on the shelf those reference titles that you use most often, so they will be within arm's reach. A hanging shelf will not take up any additional wall space, and it could add some depth to your decor. If a shelf simply will not work, consider a miniature case or bookrack just big enough for those particular books to place on the floor next to your desk.

Minor Details

Now that you have the two big issues under control, it's time to pay attention to the small stuff. If your office is like any other, there are lots and lots of little details. Anything you can do to make your work area more comfortable, easily accessible, and less confusing can only promote your efficiency, so don't neglect your duties here.

Words of the Wise

"To inform the minds of the people, and to follow their will, is the chief duty of those placed at their head."

—*Thomas Jefferson to C.W.F. Dumas, 1787*

- Make sure all those incidentals are within reach on your desk. This includes pens, paperclips, stapler, ruler, tape, and sticky notes. Regularly used items such as these should each have their own home. Any office supply store will offer you hundreds of options for storing these types of items. Or, you may want to consider designating an entire desk drawer to supplies. You can even divide the drawer into sections with something as simple as cardboard to keep the items from getting jumbled up and mixed together. Just be sure to place the items in a place that makes sense and works well within your system.

- Additional items can also work within your system. Bulletin boards can help alleviate more of the desktop clutter but still allow items to remain in sight. A desktop calendar that is large enough to pencil in appointments can be a great help. You will be able to check your schedule for the upcoming weeks at a moment's glance. It is best to get a calendar that also has the other eleven months in smaller print at the bottom; this saves you from flipping back and forth.

- Keep a small notebook or scrap paper by the phone. When you first sit down at your desk, mark the date on the top line of a clean page. Use this page to make notes of any telephone conversations you have during the course of the day. This will come in handy later on when you can't quite remember the details of the information you were given or if someone tries to back out of a verbal agreement you made over the phone. It is easy to forget all the calls you make and receive in a given day. Glancing over these notes will help keep things in check.

- Store similar items together. Letterhead, envelopes, and stamps can all be located in the same area. If you keep like items such as these together, you will not waste time running all over the office simply to mail a letter.

Multitasking

Undoubtedly, your work day will include numerous activities that don't take much thought or focus on your part for completion. These are the prime candidates for multitasking. All the other important stuff deserves your full attention, so don't let the temptation of multitasking get the better of you. The following are some suggestions that pertain to common work environments.

- Taking telephone calls while engaging in some other activity is a favorite among multitaskers. For the busy individual, it is difficult to sit still during a phone call. Some of the more popular activities to couple with talking on the phone include: straightening desktops, filing, scanning e-mail, sorting snail mail, reevaluating schedules and creating to-do lists, and gathering materials for an upcoming meeting. Of course, you must not forget to gauge the importance of the telephone call before engaging in another task.

- Business lunches are another example of multitasking. Everybody needs to eat, so pair up a meeting with a meal. Dining is a favored social pastime and nearly everyone will agree it reflects well on you to acknowledge this. Restaurants are quite a bit more relaxed and casual than offices. Depending on what the meeting concerns, it may be to your benefit to congregate in such an atmosphere.

- If you have lots of busywork on your hands, such as filing or sorting through a waist-high stack of papers, you may want to consider purchasing a tape recorder. You can use it to dictate a letter, practice your sales pitch for an upcoming meeting, or just to make notes to yourself so that whenever something crosses your mind you don't have to stop what you are doing to go write it down.

- Computers allow multitaskers a lot of freedom. You can keep several applications open at once so you can flip back and forth between them. However, you may want to keep open only those that you are currently working on. Too many

open applications can result in confusion and could possibly cause your computer to crash.

- If you have the option, keep a radio close by and schedule menial tasks to be performed during your favorite news program. You can listen and keep up to date with what's going on in the world while giving your signature to the dozen or so documents that have been lying patiently on your desk.
- When you take breaks (which you should) to stretch your muscles, consider making that nice little stroll even more worthwhile. If the fax machine is down the hall, wait until your scheduled break to send your documents. However, this works only when the break is purely for physical reasons. If you use this time to clear your mind and refresh yourself, do not multitask! It defeats the entire purpose of the break.

There are likely to be several other ways in which you personally can take advantage of multitasking. Take a look at what is piled in front of you. If you can perform a task without having to give it your full concentration, double up with a similar task. You will get more done in half the time when you choose to multitask sensibly.

Capitalize on Your Commute

Whether it takes you an hour or 20 minutes to get to work, your time on the road can be put to good use. Don't assume that because you don't have control over the amount of time you spend on the commute that you don't have control over how you spend that time. No matter if you drive or take public transportation, you can find ways to use the time effectively.

By Train, By Bus, By Subway . . .

If possible, try to take advantage of the public transportation that is available to you. That is, if it is going to be practical. If you are going to be spending two hours commuting on the train as opposed to 45 minutes driving, you are wasting your time. However, if public transportation is an option that is reasonable, consider the possibilities.

Public transportation frees you from the stress and responsibility other drivers are burdened with. This means you are free to do other things while someone else transports you from work to home or vice versa. Your hands are not tied up, your concentration is available, and your stress is reduced. So what are you going to do with this freedom?

Look at your schedule. Is there some busy work you can get out of the way? Perhaps there is a leftover item from yesterday's to-do list. If you choose to do something directly related to your schedule, make it something that is not going to need a lot of room and won't require deep thought. You mustn't forget that you will be in the company of dozens of other people. You won't always get a seat; sometimes you may have to stand in a sardine-can-like state. There is likely to be a lot of noise and a wide variety of potential distractions. Take these factors into consideration when choosing a task to complete. One way to avoid distractions is to listen to some classical music; something you won't be swept away by. It is easier to tune out outside distractions if you are tuned in to some soothing songs. Here are some more suggestions for taking advantage of your commute:

- Read the newspaper or a trade journal. It is important that you be knowledgeable about the world around you, so sit back, relax, and read. You can scan headlines and read articles of interest. By the time you reach your destination, you can recycle the paper, satisfied by your enlightenment.

- Prepare a memo to send out to coworkers or employees. Memos are supposed to be short and to the point anyway, so you don't need to spend a great deal of thought or time on this. It is easy to scribble down a draft so you don't have to concern yourself with it once you reach the office. Also, this is an activity that you need little to no room for. In most cases your lap can be a makeshift desk or you can jot down notes standing up. You can even use a napkin if loose-leaf is nowhere to be found.

- Use this time to go over your list of things to do. Make any alterations that are needed. Compare it to your schedule. Is everything accounted for? Is your day a good example of how to use time both effectively and efficiently? If not, you can make changes now before you are caught up in the heat of the day.

- If you are able to relax amidst hustle and bustle, this may be an ideal time for you to make mental preparations for the day ahead. If you can use this time as a meditation period, you will be geared up and ready to jump right into things as soon as you reach the office. Those around you will probably need a little time to catch up (and maybe a large cup of coffee). If you have already passed that point (in other words, you are on your third cup), you will be ahead in the race.

- If you aren't happy with the work you do, use this time for something that brings you pleasure. Perhaps you enjoy reading—bring along that next Harry Potter novel you've been meaning to read. If you like to do crossword puzzles, now is the time to go crazy. Whatever it may be that brings a smile to your face, this is a great time to capitalize on it. The work day will be easier to endure if it begins and ends with a little happiness.

Driving

Using commuting time if you drive back and forth to work may be a little trickier than if you are able to take public transportation. While you are driving, your concentration cannot ever be completely focused on any one thing aside from keeping your eyes on the road. You have a responsibility to yourself and those around you to take heed of the rules and regulations of driving. You don't have the same freedom as those who are riding the bus to work, but this doesn't mean that you can't put the time to good use.

Remember that your safety is the top priority here, so you need to take that into consideration.

If you are able to remain responsible and careful, by all means consider tasks you can perform while on the road. Here are some suggestions.

- Do you want to gain knowledge in a particular field of interest? Use your tape or CD player to educate yourself with foreign language instruction or biographies of famous people.

- As with public transportation, you can use this time to mentally prepare yourself for the day ahead. Think about the activities you have scheduled and what other tasks you would like to complete. Having these things fresh in your mind when you arrive at work will be just as helpful as a strong cup of coffee to get you going.

- Practice a speech or presentation you will give in the near future. Go over the outline in your mind until you are comfortable with it, and practice different ways of getting your ideas across. You can practice in the comfort of knowing that absolutely no one is going to hear you. Try out different tones of voice, pauses, and inflections to make the speech more interesting. Practice makes perfect and it also makes for a more relaxed and stress-free presentation.

- With the popularity of cell phones on the rise, more and more people are talking on the phone while driving. Although using the car as a personal phone booth is not recommended, there are times when it just makes sense to call from the car. If you are stuck in traffic and need to call the office or cancel/make an appointment, feel free. If you need to make multiple calls, it is best to invest in a headset so that your hands remain free for steering.

- Listen to a news radio show. You can catch up on current events and international affairs. If you do this every day, you may eliminate the need to buy a newspaper. Hey, that's just another way to cut off the paper trail.

Maintenance—The Toughest Job You'll Ever Love!

So now that your office is in tip-top shape and perfected to meet your needs, you are done, right? Wrong! Just like anything else, over time the system will break down and papers will pile up. Maintain your systems on a regular basis.

First, reward yourself for a job well done. Acknowledge the fact that you put a lot of time and energy into pulling everything together. You have already made it through the tough part, now you just need to sustain that momentum.

Take the Upper Hand

Stay in motion once you get in motion. This way your system will become part of your routine. By this time your office should be rather structured. Everything should have a home and items are positioned for convenience. Your goal now is to keep things that way.

Again, paper will be the biggest hindrance to keeping up with the system. All papers must be sorted, filed, or disposed of at least once a week. Magazines, newspapers, and any other literature you receive regularly are included in this housecleaning process. It is possible that you won't have had the time to read the periodicals before it is time to weed through them. If this is the case, quickly skim them for articles that you are interested in. Clip the articles and file them for future reading. Toss out the remainder of the magazine; the bulk just gets in the way.

Mail protocol can take different forms. Some people prefer to leave it until the end of the week when the rest of the paper is sorted. Others prefer to handle it on a regular basis. Your decision will most likely depend on the amount of mail you receive each day. You may decide that it would take you at least an hour if you sorted only once a week. Or it could be that all of your incoming mail for a week fits nicely in a mesh basket and it is less consuming to sort it all at once. Regardless of when you choose to sort your mail, always do it next to the recycling bin. Don't even bother opening junk mail. For the pieces of mail that you do open, you can immediately dispose of any advertisements or other unnecessary additions, hence handling paper only once.

At the end of the day, settle everything in its proper place. Replace anything you brought in from outside the office. Tidy up the area and take a look at your schedule for the day ahead. Also check over your to-do list once more. Cross off any items that have been taken care of and transfer incomplete items to a new list.

Successful Time Management

Now that you know the importance of getting organized, you are well on your way to successful time management. Here are some more tips to make your work days more efficient and effective.

- Plan your time wisely on a daily and weekly basis. You can't be an effective leader if you can't plan your time wisely. Map out the details of each day as carefully as possible. For each week, list the most important tasks you are going to handle.
- Make the distinction between which tasks are most urgent or time sensitive and which have the most impact on the company. Some tasks may be both urgent and important. For example, a proposal that needs to be written by tomorrow and that may land a new customer is both urgent and important. But more often than not, the urgent tasks are not the most important.
- Work flexibility into your schedule. Allot a chunk of time—maybe a couple of hours after lunch—for dealing with or examining those unplanned issues or tasks that arise during the day.
- Be sure the tasks that are assigned priority status are in sync with the company's strategy and its annual plan.
- Plan out your time the day before. Most people experience their greatest energy level first thing in the morning, so you want to begin your workday by delving into the tasks at hand, not determining what those tasks should be. Planning your daily schedule is a good task for lower-energy times—

the end of the previous workday or at home the night before. You want to arrive at work with a firm direction for the day's work already set in your mind.

- Try focusing on one important goal each day. Each day you may have to deal with several on-the-spot developments and emergency matters. Despite this, try to focus as much time as possible each day on one task. Don't jump from one issue to the next without realizing resolution of or progress on anything.

- Delegate. Every day, scan the list of tasks to be completed and determine who in your organization may be able to help you out. Delegate the task or a portion of the task to that person.

- Use lunchtime productively. Lunchtime meetings can be ideal for discussing certain types of issues with other employees. Try brainstorming, weighing the pros and cons of upcoming decisions, or getting a progress report from a staffer over a deli sandwich or Chinese buffet. But, never use the lunch hour to discuss highly emotional issues such as performance reviews.

- Coach others on using their time effectively. Sit down with others and help them plan their time. Emphasize the goals you have set for them and their function. But, do give people some latitude. Let them develop their own time-planning method. Some people have a favorite calendar program on their computers, while others prefer printed daily planner books.

Stop Bothering Me!

Surely there have been days when you have been heard to say things like, "Calgon, take me away!" or "Serenity now!" How can you avoid the constant stream of interruptions throughout the work day?

One of the most prevalent excuses for missing deadlines is "I got distracted." This is a widely accepted reason because each of us encounters numerous distractions and interruptions each and every day. Sometimes it may seem as though they rule our lives. A distraction is anything that pulls your attention away from what you are currently working on. Noise, lack of noise, emergencies, screeching tires outside—these are all distractions. Distractions are inevitable and have the potential to ruin even the best-laid plans. Even though they serve as a great excuse, there are ways to cut down on the damage distraction can leave in its path.

Do You Welcome Distraction?

What you have to realize is that distractions are only distractions because they are allowed to be. In other words, the constant ringing of the fax machine down the hall may very well distract you to the point of insanity, whereas the other people in the office don't even seem to hear it. If you are doing something that you don't particularly enjoy, you may subconsciously search for distractions. In this case anything that diverts your attention is welcome, though you may groan about it. But truly, you are finding a way to place blame on the environment for your momentary lack of motivation and focus. If you seem to welcome distractions, you simply need to find your focus once again.

Control Distractions

You can gain control over some of the distractions that haunt you. For instance, if you are trying to write a proposal or report:

1. Shut the door to your office (if you have an office). Also shut the blinds if necessary.
2. Position the computer screen so there is no glare beckoning you.
3. Remove all external distractions (i.e., magazines, newspapers, pictures of your coworker's new grandchild, mail from home).
4. Let others know that you will be busy and would like not to be disturbed until later in the day. (Be sure to take time later to answer questions that may have arisen.)

Words of the Wise

"You must never so much as think whether you like it or not, whether it is bearable or not; you must never think of anything except the need, and how to meet it."

—Clara Barton
(1821–1912),
American Red Cross
founder

These precautions should help to some degree, but if writing that proposal is something you really dread, your own mind can be your worst enemy.

Daydreaming is the evil culprit. It doesn't need outside influence; instead it will play on your fantasies and imagination. Since you can't very well turn off your mind, you will need to find an alternative way to stop daydreams. In this case, you may want to enlist the help of visual aids. When you start heading into the dangerous daydream zone, it is important to have something visual to bring you back to reality. Place a memo in front of you listing the reasons why this project is important to you. Make sure to put the list in eye contact. Or, if positive reinforcement doesn't work, make a list of the penalties that will ensue if the project is not completed on time.

Another suggestion is to let someone else know you are having trouble focusing. This should be someone who is at the same level of authority as yourself, not one of your employees. Ask this person to check on your progress periodically. Chances are the added pressure will be just the jump start you need to get moving. But make sure that the checkups are not too frequent or they will just serve as another distraction.

What Do Distractions Cost You?

Consider the amount of time lost to distractions. If you stay focused on the project at hand, it will be over quickly and painlessly. On the other hand, if you allow distractions to interfere continuously, it could drag out the project over a course of days. No one wants to wake up in the morning knowing they have to complete a dreaded task that could have been finished days ago. Try to focus on the positive aspects of the job, even if that just refers to the completion of the project.

There will always be some distractions that you can't avoid. Emergencies can never be anticipated. However, if you are a successful time manager, you will have time allotted for the unforeseen events. Emergencies fit well into this category and, hopefully, don't happen all too often, so you still have that allotted time for unexpected occurrences.

Keep in mind that distractions aren't always the enemy. If you have a tendency to become distracted quite frequently, this could be a warning sign. If you are in a very busy time and place, it is easy to become overloaded. Distracting ourselves may be a natural way of allowing the mind a little down time. Though it may seem like a contradiction, breaks are an important part of getting things accomplished. So pay attention to your inattention. You just may need to schedule a few more breaks.

Interruptions

Perhaps the most common type of distraction is the interruption. An interruption is any interference in your schedule caused by outside forces. Most often people are the cause of interruptions, and that can sometimes make them more difficult to deal with than other distractions. Though some don't mind dissuading people from bothering them, others find it very difficult to discourage someone for fear of hurting her feelings or alienating themselves from social encounters. Regardless, interruptions must be dealt with if you want to strengthen your time management skills.

There are different degrees of interruptions. Some you simply have to learn to live with. But the most common interruptions can be limited; it just takes a bit of skill and savvy.

Glued to the Phone

Some people just can't resist picking up that receiver when the phone rings. The curiosity of wanting to know who is on the other end of the line cannot be overcome.

Phone calls are an easily accepted distraction because they can be blamed on the caller. Track your phone usage for a couple of days. Mark down who calls, for what reason, and how long the call lasted, and rate its importance. Just a few days' time may be all that is necessary for you to realize that the time you spend on the phone outweighs the time you actually spend working. If this is the case, it is time to set

some limits. The following are some suggestions to help you on the road to a less phone-intensive day.

- Shut off the ringer and let voice mail pick up. If you are unaware of the fact that the phone is ringing, you won't feel the compulsion to answer. Even if you do it only while you are completing a project, the time saved will amaze you. Not only will you save yourself the time it takes to carry out the conversation, but also the period of time in which it is ringing and you decide to answer, as well as the time it takes to get focused again on your project.

- If you just can't bring yourself to shut off the ringer (or perhaps the silence of the phone would prove to be a distraction in itself), install a Caller ID feature that will allow you to see who is calling before you decide to answer. This won't lower the number of interruptions, but it will decrease the amount of time spent overall on giving in to them. However, this will work only if you refrain from answering every call.

- Designate a period of time in your day to return and make calls. For optimum payoff, schedule this time to coincide with your least productive time of day. It doesn't take a lot of energy or mindwork to make phone calls, and this could serve as a needed break from the project you are currently undertaking. Also, let others know that this is the best time to reach you. If they call in the time slot already allowed for phone calls, that just cuts back on the number of unexpected interruptions throughout the day.

- Once you make/answer the call, don't dawdle, get right to the point. It isn't necessary to find out how each member of the family is doing or what the weather is like in Cleveland. Be pleasant. Begin by asking what it is you can do for the person. This will encourage the caller to get right to the point without participating in the usual idle chatter. If at all possible, write down the information you need beforehand so you aren't wasting time trying to remember everything you need to say.

- Set time limits. You can easily do this by informing the caller immediately that you have only a few moments to spare. If you do this in a courteous manner, the caller will not only be aware and try to keep within the time limit, but also feel honored that you chose to spend that precious little time to speak with her.

- By all means, don't humor a salesperson or vendor. Some people feel it is rude to deny these types of callers the chance to speak. But if you think about it, the motive behind the call is to make a sale. If you aren't interested, say so right away. Otherwise the salesperson will waste your time and his by reciting the entire speech before you decline the offer.

Got a Minute?

The telephone is certainly not the only interruption faced during the course of the day. Socialization is necessary for personal comfort and happiness and plays a role in the course of the day. Interruptions from people are a tough thing to avoid, especially when you are in a managerial position. Yet, if you don't place some time restrictions, your entire day can be easily consumed by nothing more than the infamous, "Got a minute?" opening line. Because you are forced to deal with the issue face-to-face, it is easy to give up your ground. But there are always ways to dodge drawn-out interruptions without ruffling any feathers.

- Hide—yes, this sounds like silly advice, but it works. If you have a project to work on, try to find an area that is out of your traffic zone. People are more inclined to stop and chitchat if they see you. Unless they have something important to say, chances are they will walk right past you as long as you don't catch their eye. You can also subtly conceal yourself by positioning your work area behind a partially closed door. This way, you are still open to those who really need your help, but you escape the wagging tongues of those who have nothing better to do.

Leadership Tip

Dangerous Opening Lines

"I just need a second of your time."

"Are you busy?"

"Well, don't you look fabulous today!"

"Hey, how about those _____ (Fill in the blank with Red Sox, Yankees, Lakers, Penguins, Vikings, etc.)."

- Get to work earlier or stay later (depending on your most productive time of day) than your coworkers. Even if you only gain half an hour of quiet time each day, it adds up quickly.
- Stand up when someone approaches you. This will make them less inclined to sit and stay a while. Also maintain a workingman's body language. Don't relax and neither will the interloper.
- Look busy. This shouldn't be too difficult for you to do. Quite often people won't make you part of their rounds if you are visibly busy.
- Again, it is important to set time limits. Let the interrupter know right away how much time you have, if any, to spare. If it looks as though it may turn into an involved conversation, ask if you can schedule a time to sit down and talk. This is a courteous way to plan for the discussion, and it also shows that you care enough about what the other person has to say to make time to listen.
- If all else fails, place a "Do Not Disturb" or "Beware" sign outside your work area.

Schedule for Distractions

Only you know which types of interruptions will affect you the most. If you don't know, then keep a log of all interruptions that pass you in a day. Group them into categories and begin work on the biggest group first. You may be surprised to find that the technology (Palm Pilots, e-mail, etc.) that you formerly thought to be heaven sent is actually costing you more time than it is worth in the long run. If you can, try to narrow the distractions down to specific activities. This will allow you to better gauge how much time is wasted and how much could be saved with a slight change in your habits.

It is nearly impossible to get through an entire day with no interruptions. It's a good idea to allow time in your schedule for distractions. Expect them, they will occur. But you do not have to let them destroy the entire work day. By allotting time for them in your schedule, your other activities won't fall behind.

CHAPTER 8

Keeping the Peace: Resolving Conflict and Solving Problems

R esolving conflict is the eighth core concept. This will undoubtedly be extremely useful to you once you have established—or even begin to establish—your leadership abilities. Because problems can arise within any of these set concepts, you must be prepared to employ a problem-solving approach.

Every workplace, no matter how well managed, is going to have some conflict. How effectively conflicts are handled will greatly determine how productive your workplace is going to be. As a leader you want to identify conflicts as early as possible; then determine what kind of conflict is involved and its underlying causes. Actively involve the affected persons in finding solutions.

Conflict occurs on many levels between employees, managers, and across departments. If conflict is addressed effectively, it can benefit individuals and organizations by producing stronger, more resilient working relationships, improving creative output, and generating innovative solutions to problems.

Divide and Conquer

There are two types of conflict. Discerning between the two and treating them as separate breeds will allow you to "divide and conquer" the problem. The first type is unnecessary conflict. This type occurs when individuals have differing perceptions, lack of information, or hostile feelings that can appear unexpectedly, cause disagreements, and build up into full-blown conflict if signs are not noticed early enough. The second type is resolvable conflict. This will occur when two individuals' viewpoints on an issue are initially seen as opposing fixed positions but are actually based on different needs, goals, values, or interests that first need to be understood and then worked out to their mutual satisfaction.

Unnecessary Conflict

Unnecessary conflict occurs most often when an individual feels that his personal agenda is not being addressed by another individual. Unnecessary conflict can be the result of:

Words of the Wise

"The ultimate measure of a man is not where he stands in moments of comfort, but where he stands at times of challenge and controversy."

—*Dr. Martin Luther King Jr. (1929–1968), leader of the Civil Rights Movement*

- Strong negative feelings such as anxiety, stress, or anger
- Unclear communication such as misunderstandings or a lack of information
- Disagreements caused by differing perceptions and attitudes like prejudice, resistance to change, or a bias toward "the way things have always been done"

Unnecessary conflict can escalate needlessly, especially when a manager inadvertently causes the conflict or adds to it. At times, managers don't even have the control to resolve these conflicts, which can be caused by organizational constraints. Therefore they must discover ways in which they can prevent, reduce, or control such conflicts. After identifying the conflict, they must decide whether to become involved, and then determine how to conquer the situation.

Resolvable Conflict

Resolvable conflict occurs when two individuals' points of view are based on opposing needs, goals, values, or interests. An example of this type of conflict is when two employees from different departments within one organization have different views regarding the source of the problem. Each believes that the other is responsible for the problem. This type of conflict should be within a leader's control and can be resolved with a simple 10-step problem-solving approach.

10 Steps to Victory

1. Present the issue without emotion, blame, or judgment. Speak in the first person: "I see that there is an issue with . . ." then clearly convey what you know without blame to any specific person or department. Also, if you ask the employee(s) for help in solving the issue, you are less likely to face uncooperative and threatened persons.

Franklin Delano Roosevelt
(1882–1945)

Franklin Delano Roosevelt was the 32nd president of the United States (1933–1945). During his presidency, Roosevelt was responsible for leading the United States out of the Great Depression and through WWII. Roosevelt also served as both senator to and governor of the state of New York. FDR was elected to serve an unprecedented four terms in the White House and is credited with instituting the New Deal that expanded the powers of the federal government.

2. Ask for the opposing party's point of view, and listen actively so you fully understand his or her needs. Ask the other person how they see the situation and what they need to resolve it. Listen nonjudgmentally, and don't justify your position or argue against the other person(s) involved.

3. Explain your point of view clearly, and make sure the other person understands it as well. Make a strong attempt to be exact in your message; then ask the other party to review what you have said.

4. Clarify and define the issue in terms of both your needs.

5. Jointly develop an objective or condition to which you both can agree. Ask yourselves, "What result or outcome are we both looking for?" It is important to define an objective before looking for solutions.

6. Brainstorm possible alternative solutions. The goal here is to identify several possible ways to alleviate the conflict without actually evaluating each one. If you generate multiple ideas, you should find more innovative or workable solutions than the ones people typically use. If time permits, hold off choosing a solution until after this process has been completed and all alternatives have been listed and debated.

7. Select the solution that has the best chance of meeting both your needs. Now is the time to take the list of proposed solutions and evaluate them. Some of the best solutions are often the combinations of suggestions that originally seemed crazy and implausible. Write down the most viable solution that both sides would like to try. Keep in mind that revisions might need to be made later on.

8. Develop a realistic plan of action, and determine who will do what, when, where, and how. Using the written solution, plan the actions that must be taken to ensure its success. Make a schedule and give a copy to everyone involved. Schedule checkpoints to assess progress along the way. Decide how each party will know if the solution

is working and what criteria will tell you that the objective has been met.

9. Implement the plan. Implementation occurs after the problem-solving discussion. Each party must complete his or her action steps. Usually some follow-up is necessary, especially if potential obstacles had to be overcome.

10. Evaluate the success of the solution based on the joint objective. During the initial discussion, it is important that you schedule a time to meet after the solution has been implemented. Some revisions or even an alternative solution might be needed. Since those involved probably chose this conflict resolution process because they value their working relationships and want good results, it is critical that you determine its success.

The Dos and Don'ts of Conflict Resolution

DO:

- Show empathy; observe nonverbal signs that people are upset
- Confront difficult issues early on
- Be clear and continually reinforce your message
- Make eye contact
- Be open-minded and listen actively
- Try to come to a compromise
- Remain impartial
- Resist the temptation to argue
- Treat people with respect

DON'T:

- Disregard the feelings or concerns of the other party
- Contradict yourself
- Give in just to avoid further confrontation
- Be dismissive
- Settle for less than all the information
- Give unsolicited advice
- Get defensive or counterattack

Words of the Wise

"A conservative is a man with two perfectly good legs who, however, has never learned how to walk forward."

—*Franklin Delano Roosevelt, president of the U.S. from 1933–1945*

Problem-Solving Approach

Many of us naturally both prevent and resolve conflicts in everyday situations through avoiding, accommodating, and compromising behaviors. These approaches are effective in many cases; however, *problem solving* is a better approach. It is a more conscious approach that seeks input from everyone involved and often results in a creative, lasting resolution. Also called a "win/win" approach because everyone gains or wins something, this approach is often necessary so employees can maintain good working relationships.

Using this type of approach requires confronting the issues. In fact, for some, a fear of conflict is what gets in the way of resolving it. That fear can be a lack of experience, skills, or tools for resolving conflict. Managers particularly need these tools because they must resolve their own conflict with their staff, other managers, and outside clients and vendors as well as help others resolve conflicts.

Examples of Successful Conflict Resolutions

In this example, the manager (Mr. Kesi) uses the problem-solving approach to coach the younger employee (Gordon) who is dealing with a potential conflict with a higher-level senior employee. Gordon is having difficulty collecting information from the higher-level employee and is unassertive and lacking confidence in trying to resolve the conflict on his own.

Gordon (reluctantly and unassertively): For months I've been trying everything from reminders and e-mail to checklists and nagging, but I haven't been able to get the data from Mary on time. That is why my reports are late.

Mr. Kesi: Why don't you talk to Mary directly about the problem? Tell her you would like to discuss a way to make both your lives easier in gathering the data for monthly reports. Explain that you need to have the data by a certain time each month, but you find it difficult to get without pressing her, which you want to avoid. Ask her how she sees the situation, and really listen to what she says, making sure you reflect back her key points on why this is hard for her. Knowing Mary, what do you think she will say?

Gordon: That she tries but she has so many more pressing projects.

Mr. Kesi: Then tell her how you see it. What would you say then?

Gordon: That I need to get the data because the whole unit's progress and incentives are based on the information. Maybe I haven't actually talked to her about this before!

Mr. Kesi: Then you can ask if you have made it clear why it's so important to get the data, and ask if she sees the importance. Next, I would figure out how to keep both your needs in mind.

Gordon: That sounds reasonable and certainly something Mary should respond to.

Mr. Kesi: Do some brainstorming to see if you can come up with something new and creative that appeals to both of you. After you come up with some different possibilities, agree to try one, and memo it to her afterward. She reads and acts on memos faster than e-mail. You can evaluate it after the next month's report. But first get her to agree to meet one more time to see if it is working for both of you.

In this next example, the production manager (Noah) decides to approach the product marketing manager (Melanie) with a conflict that has occurred in trying to meet market demands. By bringing it up as a joint problem he would like to solve together, he hopes to foster a cooperative working relationship with a fairly new colleague.

Noah: Hi Melanie, I wanted to talk to you about last quarter's sales forecast. It seems that we, as a company,

---

Profile

Betty Friedan
(1921–)

American author and Women's Rights activist, Betty Friedan is one of contemporary society's most effective leaders. Her most famous publication is *The Feminine Mystique,* in which she challenges the idea the women can find complete fulfillment through marriage and motherhood. Betty Friedan founded the National Organization for Women (NOW) in 1966 and helped organize the National Women's Political Caucus, the International Feminist congress, the First Women's Bank, and the Women's Strike for Equality.

somehow fell short in our sales forecasting and, subsequently, our unit production run. I would like to discuss ways in which we can work together to prevent this from happening in the future. From your point of view, what happened?

Melanie: Well, Noah, the market shifted unexpectedly in favor of our product, and we wanted to take advantage of the shift. We thought we communicated that to you and that you would ramp up production to meet demand.

Noah: I'm not sure we fully understood your intentions at the time. On such short notice, it's really tough to schedule overtime and adjust to increase production. Sounds to me like you need to be able to take advantage of these marketing opportunities. I need some sort of communication system so I can provide you with the product you need.

It sounds as though we both agree that we need to take advantage of these market opportunities before they become lost sales. We also should have product ready to go under reasonable time frames so that we do not disappoint the market. Let's talk about alternative solutions that make sense to both of us.

Melanie: How about this: If we in marketing sense an increase in the market, I'll immediately call you for a meeting to prepare to ramp up and have product ready to go.

Noah: Well, Melanie, I think we need to figure out a way to differentiate between a "sense" and a sure thing with respect to the market. I would like to avoid ramping up to produce product unless I'm absolutely sure that the need is there. If we can't sell the product, it sits in inventory, which adversely affects our bottom line.

Melanie: I see your point. It would help me to understand how the production process actually works at this company so I can let you know how many unit runs you should schedule. Would you be willing to go over your production operation with me?

Noah: No problem. Let's meet next week and I'll take you on a tour of the plant. Then we can discuss the scheduling process, potential bottlenecks, and possible openings where it would be easy to fill orders within a forty-eight-hour period.

The Snowball Effect

There may be multiple smaller issues within a department or organization that alone are not huge problems but if left unaddressed may snowball into big headaches later on. Problems such as tardiness, missed deadlines, and passing the buck can become chronic and create a negative impact on the whole group. All of these issues tend to stem from other things such as a lack of motivation, lack of empowerment, or insufficient communication. Treat these smaller issues in the same way you would solve larger conflicts . . . immediately and head on. This will help prevent a snowball from triggering an avalanche.

Make It Go Away!

Many people have difficulty with confronting conflict. However, confronting a conflict or tolerating the expression and resolution of differences can be very useful. It is important in these situations to always fight fairly and ensure conditions are right for engaging in a conflict rather than reacting impulsively or emotionally.

You should always be on the lookout for underlying signs of conflict in a group. People feel safe bringing up certain issues that are, in fact, a mask for the real source of conflict. At times they aren't aware of the real source of conflict or are not sure of how to bring it up. Typical signs are chronic complaining, increased levels of stress, unnecessary competitiveness, absenteeism, failure to accomplish very much, retaliation, and undermining comments between or among team members. Address

Words of the Wise

"He [Grant] had somehow, with all his modesty, the rare faculty of controlling his superiors as well as his subordinates. He outfaced Stanton, captivated the President, and even compelled acquiescence or silence from that dread source of paralyzing power, the Congressional Committee on the Conduct of the War."

—*Joshua Lawrence Chamberlain, general in the Union Army and hero at Gettysburg*

these signs as soon as you take notice of them, and start to work on the resolution process.

Everyone involved must agree to engage in the conflict and make an effort to resolve it. If one party holds back and decides not to participate, the conflict will escalate to the point of damaging a professional relationship or causing the company some harm.

As the facilitator, you should make sure that all parties resolve the conflict by taking them through the 10 steps without explaining the steps ahead of time. As you get to each step, identify what you want each party to do, and ask clarifying questions to make sure they understand each other and agree throughout the process. This method is very effective, although it takes more time on your part; you must make sure they don't draw you into their sidetracking. They are likely to sidetrack because they haven't agreed upon a process and don't know your method for helping them.

Keep in mind, the best way to resolve conflicts is to attempt to avoid them altogether. Managers who meet regularly with their staff—individually and as a team—tend to stay abreast of conflicts and also learn more about their employees' needs. It is important to develop an active listening style that encourages two-way communication, so differences are brought to the surface easily and quickly, seen as part of the normal process of working together, and, if possible, resolved as they arise. Consistent open communication is the key to prevention.

CHAPTER 9

Coming to Grips
with Change

Accepting change, the ninth core concept, immediately follows resolving conflict. Though not all changes may occur due to conflict or problems, it is good to learn well the lessons taught in your problem-solving endeavors. The ability to accept the changes that are constantly taking place around you will help you to survive as a leader.

As change becomes the only constant in today's workplace, managing change becomes a crucial skill. Enhancing the skill requires extremely careful attention to communication, to empathy, to building trust, to being positive, and to finding creative ways for employees' input and empowerment. Today's workforce demands a clear and concise explanation of why change is happening—and it is necessary for managers to be able to articulate this.

Stage One: Understanding Change

Before discussing how leaders can help employees deal with change, it is important to establish some common ground regarding change and understand what's involved in the change process. You must first examine what exactly is changing, and then figure out how to deal with the emotional and/or psychological sense of loss of the old familiar routine. The change may involve a job, a location, job responsibilities, a team, or a manager, and it can be very significant. However, the most vital part of change is the way in which we deal with it.

Why Is Change Necessary?

The concept of staying in place or standing still in business is little more than an illusion. You're either moving forward or falling behind. It may be slow, and you may not notice it on a daily basis, but it's happening. Change is the catalyst for moving ahead. Think how boring and dull life would be without change.

What Is Causing All This Change?

The global, competitive economy is fueled by incredible changes in technology. Change is dynamic and is usually initiated by external pressures to stay competitive. It rolls downhill internally and impacts employees at all levels. Businesses that don't keep up or take the lead will surely go out of business.

Is All Change Good?

In a word, no! That's why it is so important for leaders to establish a trusting and open environment in which people can ask questions and get straight answers. The harsh light of the scrutiny of change before the process takes place often exposes incomplete thinking, poor judgment, or the need to review other options before moving ahead. This route will help avoid ill-conceived change initiatives and let people feel more of a sense of ownership of the change.

Stage Two: Becoming Aware of Change

Leaders can gain a successful change intervention by first realizing that employees have a sixth sense regarding changes about to happen. So before anything is said or passed around in a memo, they can sense it. That said, it's naive to believe that change can be hidden until it is about to happen, and the air of uncertainty and suspicion among employees leads to counterproductivity, adverse morale, fear, stress, and anxiety. The best decision leaders can make (although the gut instinct is to try to hide bad news) is to provide employees with as much detailed information about the upcoming change as possible. Be open, honest, and up front as early as you can when the need for change is recognized.

Change has always been present in business (and life), but in the past the change was much slower. We made a change, had time to adjust to it, did something the new way, and life rolled

Words of the Wise

"Cautious, careful people, always casting about to preserve their reputations . . . can never effect a reform."

—*Susan B. Anthony* *(1820–1906),* *writer and suffragist*

along. Today the pace has increased dramatically. We are literally bombarded by one change after another, with little time to adjust and catch our breath. And it is going to continue to increase, so we should devise ways to accept and welcome it rather than fight it.

Help others to feel a sense of ownership with the change. People tend to give more enthusiastic support to ideas and changes that they helped to engineer. Therefore, their help is recommended whenever possible. People don't mind change as much as they resent someone else trying to force change on them without allowing them any input.

Building Walls

Walls can be built in resistance to change. These walls will impede the progress of change and may even block it from happening at all. Most commonly, walls are built through fear, anger, and uncertainty; failure to see a need for change; feeling that all change must be negative; lukewarm acceptance of change or a wait-and-see attitude; and refusal to see the positive opportunities that may be outcomes of the change.

When change occurs, people are likely to put up all kinds of barriers, often without realizing that they are doing so. Emotion is always part of the change (both positive and negative). For example, landing a new job and being transferred to another division are both exciting prospects, but they incite very different emotions. We have to understand and allow for letting go of what is comfortable and familiar for a new situation or experience.

Failure to see the need for change may be a result of leadership's inability to explain the change and "buy into" it. The attitude that all change is negative is often a by-product of poorly handled previous initiatives. Reluctance is a very natural reaction because it signifies the loss of something familiar or comfortable. It takes time to work through this process, but it is also important to move people forward and get them involved in the new plan and working toward a more positive future.

Outright resistance should be handled aggressively. If it shows in an employee at the very outset of change, work through the process and try to get the person to see the need for modification, accept it, and move on. After all avenues have been exhausted, you must take whatever appropriate action is required to move the company in the right direction, with or without this employee. If you are not in the position to terminate an employee and you feel it may be necessary, speak to a supervisor about it as soon as possible. You don't want one bad apple to bring down the morale of the rest of the orchard.

Breaking Down Walls

If the Berlin Wall can come down, so can the walls that impede progress, growth, and change. Here are some keys that will put you on the path to successful change.

- Create an environment of openness. Okay, so you're probably sick of hearing this by now, but it is the single most important way to get employees on your side. Give people as many of the facts as possible; head off the office grapevine of gossip, which usually distorts and exaggerates the truth until it is unrecognizable. Allow people to ask questions, and give them straight answers. Employees worry when they feel their jobs or futures are on the line.
- Function as objectively as possible. Arm yourself with facts, figures, and examples that support the reason why a change is necessary and beneficial, even if it is uncomfortable.
- Be sensitive to subjectivity and emotion. We live in our own comfort zones and almost automatically reject anything that violates our zone. Remember that, above all else, change always suggests losing or giving up something that may be very important and personal to the employee. You're dealing with human emotions and always need to be sensitive to that fact.
- Encourage development of alternative perspectives. Encourage employees to find positive ways to accept change. Minimize

---

Profile

Queen Elizabeth I
(1533–1603)

Queen of England and Ireland from 1558 to 1603, Queen Elizabeth I was the first woman to successfully occupy the English throne and the longest-reigning English monarch in nearly two centuries. Queen Elizabeth I also established Protestantism in England and was noted as giving rise to the English Renaissance.

Profile

A Personal Account of the Fall of the Berlin Wall

With Berlin's population of 3 million, there were over 5 million people milling around in delirious joy celebrating the reunion of the city after twenty-one years. A newspaper wrote banner headlines: Germany is Reunited in the Streets! The East German government was collapsing. East German money was worthless. West Germany gave every East German one hundred Deutschmark, which amounted to several months wages. . . . Looking around I saw an indescribable joy in people's faces. It was the end of the government telling people what not to do, it was the end of the Wall, the War, the East, the West . . .

(continued on next page)

potential disruption. Evaluating as many options as possible is a valuable technique to open minds to the potential positive impacts of change.

- Disconnect and reestablish. It's important to allow a reasonable period of time for employees to adjust to the same old same old. We are all creatures of habit. Afterward, it is equally important to get them to focus on the new path, to begin to generate excitement and attain positive goals, and to reestablish the new comfort zone as another experience to be enjoyed and learned from as the company moves forward.

Real World Problems
Dealing with Reorganization

In this example, a manager has learned that his department is facing reorganization because of poor operating results. He is meeting with an employee from his department to share what he knows at this point. This particular employee was out sick the day the manager held a group meeting for other department members, and the manager wants to make sure the employee hears the news from him rather than from other department members.

Manager: Hi Tim, have a seat. I wanted to meet with you this morning to apprise you of the current operating situation. I believe it is important for you to have as much information as is currently available.

Tim: I heard something about an organizational shift when I came in this morning. What's happening? Are we in trouble as a company?

Manager: I understand your reaction. That's why I wanted to talk with you in private. It's public knowledge that our company results haven't met with our forecast for either revenues

or profits. While no definite decisions have been made, we're considering a company reorganization. That is why it's important for you to have all the facts, and I wanted to make sure that you heard them from me first.

Tim: What is going to happen?

Manager: Well, there are several things that we can do to prepare ourselves. One, we have to accept the fact that change is inevitable. My guess is that we will lose one, maybe two positions. While some situations are beyond our control, we at least can help the company by developing suggestions and ideas on ways to reduce costs and improve productivity. Let's brainstorm on how we can help the company through this transition.

Tim: What if we can't come up with anything constructive?

Manager: We have to be prepared for the reality; however, let's focus all our positive energies on creating alternative approaches. We may find some answers that will surprise us.

Here we see the manager acting proactively, addressing expected reorganizational change (and possibly job loss) prior to it actually happening. By doing this, he provides direct channels of accurate information, which helps derail the grapevine rumors. While he can't give an assurance of continued employment, he uses the situation to solicit ideas and suggestions for ways to solve the problem, and to help the employee consider his options and take charge of his own future. He helps the employee prepare for uncertainty by examining strengths, developing possible career options, and keeping a positive focus during the session.

Dealing with a Transfer to a New Department

In this next example, a project manager has to inform another employee that she is being shifted to another department because

---

Profile

A Personal Account of the Fall of the Berlin Wall

(continued from previous page)

Near me, a knot of people cheered as the mayors of East Berlin and West Berlin met and shook hands. . . . All people became brothers. On top of every building were thousands of people. Berlin was out of control. There was no more government, neither in East nor in West. The police and the army were helpless. The soldiers themselves were overwhelmed by the event. They were part of the crowd. Their uniforms meant nothing. The Wall was down.

Reprinted with permission. ©1989 Andreas Ramos

Abraham Lincoln
(1809–1865)

Sixteenth president of the United States (1861–1865) and a model for leadership, Abraham Lincoln overcame nearly insurmountable odds to become one of the greatest leaders in the nation's history. Through his leadership skills alone, he managed to preserve the Union, emancipate all slaves, and resolve one of the nation's greatest conflicts. All this was accomplished without the benefit of any formal education.

that department requires her writing and phone skills. This employee does not want to make the transfer.

Manager: Hi Joanne, come on in. I wanted to talk to you today about a change in your responsibilities. This just came up yesterday, and I wanted to let you know immediately.

Joanne: Okay, what's up?

Manager: I met with Tom Crowley in Public Relations this morning regarding the business needs in his department. Based on some specific skill sets required and the need for the best possible person to fill that position, I've selected you for the transfer.

Joanne: But Ed, I love my job, and I feel that I make a positive contribution to the company as a whole by working in this department.

Manager: I totally agree with you. It's because of your excellent achievement record that I selected you for this transfer.

Joanne: I hate PR! I have no interest in that department or in working for Tom Crowley.

Manager: I understand your feelings. I might feel the same way in your situation. However, as a manager, I have to balance the responsibility to the company with my responsibility to my employees.

Joanne: Well, it seems like the company wins out in this case.

Manager: Joanne, let's look at some of the positives that can come out of additional job responsibilities. Tell me: what do you see as some of the positives?

Joanne: Well, you know I am a solid writer with great phone skills. Customers love talking to me!

Manager: That's great! This opportunity might bring you closer to our customers while giving you the chance to focus on the skills you are really good at. Joanne, I want you to understand that if I didn't believe this could be a valuable career experience for you, I would not be recommending and supporting this transfer.

This situation was particularly challenging because the manager was losing a good employee to another department at the request of the vice president. It would have been easy to simply blame the vice president, but instead the manager accepted his responsibility both to the company and to the employee. He used active listening skills and empathy to support Joanne. He was firm in what he had to do but encouraged her to vent her negative reaction, listened openly and attentively, then refocused her into examining the positive opportunities for her personal growth and development.

Dealing with New Customer Service Protocol

In this last situation, a manager discusses changes in handling customer service calls with an employee who is used to helping one set of customers by himself. All calls to customer service will now be handled by an automated voice response system, and account information will be shared by several representatives. The manager must see to it that this employee successfully transitions into working on a broader range of accounts and shares information with other representatives.

Manager: Joseph, upper management has decided to implement a new system for handling customer service calls. Starting on Monday, we will use a voice response system to manage customer calls, and we will shift from having individual customer service reps handle twenty-five accounts each to a team-based approach where each rep will work on more than a thousand accounts with other representatives.

Joseph: What? I don't understand. I thought our customer service record was one of the best in the industry. Why the sudden change?

Leadership Tip

Watch Out for the Internal Grapevine

Never underestimate the power of the internal grapevine. News of impending change travels fast, and while its essence is often in the ballpark, the accuracy can be questionable. Employees' trust and confidence in you will be stronger when they hear about change from you rather than through the rumor mill.

Manager: Customers have complained that they don't appreciate busy signals or being on hold. With this new system, customers will be routed to the next available representative for faster response. You seem distressed by this news. Do you have concerns about the new approach?

Joseph: Yes, I do. I'm used to giving high-quality, personalized service to my customers, and now I am being asked to share my customers and their problems with other representatives.

Manager: I understand. Let's talk about this some more to see if there is a solution that will help you adapt to this new way of handling customer calls. One of the immediate benefits that I see for you is that you no longer need to be working in a vacuum, but rather you will have the opportunity to share information and learn from your fellow reps. Can you think of some other benefits?

Joseph: I suppose that by pooling our notes and comments on each customer, we could develop more effective customer profiles for upper management. But who takes charge of putting that together?

Manager: Change represents opportunity, Joseph. If you and your fellow customer service reps can agree on effective reporting techniques, I see no reason why you can't assume responsibility for delivering those reports. Do you have other concerns?

Joseph: I am used to giving a high level of individual attention to our customers. How will my performance be measured as a result of this change to a team-based approach?

Manager: That has not been finalized as yet, but I assure you that every representative will know where he stands with respect to job performance.

This time the manager has a difficult task. He has to convince Joseph that the change in operations will have an overall benefit for

the company. Joseph is naturally shocked and dismayed to learn of the change, and the manager quickly reacts by encouraging the employee to put his concerns on the table. The manager continues by encouraging the employee to offer suggestions on how the company might benefit from this new approach to customer service. Joseph is still concerned about how his performance will be measured in light of the new service, and the manager responds with a firm, honest, yet noncommittal answer.

Stage Three: Accepting Change

Remember that since you have been privy to the change before the other employees, you have had time to develop acceptance and direction. The others will need the same time to understand, accept, and adjust. Be patient with them, within a reasonable period of time. Change involves disregarding old habits and developing new ones.

There are ways to help the process of change to be accepted. Very often your attitude, motivation, and behavior toward change are vital in setting the tone for others. If people understand that you also share their unknowns but approach them in a positive and trusting manner, they will find it easier to follow your way. No one wants to feel alone when a change that will alter his or her professional existence is about to take place. By showing empathy and support, you will help your employees understand why change is taking place and start building support for your change efforts.

During the time period in which the change is taking place be vigilant. Look for signs of negative, destructive, or out–of–character behavior such as arguments, tardiness, low energy levels, and a casual attitude toward the quality and quantity of work produced. This is also a time to be aware of employee defections to other companies, especially competitors.

If you notice any of these red flags, speak privately with the employee and let her know what you are seeing and that you are available if she wants to talk. Often just knowing someone cares and is available to talk with is helpful to an employee. If the

Words of the Wise

"The art of progress is to preserve order amid change and to preserve change amid order."

—*Alfred North Whitehead (1861–1947), English philosopher*

situation is more severe, refer the employee to an employee assistance program or suggest that she speak with someone outside of work about the current situation. Depending on the type and amount of change, professional help may also be required.

You want to help employees to help themselves deal with change. So, it is helpful to remember that we are all "self-fulfilling prophecies." The things we say to ourselves in the privacy of our own minds, our "self-talk," largely govern our success in life. By making sure that our self-talk is a positive, supportive, I-can-do-it type of language, we dramatically increase our potential for success with change and enjoy our lives more at the same time.

In almost every situation, resistance is easier to deal with as opposed to apathy, mainly because it is out in the open and can be addressed. Even though it is not what you want, resistance shows that the employees at least care enough to take a stand. Apathy is more difficult to deal with because although you can see it, you have a harder time attributing it to change.

Communicate with your employees on a regular basis. Hold weekly meetings to keep employees updated as to the nature of all ongoing changes at the company. Any change, no matter how big or small, is bound to affect at least one or more of the people in your department, and you should have a regular forum to discuss these changes and encourage your employees to share their ideas and suggestions.

Leadership Tip

Emotional Response

In almost every instance, employee resistance is easier to deal with than apathy. Resistance is out in the open and can be addressed.

CHAPTER 10

The Classified Information on Hiring

Words of the Wise

"The best leader is the one who has the sense to surround himself with outstanding people and the self-restraint not to meddle with how they do their jobs."

—*Unknown*

iring the right person for the job, the tenth core concept, will call on your achievements with the previous concepts. The hiring process will call for a strategic plan of action that only a leader with a successful track record in communication, time management, and problem solving will be able to develop.

The future growth and development of any department or company starts from the inside. The best way to make your group or company better is to hire the best possible people from the get-go! It sounds a lot easier than it is in actuality. Hiring the right people requires a strategy, planning, and a good amount of time—but in the long run, the extra work to hire great people will likely be one of the very best uses of your time. Remember, people are your human assets, as important, if not more important than, the financial assets you have in the bank and in inventory.

The caliber of people who work for your company will arguably have more impact on the success of the company than any other factor. Hiring qualified and enthusiastic people who share your vision and your passion is the ultimate objective. As in all endeavors, you should have a plan or strategy for conducting your hiring. The idea is to spend minimal time screening out the less enticing candidates and maximum time comparing the more subtle differences between the strongest candidates.

Assess Your Needs and Start Recruiting

Before you do anything else, figure out what needs are to be filled. Think about all the responsibilities that the new hire will handle and decide what skills the person will need in order to be successful in the position. Next, draw up a job description so that both sides will be clear about the job and day-to-day responsibilities.

Armed with the newly created job description, you are ready to start casting the nets for candidates. Here are some ways to attract star candidates.

- **Newspapers:** This is perhaps the most common and traditional method of recruitment. Major metropolitan newspapers have wide readerships, and even a small ad can be fairly inexpensive yet yield numerous applicants.
- **Online:** More and more often job postings are springing up on electronic job banks like Monster.com. Often companies can place ads online for free. These types of ads are particularly effective for filling technical and career-oriented professional positions.
- **Trade Publications:** In some industries you may want to try a trade journal (publishers often use *Publishers Weekly*) that targets your industry or a specific niche in that industry.
- **Professional Groups:** Try sending a one-page job description to all professional groups and associations you belong to that publish newsletters or regularly post openings either online or at the association's headquarters.
- **Networking:** Use the phone to network among colleagues in the industry and your peers in competing organizations; ask them for ideas to use when locating candidates for your openings.
- **Career Fairs:** Check out the schedule for career fairs at local colleges and universities. Companies can reserve space at fairs and provide interested students with corporate literature. At the same time, students can ask questions and submit resumes. This is a good way to increase the size of your applicant pool for both full-time and internship positions.

Words of the Wise

"Whenever you are asked if you can do a job, tell 'em, 'Certainly, I can!' Then get busy and find out how to do it."

—*Theodore Roosevelt, president of the U.S. from 1901–1909*

You will now need to make some firm decisions about your hiring strategy. The following is a sample outline of a recruiting, interviewing, and hiring strategy for a fictitious company we'll call Imagine Nation.

Imagine Nation has a number of locations and has been experiencing significant growth over the last few years. Corporate expansion has created a demand for additional workers. The mission of the company promotes high levels of customer service and employee involvement.

Imagine Nation does not have a formal human resources department, so the CEO created a task force to help develop a strategy for recruiting new employees. By creating a structured, clearly defined process, they will have a greater incidence of continued success. The following represents an outline of the plan that the task force wants to institute. You may want to adapt a similar plan that is targeted to meet the specific needs of your organization.

Sorting Those Resumes

Every organization receives unsolicited resumes. When a help-wanted ad is placed, the number increases dramatically. It doesn't make sense to have the supervising manager read through all the resumes to do the initial screening. A trained clerical administrator can do this very well if he is given the right tools. Using specific criteria designed for the open position, the clerical administrator will be able to screen resumes for qualified candidates. In the case of Imagine Nation, the clerical administrator is looking for candidates with:

- Five or more years' experience in the advertising industry
- Proficiency in graphic design programs including Quark and Photoshop
- Experience working with a diverse group of retailers
- Job responsibilities that are comparable to the position in question
- Salary level within 20 percent of the posted job range, higher or lower

Based on the training given to this clerical administrator, they will be able to review hundreds of resumes and conduct initial screenings to capture those candidates who have the basic requirements for the position.

In many cases companies are swamped with more resumes than any one person can be expected to handle all at once. When this occurs, it is a good idea to conduct the initial screening as previously mentioned, and then send the following letter to candidates you plan to interview. This letter will explain that you would prefer to conduct a telephone interview first, to be sure it is worth both parties' time to have a formal interview.

Recruiting Project Plan of Action

PART I: Implementation Support Services
A. Installation of 1-800 number
 1. Compose script: When candidates call, a scripted interview is conducted on the telephone by a trained clerical person.
 2. Compose telephone screening questions.

B. Send letter to local colleges and universities, et cetera, to reach as many free sources of potential labor as possible.
 1. Create marketing packages for each location.
 2. Follow up on mailed information. A representative from the company will visit various schools to begin developing an ongoing relationship that will generate more candidates in the future.
 3. Identify a contact person. This information will later be entered into a database.

C. Recruiting print advertising. An ad or series of ads will be developed to advertise for the positions needed.
D. Resume response letter. Every resume submitted to Imagine Nation will receive a reply. The reply creates a positive image for the company.
E. Overview of strategy to managers. All management personnel are kept informed of the recruiting process in an ongoing manner.

PART II: Telephone Screening of Candidates
Once all resumes have been screened, selected candidates are first interviewed by telephone.

PART III: Interview of Selected Candidates
A. Interview packet created for on-site interviews. Each candidate will receive a package explaining how the interview will be conducted and other information about the company.
 1. Welcome to Imagine Nation. This is a letter from the owner or CEO of Imagine Nation.

(continued on next page)

Recruiting Project Plan of Action

(continued from previous page)

2. Contents of package: The package contains everything the candidate needs to know about the company and the interview process.
   a) Application
   b) Information about the company and positions
   c) Summary of generic benefits
   d) How the interview process will be conducted

B. Appropriate candidates are directed to designated manager for on-site interview.
   1. Compose structured interview questions for recruiter. Each manager is given specific questions to be used during the interview to ensure that all candidates are treated fairly and can be evaluated based on similar circumstances.
   2. Appropriate job description presented in interview for review.

C. Senior managers interview candidates following manager interviews. At least two people will interview each potential candidate for a position to ensure the best possible decision has been made.

D. References are checked. The candidate who is selected to be hired will have references checked prior to the offer being made. The intent of the reference check is to determine if the candidate was truthful and to obtain any other information. Due to legal constraints it is difficult to obtain accurate information about employees.

PART IV: Selected Candidates Hired and Oriented
A. Manager makes final determination. The manager for whom the candidate will work makes the final determination about the hiring.
B. Manager makes hiring offer to candidate. The supervising manager is the one who makes the actual offer.
C. Manager completes all paperwork to hire new employee. The supervising manager is responsible for all paperwork to enroll a new employee in the system.
D. Manager orients new hires to company and operations. Depending on number of new hires, group orientations may be planned.
E. Managers orient, train, and monitor performance and skill level while continually motivating and evaluating employees. The supervising manager maintains a high level of interaction with the new employee.

January 15, 2001

Karen Halsey
29 Ferncroft Drive
Milton, Vermont 05468

Dear Ms. Halsey:

Thank you for your interest in Imagine Nation. We are always interested in meeting qualified candidates who share our philosophy and mission.

We want you to know that we have received your resume and we will contact you during the next few weeks. Due to the large number of resumes we have received, our first contact will be to schedule a brief telephone interview between you and Mr. Buddy Recruiter, Creative Talent Coordinator.

Please be assured that Buddy will be in touch with you and there is no need for you to call our offices. I hope we have the opportunity to meet in the very near future.

Sincerely,

Hope Springs

Hope Springs
Media Manager

The Interview Process

Okay, now comes the fun part. You have been charged with the task of hiring the best possible person for the job. Your ability to select someone who fits the position well will have a dramatic effect on the department and the company as a whole. Do not take your responsibility lightly, but don't take it too seriously, either. When you are skilled in the process and technique of interviewing candidates, you will begin to notice a higher incidence of successful candidates. This is something you can learn to do, and do well.

The Atmosphere

An interview is a very traumatic time for the candidate, and it can be a stressful time for the interviewer, especially if proper planning for the interview has not been done. Please don't interview a candidate unless all the following are in place and you are comfortable with the situation.

1. Pick an appropriate site for the interview.
2. Do not allow any interruptions to occur during the interview.
3. Pick *your* best time, not the best time for the candidate.
4. Read over the cover letter and resume carefully prior to the interview, but not as the candidate is waiting for you.
5. Allow enough time to give a proper interview.
6. Use a seating arrangement that makes the candidate feel comfortable and not like he is at an interrogation.
7. Smile sincerely.
8. Take a few moments to build rapport and assess the nervousness of the candidate.
9. Don't rely on the resume sitting in front of you.
10. Take notes during the interview.
11. Tell the candidate how the interview process will proceed. Let the person know what to expect and how it all fits together.
12. Let the candidate do the talking. Listen and ask questions to collect the information you need.
13. Present your company in an honest and direct fashion to ensure that the candidate obtains an accurate picture of the company.

For the interview to achieve the objective of selecting a qualified candidate and ultimately the best-qualified candidate, you must have a plan of action that will keep you in control of the situation.

One Step at a Time

All interviews can be broken down into four basic parts. Let's go through each part one at a time.

Part I: The Opening

Here is your chance to calm the nervous candidate and create an initial rapport. Introduce yourself. Offer the candidate a beverage (usually water, coffee, or soda). If the candidate has traveled a long distance to meet you, it is also nice to offer her a few minutes to freshen up. Continue to set the tone with small talk that is safe (i.e., weather, driving conditions, etc.).

Part II: Describe the Interview Structure

By giving the candidate a better idea of what he can expect over the next hour or so, you allow him to relax a little more. This stage also shows that you are setting the tone and pace of the meeting. In other words, you are showing the candidate that the interview is under your control.

- You will ask the questions.
- You will describe the position and the company.
- You will review the job description and go over every task carefully.
- You will answer any questions the candidate may have.
- You will take notes.

Part III: The Body

It is during this part of the interview that you put your research skills to use by asking questions, listening, and taking notes. Begin with a request for a brief "oral resume." Try "Tell me a little bit

---

Profile

Aretha Franklin
(1942–)

Also known as the Queen of Soul, Franklin began her singing career in her father's choir when she was 14. Strongly influenced by visiting gospel singers, she was singing professionally and recording by the time she was 18. Among her many awards are two lifetime achievement awards, one from the Kennedy Center Honors, the other a Grammy Lifetime Achievement Award.

about yourself." Once the candidate has given you some information on her background, you can lead with a very well structured probing question about job-related situations. Continue with other relevant questions. Next, highlight all the positive aspects of your company; remember to be direct and honest. Then answer any questions the candidate may have at that point.

The most important parts of the interview involve the questions you ask and the interaction between you and the candidate. There are a variety of different kinds of questions you can ask (see samples later in the chapter); your objective is to ask a mixture of questions that elicits a broad range of information from the candidate.

When conducting an interview, there are three basic kinds of interview question categories that will generate the greatest decision-making information.

> **Self-evaluations:** These are questions that allow candidates to make comments about themselves. However, the answers are not very reliable, since you have no way to measure accuracy.
>
> **Experiences and activities:** These are questions that let candidates tell you what they have done. Here they can tell you anything they think you want to hear; you don't have any way to verify until you check references.
>
> **Behavior descriptions:** These questions tell you how the person has behaved in previous situations. These questions offer some insight into the way a person thinks and what drives the person to accomplish specific tasks.

To really make an interview effective, you must be skilled in the process of asking the right questions. All questions are either open or closed. Open-ended questions encourage wide-open conversation and allow the person to say whatever he considers to be appropriate to the question. You get to listen to lots of previously unspoken information when you ask an open-ended question.

Closed-ended questions encourage specific answers with simple yes or no responses. These questions do not allow the person to do a lot of talking. You, the interviewer, can take back a conversation if the candidate is talking too much.

As you consider the information garnered from the interview, remember that the best predictor of future behavior is past behavior in similar circumstances. Behavior is what a person says and does. It has a beginning and an end. It can also be measured, evaluated, and modified. Attitude is what a person believes and thinks. It reflects perceptions, what is in the head and heart. They cannot be seen, cannot be evaluated, and are very difficult to change.

Part IV: The Closing

Now is the time when you clarify all issues presented and you inform the candidate about how the follow-up process will be handled. You should maintain the rapport you have developed right through to the conclusion of the interview. Clearly explain the next steps that will be taken in the hiring process. Explain the role the manager and senior manager may play and the time frame in which a decision will be made. Be sure you are able to follow through on promises made to the candidate, even if the person is not selected for a position. Even people not hired can serve as ambassadors of goodwill if they are given a high-quality interview experience. Following is a sample letter that you may want to adapt to suit your own needs.

January 20, 2001

Karen Halsey
29 Ferncroft Drive
Milton, Vermont 05468

Dear Ms. Halsey:

Thank you for taking the time to meet with me regarding employment opportunities at Imagine Nation.

Although your experiences and skills as discussed in the interview are interesting, they do not match our present needs. Our recruiting and interviewing strategy is directed toward ensuring the individuals we hire are the most suitable candidates for the available positions.

We thank you for your interest in Imagine Nation and wish you well in your search for a suitable and challenging career opportunity.

Sincerely,

Hope Springs

Hope Springs
Media Manager

Sample Interview Questions

Probing Questions

Try to form most of your questions into three-part probing questions, using adjectives such as best/worst, hardest/easiest, or longest/shortest and time references such as first/last or most recent/next. Here are some sample questions to illustrate the way an effective probing question can be constructed. These questions are constructed to address a defined need or a skill or ability the candidate must demonstrate to be successful in the position.

Communication

Tell me about a time when all your skills as a communicator failed you. What were the circumstances? How did you feel following this experience?

Culture

Tell me about the most horrible environment you have ever worked in. What did you do to deal with the situation? How did the situation end?

Experience

Tell me specifically about the store volume you were responsible for in your previous positions. Who assisted you with the management of this volume? Describe the margins you achieved.

Tell me about a company you have worked for that had the most favorable company culture. What made it the best? How did this culture impact you in your job?

Hands-On Operator

In your present position, tell me about a typical week and how you plan the time you spend doing various functions of your job. How would you like to change this? What obstacles stand in your way?

Profile

Walt Disney
(1901–1966)

Walt Disney was a pioneer in the field of animated cartoons and films. Through the establishment of the Disney Studio, Disney created some of the world's most beloved characters—foremost among them Mickey Mouse. Walt Disney and his partner Ub Iwerks were responsible for the creation of the first animated film to incorporate sound (*Steamboat Willie*, 1928) as well as the first feature-length animated film (*Snow White*, 1937). Walt Disney had the dream and vision for the creation of an enormous amusement park in Los Angeles. Walt Disneyland was opened in 1955 and Walt Disney World in Orlando, Florida, followed in 1971. Today, these two theme parks combined welcome billions of visitors each year.

Leadership Tip

What Not to Ask: Illegal Questions

1. Are you married?
2. Do you have children?
3. How old are you?
4. Did you graduate from high school or college?
5. Have you ever been arrested?
6. How much do you weigh?
7. What country are you from?
8. Are you a U.S. citizen?
9. What is your native language?
10. Are you handicapped?

Interpersonal Skills

Describe the worst employee you have ever managed or supervised. What was the problem with this employee? How did you deal with it? What was the final resolution?

Tell me about the first time you were ever involved with a legal issue involving an employee at work. What were the circumstances? How did you feel following this experience?

Recruiting

Tell me how you recruited and hired staff at your former job. What was your role in the process? How well did the process work?

Training

Tell me about the last time you developed a learning or training plan for an employee. What was the training need? How did you create and implement the program for the person? What were the results of your efforts? Who was the most difficult person you have ever had to train? What were you trying to teach that person? How did the whole process end up? How successful was the training?

Self-Evaluating Questions

What is your greatest strength and your weakness?

What trait or characteristic offers you the greatest opportunity for improvement?

What motivates you the most?

What would you do if you were hired to be the manager of this company beginning next week?

How resourceful are you?

Tell me something about yourself that I wouldn't know by reading your resume.

How good are your writing abilities?

Did your clients at your last job enjoy working with you?

Why are you the best candidate for this position?

Prove to me that your interest is sincere.

Questions about Experience and Activities

Describe each of the jobs you have had in the past.

Please give me a summary of what is listed on your resume.

Which part of your job do you like the most? Why?

Which part of the job do you dislike the most? Why?

What would you change about the way your present company is run?

What new skills do you bring to the job that other candidates are not likely to offer?

What are your key skills?

How is your experience relevant to this job?

How do you explain your job successes?

Tell me about a good process that you managed to make better.

Tell me about a major achievement.

Questions about Behavior

Tell me about the last time you had a difficult customer service situation. What did you do? What were the final results?

When was the first time you ever had to confront an employee you supervised due to a major violation of company policy? What did you do? How did the person respond? What was the final outcome?

What was the greatest disappointment you ever had? What did you do about the situation? How has this decision affected your life today?

Make 'Em an Offer They Can't Refuse

Once a decision is made based on the interview, reference checks, and conversations among the people who interviewed the candidate, an offer is made. Whenever possible, make the offer in person at a follow-up meeting. If that is not possible, call the candidate and make the offer.

In either case, be sure to send a letter confirming the offer so that there is no misunderstanding. The offer letter should clearly explain that this is not a contract, nor does it represent any agreement beyond identifying the salary and benefits for the position. Most companies have a standard offer letter that they send to all new employees.

Words of the Wise

"Walt was our father figure. We both respected and feared him. He ran the studio as a sort of benevolent and paternal dictatorship . . . but we all knew he was a genius . . ."

—*Ward Kimbell,
Disney animator*

What If They Decline?

If you offer the position to someone, prepare yourself for the possibility that they may say thanks, but no thanks. Now, you need to offer the position to someone else. It is good business practice to never tell candidates they do not have the position until you are sure you have hired the person you want. In the event that your first choice turns you down, you can still call the second choice and offer the position to that person. If you don't have a second candidate due to a small applicant pool, then you will need to begin the process all over again. It will be beneficial to know why the first person decided against taking the position. You can learn a great deal by simply asking questions and listening.

Employee Orientation

You have only one chance to make a good first impression. When a new employee accepts an employment offer from your company, the real work begins. To maximize all the time and effort you have put into the process so far, you must begin this new relationship in the best possible manner. Keep this objective in clear view as you design your orientation program for new employees.

New employees may bombard you with a laundry list of questions such as:

- Who is my boss or supervisor?
- Are we allowed to take coffee breaks?
- How should I dress?
- Can I eat lunch at my desk? When can I take lunch?
- Who are our biggest clients?
- Where are the restrooms?
- Do I need a parking sticker for the parking lot?
- Are we allowed to make personal phone calls?

These individuals may have a difficult time getting down to work because there are so many distractions as they attempt to

acquire the missing information. By anticipating as many questions as possible and incorporating these questions into the content of the new employee orientation, you will help your new employees become assimilated faster and more easily.

Have a Plan

Develop a detail-specific plan for orienting employees. First, come up with a welcome letter defining what will happen on the first day of work. Include the following: time and place to meet, name and title of person to meet, description of materials the new employee should bring, schedule for the day, basic paperwork (payroll, benefits, etc.), company policies, information about time off, departmental procedures, company culture description, job description, and anything else you think is important.

As you design your orientation, try to include as many different people as possible in the process. Let the new employee learn about the company through existing employees. Be sure that one person, generally someone with authority, is the coordinator for the orientation. You do not want the process disrupted because an existing staff member decides he has more important things to deal with.

To make this orientation a positive experience, the new employee must feel that she is considered a valuable member of the organization.

Don't keep this person waiting. Be prompt and set a good example. When you are working with this individual, let all calls go through to voice mail. A new employee on the receiving end of this behavior will immediately recognize that you are validating her as an individual. Invariably the new employee will replicate this behavior with others when they interact.

People want to fit in; it's only natural. People want to be accepted into a new organization. As you plan an orientation, don't skimp on time. Do this orientation properly the first time and productivity will increase rapidly and the incidence of employee turnover will reduce dramatically.

Profile

Samuel Walton
(1918–1992)

Samuel Walton was the founder of Wal-Mart Stores, Inc. Against the advice of others, Samuel Walton decided to operate his stores in small-town areas, offering brand-name goods at discount prices. He opened his first store in Rogers, Arkansas, in 1962. Soon, a prospering discount-store chain was created. With little competition from retail chains, Walton's stores flourished in these small towns. Now Wal-Mart is the largest retailer in the United States.

CHAPTER 11

Evaluating Employees

Once your leadership duties have taken you beyond the hiring process, you will need to incorporate the eleventh core concept, evaluating employees. You may have found the perfect employee during the hiring process, but your interest in that employee does not stop there. A good leader will need to continue to assess the employee's work and skill level.

To make employee evaluations work and have value, you've got to have a true two-way dialogue—not just a chance for the employee to offer a rebuttal at the end of your summation of his shortcomings! You've got to hear his perceptions about his performance—and you've got to address his perceptions during the review. You also need to work with the employee in developing goals and objectives for future reviews.

Each employee is unique and that fact should not be overlooked. Jane most likely got her job because of her unique and creative out-of-the-box thinking style, and Zack got his job because he loves to crunch numbers. You want to make the most of each person's talents and individual skills. Accept the fact that each person needs to be handled with a different approach. Some need more instruction and need to be more closely monitored, while others will need to be held back from their overzealous attempts to reinvent the department. Neither of these employees is "bad" . . . each just needs different guidelines. Keep this in mind when you are evaluating.

What's the Point of Formal Evaluations?

Individuals both want and need clear statements of goals. This is the idea behind employee evaluations. You need to develop a well-thought-out evaluation system or people will begin to judge others inappropriately. Other important reasons for formal evaluations:

- To review compensation issues
- To make sure both employer and employee are happy in the working relationship
- To make improvements or changes in the job or workplace

- To ensure that each side understands what is expected and how performance matches up with expectations
- To identify weaknesses and strengths
- To identify poor performers and make the decision to terminate or demote as appropriate

Performance Evaluation Objectives

A performance evaluation can be one of the most positive and proactive tools a manager has to communicate with employees. Yet, most managers dread conducting reviews, and most employees fear receiving them. A major reason for these feelings is that many managers don't know how to give good reviews. As a manager, remember that evaluations are the times to provide feedback, direction, and leadership to your employees. Use these times wisely, and you'll reap the benefits a hundredfold.

When preparing for and conducting the actual review, keep in mind that your role is to guide the employee. You must not only encourage and support but also educate in the areas that need improvement. At the same time, you must ensure that she feels positive about her efforts and understands what must be done in the future. The employee should walk away from the review with a good feeling about her accomplishments and an understanding about what still must be done and how to go about doing it.

Giving a good review is easy if you prepare for it throughout the year and put forth the effort to make it a positive experience. This section will introduce the steps needed to prepare for and conduct a review and present both a positive and a negative approach to conducting a performance review.

Preparing for the Process

Performance evaluations can be positive experiences for both managers and employees if they are conducted properly. During the

---

Profile

Sir Winston Churchill (1874–1965)

Former prime minister of Great Britain (1940–1945, 1951–1955), Winston Churchill served as an author, orator, and statesman throughout his life. Although much of Churchill's political career was filled with strife, his leadership of Great Britain during World War II forever revered him to the Western world. Through his oratory skills, Churchill managed to rally the English people to persevere against continuous German air raids. Churchill also pressured President Franklin Roosevelt for American support and protected his nation by insisting that the defeat of Germany must take precedence over the battle with Japan. During his lifetime, Winston Churchill was awarded both the Nobel Prize for Literature and the Order of the Garter (the highest British civil and military honor). In April 1963, he was declared an honorary American citizen by an Act of Congress.

review, the manager should work with the employee to provide constructive feedback, analyze strengths and weaknesses, and set goals for the coming year. If the review is objective and constructive, the employee will gain insight as to how his performance contributes to the company's mission, what the manager's expectations are, and what are the areas in which he excels and/or needs improvement.

- **Review the Job Description**

  Since the purpose of a good performance review is for the manager to objectively evaluate an employee's ability to perform a specific job, managers must remember that the best evaluations focus on issues that are relevant to the job and not personal factors such as length of service or personal biases. The evaluator must also avoid the "halo effect" (in other words, giving a favorable rating for the year based on performance during the previous month or so).

  To ensure complete objectivity, managers must first have an understanding of the employee's job. A good way to gain this understanding is to review the job description with the employee before the evaluation. The manager can learn what the employee has actually been doing, what she likes or dislikes about the job, and what she wants to do in the future. This is also a good time to work with the employee to revise and update the job description to reflect current duties and responsibilities.

- **Review Previous Documentation**

  The second step in preparing for proper appraisal is the gathering of information such as the prior year's appraisal, reports, letters of commendation, or complaints and warnings. Review previous evaluations to search for any dramatic changes in performance as well as to determine whether goals were achieved. Properly set goals should have had measurable criteria set with them, making it easy to determine if the goals have been fully, partially, or not achieved.

- **Gather Support Materials**

  Review notes kept during the year to look for concrete examples that support statements you will make in the review (especially critical ones). Employees appreciate examples, particularly when you have critical comments.

  Of course, these types of comments should be discussed as they occur with the employee rather than after the fact.

- **Be Concise but Precise**

  When you actually sit down to write the evaluation, limit comments on specific items or objectives to one or two short paragraphs, but be sure to use the examples you have gathered.

- **Involve the Employee**

  To get the employee involved in the evaluation process, ask him to do a self-appraisal, using the same form you will use. This helps keep communication lines open and gives you valuable insight as to how the employee perceives himself. If the perception is very different from yours, you have not been a successful communicator with the employee. Obviously, the areas of greatest difference are the ones you should focus on during the appraisal interview. Also, for more employee involvement, ask the employee to be prepared to answer questions like:

  - What do you feel your major accomplishments have been during the year?
  - What do you feel you could have done better?
  - What could I have done to make your job easier?
  - What things would you like to see changed in your job?

- **Set Goals and Objectives**

  Once the current year's employment is evaluated, you should begin to set goals and objectives for the next year. It is vital that you have a clear idea of what needs to be accomplished by your department before you can help

employees set individual goals. You must also be able to communicate your needs and the department's needs so that the employee can see where his responsibilities fit into the big picture.

Performance objectives and goals represent the results you would like the employee to accomplish within a specific time frame. Objectives should be easy to understand and measure; they should be challenging but also within the employee's realm of achievement. Objectives generally fall into four categories:

- Innovations are new results that the employee will attempt to create as part of her job. For example, she might take on a new job function or responsibility for a specific program, such as opening a new sales territory.
- Solutions involve situations that require objective analysis to solve a problem, such as getting an item from manufacturing to the customer more efficiently and with less cost.
- Routines are improvements in the existing job standards, such as increased turnaround time on purchase orders.
- Learning opportunities are objectives that give employees the chance to grow in their careers, increase their responsibilities, or learn new tasks. For instance, an employee might learn desktop publishing so that marketing materials can take on a more polished and professional look.

You may even want to determine more specific goals or skill levels that need to be reached at a designated time and go from there. Many companies have a 30-, 60-, or 90-day trial period. During this time, if either the employee or employer feels that the situation is not working out, the employee can leave with no hard feelings or future ramifications (hopefully).

As a manager and a leader it is your job to work with the employee to decide what will be achieved each year and to ensure that the employee phrases each goal as clearly as possible. After the goals have been decided on, take the following steps:

- Agree on the ways the employee will reach the set goals.
- Agree on the method to measure the achievement of goals.
- If appropriate, agree on a budget.
- Agree on benchmarks throughout the year to monitor progress toward achieving the goals.

- **Deliver the News**
  At this point in the review process, communicate to the employee where he stands with respect to the prior year's performance. Was performance average, above average, superior, or weak? Depending on what measuring tools your company uses, it's critical that the employee knows not only his strengths and weaknesses, but also how you feel he has performed. Before you "deliver the news," the employee should have, at the very least, a sense of the scope of his contributions to the company's success.

  Delivering the news also means bringing up dreaded salary discussions. This is often a sensitive and delicate area for managers who are not tied to a strict grade-level performance pay scale. Annual salary increases usually average between 3 and 5 percent for average performers, while those individuals who are above average or even superior performers can expect increases between 7 and 12 percent or more.

Writing a Review

Because performance reviews can be highly emotional, especially for the employee, it is best to approach a review with a specific agenda in mind. Plan in advance what you are going to say during

---

Profile

Nadia Comaneci
(1961–)

At the tender age of six, Nadia Comaneci was recruited by famous gymnastics coach Bela Karolyi. At the 1976 Olympic games, when she was only 14 years old, she received perfect scores (the first ever) and three gold medals for her talent and skills. In 1989, Comaneci made a daring escape from Romania to Hungary, and then defected to the United States. Today she stays active in the sport of gymnastics through coaching at a school she and her husband, American gymnast Bart Conner, founded.

each part of the review. Be sure you can successfully deliver the message you intend, regardless of the employee's response.

- **Greeting**
  Start the review with a warm greeting and perhaps some very brief small talk to help relax tensions and create an atmosphere more conducive to the review.

- **Summary**
  Be sure that each employee knows how her overall performance ranks. Summarize the overall performance first, and then explain what the ratings mean. Don't announce any salary changes at this point. If you don't give the summary at the beginning of the review, the employee will spend the rest of the review trying to figure out what her total performance is, based on your comments.

  The employee may want to discuss the rating immediately after you offer it. Try to put this off until you have been able to thoroughly review the employee's strengths and weaknesses.

- **Strengths**
  Unless an employee's performance is unsatisfactory, compliment him on both major and minor strengths as they relate to the job. Avoid saying anything negative until you have reviewed his strengths. You can be either specific or general when describing strengths.

- **Weaknesses**
  Unless an employee's performance has been truly exceptional, you should provide feedback on areas of weakness, or at least suggest room for improvement. In stating weaknesses, be as specific as possible. For example, rather than saying "you have a poor attitude," cite a specific example of behavior, such as, "you are often late for company meetings and several times throughout the year you complained excessively about company policies."

- **Feedback**
  After you have discussed an employee's weaknesses, you should give that person an opportunity to air her thoughts.

Listen politely until the person is finished. Avoid being argumentative, but do let the employee know that the feedback she has given is not going to affect your review. For example, you may want to say, "I understand that you don't agree with what I have said, but my perception of your overall performance remains as I have stated it."

- **Salary**
  Recap the employee's overall performance rating. Announce the new salary, if any, and the date on which the new salary will be effective.

- **Closing**
  Unless the employee's performance is substantially less than satisfactory, try to end the review on a positive note. You might say, "The company and I very much appreciate your work, and we are glad to have you as part of our team!"

Other Things to Keep in Mind

Evaluation of an employee should be based on how well she has performed her duties. Make sure to clearly define all tasks and responsibilities in detail. Make sure to clarify to yourself and the employee how/why/when the tasks are to be completed. Determine the skill level and competency of the employee. Give her the appropriate training and guidance she needs to become self-sufficient.

Check on progress along the way. Give constructive feedback. Give directions both verbally and in writing. Some people comprehend the written word better than the spoken word, or vice versa. Adjust the work so it is appropriate to the individual. Having all the training sessions in writing will help in pulling together performance reviews. You will have written documentation with dates and specifics that were taught. This way, you can prevent any future backlash. For example, if an employee said, "I was never told that" or "You said to do it this way," you have proof of what actually occurred.

It is also a good idea for the employee to take notes along the way. This will help him to create a reference guide and may lead to fewer questions for you in the long run.

Profile

Jonas Salk
(1914–1995)

An American physician, Jonas Salk dedicated his life to searching out cures for epidemic diseases. In 1955, Salk discovered a vaccine for polio, a crippling disease that affected thousands, including President Franklin Delano Roosevelt. In 1963, he became the fellow and director of what is now known as the Salk Institute. In 1977, he was awarded the Presidential Medal of Freedom. Salk spent the last years of his life researching a possible vaccine for the AIDS virus.

Leadership Tip

Legal Eagle Tip

The biggest job-related legal problems are often a direct result of unrealistic employment reviews. Managers often avoid conflicts by failing to appraise poor employee performance accurately and truthfully. Later, if the company fires the employee, it is easier for that employee to claim discrimination and offer her performance reviews as evidence of adequacy to carry out the job requirements.

- Make sure that all employees are given a realistic review.
- All reviews should be issued in writing.
- The reviewed employees should receive a copy of the review.
- Develop consistent review criteria and be absolutely sure to adhere to the performance criteria.

(continued on next page)

The Elements of Successful and Not-So-Successful Evaluations

After a review, both the evaluator and the evaluatee should come away feeling better about the job and the future. An organized and thorough evaluation delivered in a friendly and supportive way encourages the employee to improve.

In a successful evaluation, the manager . . .

- is friendly and interested in the well-being of the employee.
- takes the time to give an overview so the employee can mentally prepare for what is ahead.
- begins with positive feedback and a discussion of the previous goals achieved.
- reminds the employee about negative issues that have been discussed over the past few months and gives an opportunity for discussion about correction of the problem.
- involves the employee in the goal-setting process, allowing him to formulate solutions and measure accomplishment.
- evaluates the employee (unsatisfactory–exceptional) and indicates the salary and bonus schedule.
- articulates the goals that have been set for the next 12 months.

In a not-so-successful evaluation, the manager . . .

- indicates that she wants to get the process over with as quickly as possible.
- refuses to answer questions posed by the employee.
- takes no time to think through the evaluation process or ways to do it better.
- shows a lack of commitment in working with the employee to develop goals and skills.
- does not give the employee an incentive to improve his performance.

In order to ensure that your evaluation is a success, remember that employees need to feel that they have some opportunity to affect your evaluation of their performance through open communication.

Let's Answer Some Common Questions about the Evaluation Process

Q: **Why should the employee complete a self-evaluation?**

A: It helps to open the lines of communication. If you've been consistent during the year with both praise and constructive criticism, you'll see that the employee has a fairly good idea of where he stands. By completing a self-evaluation prior to the review, the employee will have the opportunity to look at what he has accomplished in concrete terms. Your expectations should closely match and provide a solid basis to proceed with the review.

Q: **How can I find time for "mini reviews" throughout the year? I can barely find time to get my other work done.**

A: A "mini review" is exactly as it sounds—quick and to the point. It can take fewer than five minutes and should be well worth the time spent; if you keep good notes, you'll be better prepared for the annual review.

Q: **Employees always seem to complain about their raises after their reviews. What can I do to prevent constant complaining?**

A: Don't schedule the raise at the same time as the evaluation. Or make sure that if you give an above-average review, you give an above-average raise. There is a tendency to say only good things about an employee, and then to give what she perceives to be only an average raise. By doing this, inconsistent messages are sent.

Leadership Tip

Legal Eagle Tip

- Reviews should contain specific examples of negative and positive performance, not just generalizations.
- Establish grievance procedures.
- Involve other managers in determining each employee's overall performance rating or at least allow them to provide input during the preappraisal process.
- Give employees feedback throughout the year, as appropriate, to avoid performance review surprises.
- Encourage other managers to work with employees who are underachievers in an attempt to raise their performance to a satisfactory level.

Mikhail Gorbachev
(1931–)

President of the Soviet Union from 1990 to 1991, Gorbachev encouraged and promoted a policy of "glasnost" (openness) and "perestroika" (transformation) that helped modernize the country and move it in the direction of democracy. In 1990 Gorbachev was awarded the Nobel Peace Prize for his efforts.

Q: **How do I ensure that the review is objective and not subjective?**

A: Document, document, document. You can never take too many notes. If you take the time to speak to employees and to take notes on what happens, you are fast on your way to presenting an objective review. Also, keep personality conflicts and personal biases out of the review. If you set goals and criteria to evaluate employees, you'll be on the mark.

Q: **I tell employees when they do something wrong, but they don't seem to make any improvements. What am I doing wrong?**

A: When you are critical of an employee's work, be sure to give a recommendation as to how the employee can fix the problem. It's important to remember that not everyone thinks the same way, and some people need more guidance. If you are patient and encouraging, most employees will catch on and learn how to solve problems on their own.

Q: **How do I decide what goals to set for the employee?**

A: If you don't have any specific goals in mind, ask the employee what he would like to accomplish. You'll be surprised by the problems employees see and want to work on but have been afraid to mention.

Q: **Some of my own reviews have seemed negative even though they turned out to be not so bad. How can I avoid this with my employees?**

A: Discuss performance positively in terms of what the employee has accomplished. Here is an example:

"I like your willingness to help when we are running behind schedule. But, I would like it if you would volunteer to stay late when you notice things getting out of hand."
Avoid negatives like "you never" and "you didn't."

Q: What are measurable criteria?

A: Measurable criteria are the methods you use to judge whether the employee has accomplished what you asked. The criteria can be expressed either as an objective that can be concretely measured—such as increase sales volume by 20 percent—or as desired behavior—such as maintain a friendly demeanor when answering the phone or follow up orders without complaining.

Q: How do I prevent an employee from arguing with me during a review?

A: Use concrete examples to support your statements. The employee can't argue with you when she knows you're right. Also, don't allow yourself to get sidetracked. Stick to the point, refuse to argue, and don't let the employee take charge of the review. Make sure the employee clearly understands what your overall rating for the employee really means, especially with respect to salary increases.

Q: What can I say in an average-performance rating other than "average" and "satisfactory"?

A: You can say something like "fully meets the job requirements with work of good quality." This type of response explains that the employee is meeting expectations. Be careful not to over-hype whatever you say, as you may easily create a false set of expectations for the employee regarding salary and bonuses based on your statement.

Q: What percentage of employees fall into the average category?

A: Most of them. You probably have a few superachievers and rising stars; however, most employees do a good job and are satisfied with that. Your job is to make sure they maintain or improve their performance.

Words of the Wise

"The country received freedom, was liberated politically and spiritually, and that's the most important achievement."

—An excerpt from
Mikhail Gorbachev's
resignation speech, 1991

Q: **What do I do about employees who are less than average?**

A: First, don't reward them with high or even average raises. Second, if they don't meet your expectations, work with them to improve their performance. Include any warnings and advance notices as evidence of poor performance. If you must terminate the employee, follow the legal and accepted termination policy of your company. If you are unsure about it, ask your human resources department or manager for clarification.

Q: **Why must the employee sign the evaluation?**

A: The employee's signature indicates that the employee has received the evaluation, even though he may not agree with it. The signed appraisal protects you if he ever accuses you of not giving him notification of a problem.

CHAPTER 12

Dealing with
Difficult Employees

T he twelfth core concept, dealing with difficult employees, may not be all that appealing to you. However, if you have gone through the hiring process and continuously evaluated your employees, undoubtedly you have run across a difficult employee. As a strong leader, you need to know the best course of action to take.

With a little determination and a lot of hard work, you can turn around the performance of almost any employee. Pay attention to the word "almost" in that sentence. There will always be exceptions. Virtually everyone wants to succeed at work, give it their best effort, and get along with people. When shortcomings or problems arise, they can almost always be overcome with some additional coaching or with a positive but frank discussion. As much as possible, you want to leave people with the feeling that you are helping and supporting them, not reprimanding them.

In any situation, as part of a manager-employee relationship, the potential for a clash of motivations, fears, competencies, and communication styles is always present. For instance, you might be a direct communicator who takes action quickly. But an employee who reports to you may need time to methodically weigh alternatives before responding to your question or inquiry. As a result, you may mislabel this employee as slow, incompetent, rigid, or the all-encompassing "difficult."

When you have a disagreement with a difficult employee, the impact can be felt throughout the company, even more so by employees who are not vocal about their unhappiness over any particular issue. Your difficult employee will ignore your message and obviously make it tough for you to lead and ensure continued productivity if the disagreement spreads and affects other employees. This is especially true if other employees, whether or not they are vocal, view you as the *source* of the difficult employee's problems.

Take Control of the Situation

Don't play victim to the problem or misunderstanding. If not dealt with, it will only fester and grow until it overtakes everyone. You need to take control—that is, take control of the situation.

You can be proactive by learning techniques to head off difficult situations before they turn into disasters. By learning to "read" others, you can objectively describe behaviors, then create and implement solutions. Think of resolving these one-on-one situations as a dance; until now you and your partner (the difficult employee) have been tripping each other up. Now you must take it upon yourself to lead and hope that your partner decides to follow. By taking the lead, you can work to find the best solution with minimal damage to the rest of the company.

You take control of a difficult situation when you commit to learning results-oriented communication skills such as listening proactively, asking open-ended questions, and matching your words with your body language. These skills will enable you to persuade your difficult employee to buy into your goals and objectives.

Back to Basics

Before you actually sit down to address the problems at hand, it is a good idea to review the skills that will help you succeed in this situation. We've gone over them a thousand times because they are important, so they are worth mentioning again.

Communication is going to be your best weapon of defense. But remember, communication is a give-and-take that involves both sending and receiving information. Empowered communicators learn to receive signals so that they can be proactive rather than reactive in a situation. When communicating, step into the shoes of the other person. Read body language, tone of voice, statements, and silences. Investigate the employee's motivation and fear.

Body Language Speaks for Itself
- Arms crossed over chest—Defensiveness or anxiety
- Swinging arm—Wants to walk away from a situation
- Eye blinking—Fast blinking signals stress
- Downward gaze—Feeling defeated
- Taking notes—Shows interest or involvement

Geronimo
(1829–1909)

Geronimo was the infamous Apache Indian who fought for more than 25 years against the U.S. government to prevent Native Americans from submitting to life on reservations. Geronimo was the last of his group to surrender and lived the remainder of his years as a prisoner of war.

- Hand over mouth—Can mean boredom
- Arms behind head and leaning back—Looking for power or control
- Unbuttoning coat—Openness
- Buttoning coat—Feels trapped and wants to leave
- Standing with hands behind back—Confidence
- Clearing throat—Nervousness
- Rubbing back of neck—Defensiveness
- Hands flat on table—Ready to agree
- Stroking chin—Evaluating or thinking
- Foot tapping—Impatience
- Rubbing the eye—Doubt or disbelief
- Rubbing hands—Anticipation
- Tilted head—Interest
- Pulling/tugging ear—Indecision

Ask Questions That Allow for Informative Answers

Your goal is to get enough information so you can work with the person to resolve problems and increase productivity. A yes/no answer isn't going to help you here. A question that begins with "why" puts people on the defensive. Think about how you react when asked questions like, "Why were you late?" "Why do you act like that?"

"Who," "what," "when," "where," and "how" questions involve the other person. "What led you to make that decision?" "How would you handle the situation if you could do it over again?" "Who else is affected when you are late?" "When do you think you can start working toward this new goal?" It takes practice to self-edit and rework your technique. We are conditioned to accuse and assume, not to accumulate information.

Listen Intensely and Avoid Solving Problems for Other People

So often our good intentions prompt us to provide solutions to people's problems, when they don't actually want advice but simply want to be heard. Comments such as, "That must be painful for you," "You sound angry," and "It seems like you're feeling frustrated" might seem weak and even ineffectual if you're used to communicating directly and giving orders. But the up-front investment is worth the results generated by this kind of listening. Once people feel genuinely heard, they'll entrust you with more information, which is what you want because it gives you control.

Frame Your Responses Using the "I" Language Technique

Essentially you are taking responsibility for your feelings. You are not, I repeat NOT, blaming the employee for her actions, but you are pointing out how her behavior affects your feelings. To begin, comment on observable factual behaviors and state the consequences. Finish by involving the employee in a collaborative resolution.

Match Your Words to Your Body Language

If you're honest, your body language will confirm it. If you're feeling angry and denying it, your tone of voice might give you away. Be honest; then do a quick check of your body language to make sure your words match your nonverbal gestures. Otherwise you won't be taken seriously.

Learn as Much about Yourself as Possible

Know your own "hot button": What is your threshold for tolerating different behavior patterns? Establish what motivates you and notice how it differs from what motivates your employees. For example, you may be motivated to get recognition for doing excellent work; an employee who works for you may be motivated to come to work for the socializing rewards. Remember, it takes all types. What type are you? A driver? An influencer? A people pleaser? A perfectionist? Be aware of the differences and try to use them to create a more flexible working relationship between you and your employees.

Be Assertive

Assertive is neither passive nor aggressive. It's simply communicating directly and appropriately. It's about knowing what you want and thinking enough of yourself to assert your needs. When you are honest and up front with your words and actions, you're neither lying in an attempt to be overly nice and protective (passive), nor are you denying your anger to the point of one day blowing up (aggressive). Asserting yourself allows you to hold your ground without pushing the other person down. This creates a win/win situation for both parties.

Do Not Try to Solve a Problem That Is Too Tough to Handle

Ask for help from resources with more expertise than you have. Don't feel you have to solve your employees' problems. You might be a terrific line manager but an inadequate therapist—and that is because you are a manager, not a psychological expert. Don't bite off more than you can chew. If you have listened, asked caring questions, involved the person in a possible solution, but still failed to reach a resolution, call for backup. The human resources department, your company's employee assistance program, or your own manager are all good places to start.

Learn to accept that you cannot change others. You can only change your own behavior and hope that by serving as a role model, you will inspire others to follow your example. Do yourself a favor and understand that ultimately people do what they want to despite your best wishes and intentions. Protect yourself by learning to deflect their negative behaviors, and don't take them personally. So often, out of self-defense, we make false assumptions. It takes a self-assured person to dig in and ask information-gathering and constructive questions that lead to mutually satisfying results.

Be Flexible

When you think about all the ways we are different as human beings, it's easy to see how we view the world through different glasses. We are different in age and gender; our upbringing, environment, education, values, and culture all define us one way or another. Learn to accept the differences even if you don't agree with or condone other's choices. Your life will be a lot less stressful that way!

The Problems You Will Face

Lack of Skill

First make the distinction between a person who simply lacks the skill to accomplish the job versus someone whose progress is impeded by other factors. Often, when a manager assumes that someone cannot do the job due to a lack of skill, the real problem is centered on sloppiness. And sloppiness is curable in 99 percent of all cases.

If the problem is skill oriented, decide whether there is something you or the company can do to help the employee. Can a coworker bring the employee in question up to speed? Would a professional seminar be worthwhile? Would studying a book or using instructional software help?

You also need to evaluate how important the deficient skill is within the scope of the particular job. Consider how strong the person might be in other aspects of job performance. A shop floor manager, for instance, may not be great at giving performance reviews but absolutely terrific at scheduling and maintaining production runs and inventory management. Obviously, her strengths far outweigh the weaknesses in effectively carrying out the primary responsibilities of the job. It is okay to have an employee with a serious weakness, as long as you are aware of the problem area and the employee compensates for one skill deficiency with superior skill strength in another area.

If, despite all these considerations, you feel that an employee should not remain in the current position, think about moving him to another area or level of responsibility within the company. There are two advantages to this strategy. First, since you already

PERSONNEL DEPT

know where the employee's strengths and weaknesses lie, you have a good idea of what capacity he can perform at—this is more than you would know about a brand-new employee. Second, it is demoralizing for other employees to see a coworker fired, especially if that employee was trying hard to succeed at the job.

A Snail's Pace

A slow work pace can be among the most difficult problems to resolve unless you have standards or goals against which to compare actual performance. For most nonprofessional positions, you can create standards or measure the work output. For example, warehouse workers may be expected to pack so many orders a day. Data-entry people may be expected to process a certain number of entries each day. Salespeople may be expected to make a designated number of phone calls to new accounts, make some face-to-face contacts, or close so many deals per day.

The work of professional employees, on the other hand, generally does not lend itself to quantitative performance standards. However, you can usually set specific time goals for when you expect projects to be completed. For example, you may expect an accountant to accomplish month-end book closings within a three-day period at the end of each month. You may expect a software engineer to write a particular program within two weeks. You may expect a graphic designer to lay out a specific small catalog within a three-week time frame.

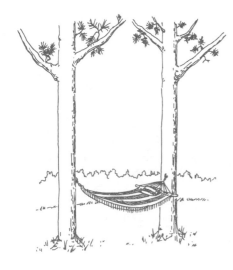

If an employee consistently fails to get things done in a timely manner, then it is time to have a closed-door meeting with that person. During this meeting, present, in an encouraging manner, the facts in as simple a manner as possible. For example, you may say, "You are packing ninety-three orders per day, whereas our standard is one hundred thirty-five. How do you think you can increase your output?" Or, "Together we set a time frame of three days at the end of the month in which to close our monthly accounting books. It is typically taking four. Is there some way in which we can work toward the original goal?"

If you are pleasant and encouraging, the employee will probably say something like, "Gee, I thought I was working at a pretty good pace, but I am confident that I can work a little faster." In this case, say, "That would be great. I'm glad to hear it!" Then follow up and be sure the employee knows exactly where she stands at the end of each day. Chances are, such employees will reach a higher performance level. If not, have them monitor themselves and record their progress every hour or day, as may seem applicable to the task. Consider having peers work with them and help them along. Or consider having the employee make progress reports to you at various intervals.

Sometimes an employee will tell you during your first meeting or during subsequent meetings that the standards or goals that have been set are unrealistic, unfair, or impossible. In this case, (assuming you don't agree with the assertion), promptly issue the employee a written warning and plan on terminating employment unless her attitude and performance improve quickly.

Sloppiness

Sloppiness is one of the most common workplace problems. Examples include missing errors when proofreading company literature, mispacking orders, entering shipping addresses incorrectly, and performing inaccurate accounting work. Sloppiness most quickly surfaces in clerical work, but it is also prevalent in the work of many professionals—although it is much more difficult to detect!

For the first incidence or two of minor sloppiness, you should kindly point out the error to the employee. Don't comment, but do watch the person's work more carefully.

If the problem proves to be recurring or is more serious in nature, you need to sit down with the employee out of earshot of his coworkers. Be positive. Remember that the employee probably has no idea that his work is sloppy. Most people take pride in their work. But be candid. Tell the employee that you are concerned about the work he has been doing and cite specific examples of sloppiness. Relate the clearest or most serious infractions that you have evidence of. Don't discuss marginal problems or ones that you

Profile

Benazir Bhutto
(1953–)

Benazir Bhutto served as prime minister of Pakistan from 1988 to 1990 and from 1993 to 1996. She was the first woman prime minister in any modern Islamic state. Known for her dedication to social issues, Bhutto champions causes such as health, education, clean drinking water, sanitation, energy, and women's rights. Benazir Bhutto was awarded the Bruno Kreisky Award for Human Rights in 1988.

have little evidence of. This can lead to arguments and a feeling of unfair treatment. The point is to assist employees in performing up to standards, not demoralizing them.

Encourage feedback, but expect to hear something like, "These are isolated examples. Everyone makes mistakes and basically my work is fine." Or "No one ever told me that I had to do that." At this point, don't get into a long discussion about how serious or representative the cited problems are. Instead, shift to telling the employee how important his work is to the company. Let the person know how important it is to eliminate all errors and sloppy work, no matter how infrequently it may occur or how minor it may seem. Try to end the meeting on a positive note if possible.

Keep observing the employee's work. If, after a few days, the work patterns are improving, be sure to compliment the person on a job well done. If the sloppiness and carelessness continue, conduct another closed-door meeting. There is a good chance that the person is capable of better work and is simply refusing to recognize the existence of an ongoing problem. In this second meeting, make a judgmental statement like, "I am concerned about the overall errors or sloppiness in your work." Again, bring up the most clear or flagrant examples.

For a nonprofessional or entry-level employee, assign someone with good or exemplary work habits, especially in the problem areas, to work side by side with the problem employee for a small portion of each day. Have the monitoring employee suggest specific steps for achieving performance improvement. Have the monitor provide continuing feedback. Personally monitor the work of a professional employee. Discuss any progress or lack thereof every few days.

As long as an employee has the basic skills necessary to effectively perform in the job, sloppiness can be overcome in almost every case. If for one reason or another the employee refuses to improve, then termination needs to be carefully considered.

Why Can't We All Just Get Along?

Sometimes a person can be just plain difficult to manage, making your life miserable. Such a person can be as disruptive to the forward progress of your company as an employee who lacks the skills or initiative to do the job well.

The first thing you should do with a difficult employee is bite your tongue and try to woo him. Go out to lunch and try to develop a positive rapport with the person. Often there is some issue that is causing the negative behavior. Many times, the employee will be very reluctant to discuss this issue, whether it is professional or personal in nature. A casual, relaxed setting may put him at ease. He may open up and tell you what's really been going on.

Often the underlying cause of a person's behavior pattern is quite simple. She may have the perception that she is not appreciated. She may feel that she deserves more attention. She may feel that she has not been complimented for work done well in the past. Remember, you should always be liberal with compliments. Key employees especially need attention from you. But, this is advice that is easier to give than heed.

On the other hand, sometime a difficult-to-manage person is suffering from personal problems (an ailing parent, a rebellious child, a divorce, or financial difficulties). If this is the case, you want to show that you understand the predicament. If at all possible, offer the employee time off or an adjustment in work hours so she can focus on solving the personal issue. However, if the problem is ongoing and is having a serious negative impact on your workplace, you need to let the person know that some sort of resolution is imperative.

If the problem persists, have a formal, closed-door meeting with the employee and address in a forthright manner the most obvious examples of inappropriate behavior. If an employee remains difficult despite all attempts at building rapport or providing help, you need to make a careful assessment. Be honest with yourself. Do you simply dislike the employee in question? Are the difficulties you are experiencing perhaps minor in character? If this is the case, drop the matter. But if the employee is truly a disruption to the workplace, you need to take further action. Consider issuing a written warning that details the specific problems as clearly as possible.

George Washington
(1732–1799)

As one of America's Founding Fathers, George Washington served as the first president of the United States (1789–1797). The presidency was just the crowning moment for a life of leadership both on and off the battlefield and in and out of the political arena. Washington served in Virginia's House of Burgesses (1759–1774) and was outspoken in Virginia's opposition to Great Britain's colonial policies. He also participated as a delegate to the First and Second Continental Congresses.

(continued on next page)

If, after issuing such a warning, the employee's bad behavior persists, you may feel that the only solution is termination. Consult with an attorney before dismissing an employee. You need to know whether you have a strong enough case to withstand a potential lawsuit for wrongful firing. An employee who has been fired for issues relating to difficult behavior is much more likely to sue you than an employee fired due to poor work performance.

Always Late

Many good, hardworking people have a tendency to be habitually late. Unless being precisely on time is crucially important, don't bring up the tardiness issue with an employee who is occasionally late. Such employees will appreciate your tacit understanding and they will take it as a sign of your trust in them. Of course, if the person is supposed to be the security guard and you are operating a division of the Federal Reserve Bank, the tardiness could cause a problem . . . and may result in a major robbery! In all cases, use your best judgment.

In some cases, an employee who is habitually late can have a demoralizing effect on other employees who manage to be on time every day. Furthermore, habitual lateness is an infectious disease. Soon many employees may exhibit tardy behavior. Why do some otherwise great, hardworking employees have a problem being on time? Who knows?

The key idea is to figure out where to draw the line. If a person is 10 or more minutes late more than five times within a given month, it's time for a chat. Assuming that the employee's job performance is satisfactory in all other respects, say something like, "Linda, overall I really enjoy having you on our team. I would appreciate it though if you could cut back on your tardiness. I can understand being late once in a while but enough is enough. Can I count on you for a little improvement in this area?"

Virtually all tardiness problems disappear after a gentle yet firm talk. Unless the problem is extremely severe, stick to a very light approach. But sooner or later you will encounter a person who absolutely refuses to be constrained by a schedule. Not a fun prospect!

Some Common Problems and Some Plausible Solutions

Problem One: You've Got a Tortoise but You Need a Hare

You are the chief editor of *What's the Scoop?* a newspaper for twenty-somethings. A few months back you proposed a new format to help reporters get their stories done faster and with less hassle. Grant, the arts and entertainment reporter, has not followed the new format since it was instituted.

The voice inside your head says: Grant is slow and obviously not smart enough to understand the new format. He always misses his deadline.

What's the deal? In reality, Grant is just focusing too much on minor details. In addressing this problem with Grant, you will need to:

- state the situation in measurable and observable terms
- involve Grant in developing a solution by asking for feedback
- take the time to hear Grant's explanation

The result: Grant will feel motivated to change because a level of understanding has been reached instead of an accusation or demanding "why" question.

Problem Two: There's More Gossip in the Office Than in a Tabloid Newspaper

As the manager of the department you have to deal with Alexandra, the office gossip and general troublemaker. She doesn't mind stirring the pot and takes shots at management for what she sees as a lack of attention to important issues.

Profile

George Washington (1732–1799)

(continued from previous page)

In June 1775, the new Congress unanimously elected Washington as Commander in Chief of the Continental Army. After successfully defeating the British, he was again unanimously elected to serve as the first president of the United States of America. Under George Washington's leadership, a precedent was set for a solid and united federal government, the new country's financial system was firmly established, and U.S. territory was expanded under foreign treaties.

The voice inside your head says: Don't trust Alexandra. She is out to get the company, and she is bringing morale down.

What's the deal? In reality, Alexandra is just looking for attention. She doesn't feel that the good work she does gets noticed, so she tries to get management's attention in destructive ways. She feels underpaid and underappreciated. In addressing this problem with Alexandra, you will need to:

- establish an environment of trust to gain insight into Alexandra's true motivations
- ask Alexandra directly to establish the issues
- be consistent with responses and actions

The result: Either Alexandra will start to feel more comfortable and open up in an attempt to resolve the situation, or she will leave because she is unhappy with the job. Alexandra's leaving might even be the best outcome for everyone. Managers should not feel like they have to save the world.

Problem Three: The Skills Are Lacking

Cecilia, an accounting clerk who lacks verbal communication skills, is asked to take the responsibility of calling on delinquent accounts to collect funds. When you gave Cecilia this assignment you were unaware of her fear of rejection and lack of verbal skills. You assume she is fine with the assignment and berate her for not getting the job done.

The voice inside your head says: Cecilia isn't trying hard enough. She is being asked to do the same thing as everyone else, yet she doesn't put in even an ounce of effort.

What's the deal? In reality, Cecilia is "phone phobic." She knows that she could use some verbal communication coaching but is afraid to ask for help, so instead she just avoids the work no matter what the consequences. In addressing this problem with Cecilia, you will need to:

- be patient

- walk Cecilia through the steps that will increase her confidence in performing the task at hand
- focus on the problem rather than the person

The result: You have focused on the problem rather than the person. So as Cecilia gains more confidence and self-assurance, her productivity continues to increase. In the long run, she also learns to respect you as a teacher, not a disciplinarian.

Problem Four: He's Late, He's Late, for a Very Important Date

Now let's take a closer look at a situation where you have to confront an employee who is habitually late for no apparent reason.

The voice inside your head says: There is no reason for Jared to be late every day. He needs to manage his time better and make an effort to get here when everyone else does.

What's the deal? Before confronting Jared, you did not have the complete information about why he is late all the time. After talking to him, you find out that he and his wife have just moved an hour and a half away, and with traffic, he is lagging behind. With the sale and purchase of houses and getting used to a new commute, it is no wonder Jared is always running behind. In addressing this problem with Jared, you will need to:

- ask for all the facts
- be supportive and offer assistance in whatever capacity is possible
- ask to be kept posted as time goes on
- make the necessary accommodations in Jared's schedule

The result: Everyone wins in this situation. Jared's schedule has been adjusted to accommodate his needs and to suit the company's needs. He is still working the same amount of hours but will no longer be stressed about coming in late. The other staff members will surely be able to understand the situation and support Jared.

Profile

Catherine the Great (1729–1796)

Former Empress of Russia (1762–1796), Catherine II overthrew her husband, Peter III, to become the monarch of the largest empire in Europe. Catherine the Great attempted to follow in the footsteps of Peter I (Peter the Great) by bringing enlightenment and Westernization to Russia. During her reign, she established the first Russian schools for girls and sought improvements in agriculture and health care.

Nadia Boulanger
(1887–1979)

French composer, conductor, and educator, Nadia Boulanger was the first woman to conduct an entire program of the Royal Philharmonic in London (1937). She was also the first woman to conduct the Boston Symphony, New York Philharmonic, and Philadelphia orchestras.

Problem Five: Green with Envy

This time you have to deal with Nerissa, who was formerly a peer but now reports to you. You are upset because Nerissa displays an indifferent attitude and doesn't seem to take direction from you very well.

The voice inside your head says: I don't understand why Nerissa is refusing to follow the new policies I am implementing. We used to work together very well. Now I don't even want to go out for coffee with her.

What's the deal? Nerissa is jealous of your promotion. At the core of her resistance is fear. She feels that she works hard and is worthy of a higher position as well. In addressing the problem with Nerissa you need to:

- encourage open dialogue about the "real" issue
- refrain from making judgments and placing blame
- admit that the changes are going to be difficult to adjust to

The result: With an open dialogue established, Nerissa will learn a lot from you. Soon the friendship both inside and outside the office should get back on track. Change is difficult, but it can be worked through to the benefit of all. Once again, communication is key!

Leadership Worksheet

Use the following worksheet to see if your perception of how individuals respond to particular questions and statements matches with their true response. Choose the answer that matches your gut reaction to each statement. Then take a look at the explanation that follows the question to better gauge your level of effective communication.

Leadership Worksheet

What generally happens when you start a question with "why"?
A) The person gets defensive.
B) You get a direct answer quickly.
C) You begin to open a dialogue.

When you start a question with "why," employees feel threatened or, at the very least, defensive about their actions and look to confront you rather than explore the issue with you. You may get, from time to time, a direct answer such as "I don't know" or "I'll have to look into that," but from a purely emotional standpoint, employees will feel like you are backing them into a corner. Thus, A is the most appropriate response.

Asking people to get involved with providing a solution to a difficult situation . . .
A) Takes too much time.
B) Gives away authority.
C) Motivates them to achieve.

C. One of the most rewarding aspects of managing a difficult situation successfully is cooperatively working toward a solution with a difficult employee. He will feel like a part of the solution rather than the source of a problem and will be more motivated to work out solutions for future problems with you without resorting to difficult behavior.

Comparing someone's actions to those of a controversial, well-known figure . . .
A) Provides a point of reference.
B) Belittles the person.
C) Puts the person in her place.

It is not a good idea to make light of a well-known or controversial individual in the context of a conversation with a difficult employee and her actions. It only serves to make a difficult situation go from bad to worse. Thus, B is the most appropriate answer in this case.

(continued on next page)

Leadership Worksheet

(continued from previous page)

Asking an employee a question such as "What's the real issue?" . . .
A) Gives too much credence to his bad behavior.
B) Can reveal more problems than you want to deal with.
C) Opens dialogue and holds the person accountable for his behavior.

C is the best response because by using the word "what" you immediately open a dialogue with your difficult employee and avoid a hostile confrontation. It is also possible that your difficult employee may reveal problems that you do not want to hear about or deal with immediately, so answer B is possible but not as likely.

Describing someone's performance as "weak and unacceptable" . . .
A) Provides valuable information.
B) Focuses her attention on performance issues.
C) Is considered, in part, a value judgment.

If you simply labeled someone's performance as "unacceptable," then the second response would be appropriate. By adding the word "weak," however, you enter the realm of making value judgments with respect to an individual's performance, without any clear reasons behind the comment. Thus, C becomes a valid response.

Providing step-by-step instructions . . .
A) Is rarely appropriate and necessary.
B) Is too time consuming.
C) Provides measurable results.

Because our professional lives are becoming more hectic with each passing day, as managers, the second response might seem to be most appropriate. However, when working with a difficult employee, you sometimes need to provide additional guidance to help that individual succeed in her position. For that reason, C is the best response.

(continued on next page)

Leadership Worksheet

(continued from previous page)

People who let their personal problems affect their personal work are . . .
A) Undisciplined.
B) Unprofessional.
C) Human.

While you may feel that anyone who brings his personal life to work is unprofessional or undisciplined, the third response is most appropriate because there will always be times when even the most disciplined employee will carry some personal baggage to work. It is unavoidable.

Accommodating and changing the rules for one person . . .
A) Causes everyone to feel entitled to special privileges.
B) Paints the organization as compassionate.
C) Hinders organizational progress and productivity.

The normal tendency here is to go with the first response because one's natural reaction is, Why should the company bend the rules for any one individual? However, the most appropriate answer is B. The fact is that by demonstrating the ability to be flexible and recognizing an individual employee's special needs, a manager will go a long way toward turning a difficult employee into a more cooperative and productive employee and help everyone feel the company is a compassionate, caring organization.

Communicating assertively . . .
A) Means being aggressive.
B) Means that you are being straightforward with a person.
C) Puts your needs before that of the employee.

Some people equate being assertive with being aggressive. Rather, communicating assertively suggests that you are being open and honest in a direct manner with your difficult employee. Thus, B is the best response to this statement.

If you selected all or most of the right answers, congratulations. You can consider yourself an effective communicator. You read people well, are perceptive, and deal with difficult situations appropriately.

If you answered only some of the answers correctly, challenge yourself to learn all you can about listening empathetically, making nonjudgmental statements, and taking time to resolve conflicts in a win/win approach. Remember, there are more viewpoints and approaches than just your own.

Firing a Problem Employee

No one enjoys firing people. But getting someone out of the organization who just can't do her job or who is a demotivator can give a huge boost to the performance of the business. The general tendency is to put off the decision to fire someone, because it is not an easy decision to make. But procrastination just makes it worse for everyone involved.

Of all confrontations with an employee, the response you get from firing someone is the most difficult to predict. One employee may thank you, while another may attempt to engage you in a fistfight.

You need to prepare carefully before firing someone. You need to be ready to become fully engaged in what may become a very demanding encounter. How you handle a firing will have a tremendous impact on how the employee feels about himself, you, and your company. This will, in turn, affect your chance of being sued. In addition, a poorly handled firing will have a negative impact on morale throughout the entire organization.

Holding Off

There really aren't any specific guidelines to determine how much time you should give an employee to improve on performance. One thing to take into consideration is the employee's length of service with the company. Loyalty does count. Give an employee who has served you for several years a few months to work out any performance issues.

Remember, too, that when you fire a long-term employee, the negative effect on the morale of other employees will be far greater than if you were to fire a recent hire. And when you work together with long-term employees in an effort to help them improve their job output, and ideally keep them gainfully employed, you create goodwill throughout the company.

On the other hand, if an employee shows poor work habits, has unsatisfactory skill levels, or displays attitude problems during the provisional 90-day trial employment period, don't hesitate to fire her. (But beware of the legal risks—the courts do not recognize "provisional" employment periods.)

Last Resort

As demonstrated throughout the section on problem employees, carefully working with an employee can resolve many performance shortcomings. An employee's job achievement can be improved through care.

If these "gentle" tactics don't work, however, you must move on to a firm verbal warning that makes mandatory a work quality or attitude improvement and cites specific suggestions for effecting such an improvement. If that fails, issue a written warning. Some people just require the jolt of a firm warning to shift their performance into high gear.

Of course, during the period when you are working with an employee in an attempt to improve her performance, you run the risk of having her decide to seek another job. This risk increases if a written warning is handed down. If the employee quits or submits her resignation, that's okay. It is a lot easier to lose weak performers through their own proactive decisions.

Let Them Down Gently

After you have taken all the preliminary steps; considered all of the potential ramifications, legal and otherwise; and have made the difficult decision to let someone go, stick to the plan. Don't torture yourself and don't prolong the firing.

Only the worker's direct supervisors, and any witnesses that will be present at the termination meeting, should be told about the termination decision in advance. An advanced leak of a firing can only worsen the situation.

In the past, late Friday afternoon was considered the best time to let someone go. Now, earlier in the day, or even the week, is deemed appropriate. Some companies that take this approach offer the employee the option of either remaining for the rest of the day or leaving immediately with pay for the work day.

When you are ready to proceed with the termination, call the employee into your office and tell him you have something to discuss with him. After the employee and the managerial personnel or witnesses have gathered in your office, get to the point quickly. Briefly explain to the employee that he is being fired. Summarize the main reasons for the firing and recap the warnings that have been given and the opportunities extended to improve performance. Give the person a check for monies due. If you are offering severance pay, detail the severance offer and present the employee with the forfeiture document to be signed if the severance is to be paid. Explain any continued work options. Offer him a choice between cleaning out his desk now or having you mail any personal belongings to him later. If the employee elects to have you mail his belongings, have two people oversee the cleaning process to be sure that all of the employee's personal belongings are mailed.

Show appropriate sympathy for the employee, but not empathy. Do not waver or change your mind. Do not overstate any aspect of the employee's performance.

Answer any questions the person may have, even if he interrupts you to ask them. A termination is extremely emotional, and often the person doesn't hear a lot of the information that is being given to him. You may have to restate all or part of the information.

As long as the employee doesn't lose control, extend him every reasonable courtesy. Certainly give the person an opportunity to say good-bye to coworkers. If the employee does lose control and become verbally abusive, ask him to leave the building. Don't get upset. Remember, no matter what you think of the employee, that person is being terminated. He is leaving, not you.

Severance

By law you need to immediately pay a terminated employee for any unused vacation or personal time, all regular and overtime hours worked, and previously unpaid earned bonuses and other earned pay.

When you fire an employee, no matter how long she has been with the company, you should pay severance. It is decent, remaining employees expect you to have done it, and it makes you look better in the worst of situations. It also decreases your risk of a lawsuit.

Many firms that pay severance offer two weeks' pay. Others provide two weeks plus one week for each year of service the employee has given to the company. Still others are considerably more generous, particularly to employees who held senior positions. In this case, six months' to a year's pay is not atypical and is predicated on the assumption that a senior-level employee will have a more difficult time obtaining a new and equal job than will an entry-level employee.

While it is nice to pay out a lot of money to departing employees, if you own a small business, you need to be concerned about staying in business and paying your remaining staff members. But whatever you decide to do regarding severance pay, in all termination situations, severance for similar positions with similar service time should be consistent. If you continually change your severance policies, you are only adding to your legal risks.

You should pay severance, however, only if the employee agrees to sign a document that forfeits her right to sue you for wrongful termination. Don't be cheap in this lion's pit of potential danger. Have a lawyer draw up the release document so that it is, as much as possible, bullet proof. You should give the employee 24 hours to review, sign, and return the document to you, otherwise it may not hold up in court should the employee decide to sue you anyway. If the employee is age 40 or over, you must, by law, grant the person 21 days to review such a document.

Words of the Wise

"I never give them hell. I just tell the truth, and they think it is hell."

—*Harry S. Truman, president of the U.S. from 1945–1953*

CHAPTER 13

Retention and Recognition

etention and recognition is the thirteenth core concept. You may have succeeded in pulling together the most efficient and effective team in the company's history, but unless you are able to keep your employees happy, your team may soon fall apart.

When the economy is booming, it becomes increasingly difficult to retain employees. People are always assuming that there is something bigger and better waiting for them at another company. Now there is a lowered sense of loyalty between employees and their employers. The fact is that employee turnover costs money, time, and energy. Good employee retention is more than cost savings. It is the value of keeping the knowledge base within your company. So, in order to prevent a vicious cycle of turnover, do everything possible to retain and recognize employees before it is too late.

What's All the Fuss about Retaining Employees?

Good managers should be concerned about the impact of losing not only employees, but also the information and skills they take with them. It's not as if every employee can return all his knowledge when he turns in his keys, uniforms, and materials. The information, knowledge, and skills he developed while working for you are important assets—sometimes more important than you realize.

Have you ever thought to calculate the value of the information and knowledge you have supplied to your fellow employees? Sometimes you might even think about charging a fee for all the training you have made available. How long did it take you to finally get a particular employee trained to perform at a high level of productivity? In some cases it may have taken months. Consider the product knowledge you supply to your employees. Think about the team-building and supervisory training you have supplied. Think about the lost revenues for your company. Think about the impact on you as you support the slow, methodical process of training the replacement employee to be a fully contributing member of the organization. There is an impact, and it is very important.

It is almost impossible to record and classify all the information each employee has accumulated. The good employee has developed relationships with customers and coworkers that may have a profound impact on the productivity of the group. As we all know, certain people make a greater difference than others when working together in a team environment. Certain clients and customers also demand a level of skill, service, and consistency when doing business with your company. When individuals leave your company and these individuals have developed positive relationships with your customers, the potential for problems is very great.

In many cases, clients and customers actively seek out former employees to replace your company for the product or services your company has been supplying. The clients or companies likely have no allegiance to your company; their allegiance is to the employee. Your potential loss is enormous.

When you lose an employee, you are losing a part of your company. But, you are losing a part of the company that you cannot identify. It is the ultimate paradox of business that the obvious individual contributions of employees are frequently enhanced by unknown and undefined contributions. Frequently it is the undefined contribution that makes the employee so valuable. In effect, it is this long list of undefined and unknown contributions to the organization that makes the retention of employees so important.

What Is Turnover Anyway?

Once you have an employee on the payroll, it is in your best interest to keep him working with you. Of course, you must ensure that this person is operating at a high level of productivity within the organization.

According to the department or company budget, how many employees should you have in a given year? In other words, what are your budgeted staff requirements? In the past year, how many employees left your department or company for any reason during the full 12-month period?

Words of the Wise

"I don't pay good wages because I have a lot of money; I have a lot of money because I pay good wages."

—*Robert Bosch (1861–1942), German inventor and industrialist*

Look at these two numbers and compare them. If you are budgeted for a staff of 10 and you have only 5 people working in the department, you need to take a closer look at why you are only half-staffed.

The High Cost of Turnover

Every time you are faced with replacing an existing employee due to turnover, you are wasting money that could be spent in more productive ways. When you are looking to turn the red bottom line into the black bottom line, you may find some black ink with better retention of your employees.

To reduce hiring costs, you must begin to think more strategically. Consider the long-term goal of your company and how you will get there. What are the incremental steps along the way? What can you do independently? What will need the assistance of other people to be accomplished? How much of your budget can you dedicate to this effort? Will you be able to measure your success?

When you have gone through the strategic thinking process, you can then begin analyzing specific situations. The details of these situations will change, but your strategy will remain the same. For example: Have you priced classified advertising in local newspapers recently? If you have, you know how expensive it can be to advertise in the help-wanted section of the newspaper. The greater the distribution, the more expensive the advertising.

Print advertising is the most prevalent form of first-line recruiting for companies. Scan any help-wanted section of a newspaper and you have an immediate snapshot of which companies are growing rapidly and which companies are managing poorly. Companies place ads for one of two reasons:

- To staff vacated positions
- To fill newly formed positions

The up-front cost is the same for both cases, but the return on the investment is dramatically different. Let's explore the difference.

Case One

A growing company has forecast future sales and recognizes the need to support these sales with additional staff. The company identifies the staffing need; develops a job profile, job description, and job specifications; and then moves into recruitment mode.

Generally a classified ad is placed with the local urban and suburban papers. Sometimes a headhunter is hired to help in acquiring new talent. The cost for a service such as this can run between 10 and 40 percent of the new hire's first-year salary.

This company is planning ahead to ensure that the increased sales forecast will be appropriately supported by additional staff. The new employee salary and benefits, as well as the cost of recruiting for this position, have all been included in the business forecast. A talented person has an exciting position and a well-run company has a quality new employee. Everyone wins!

Case Two

A company needs to replace an existing position from which an employee has resigned. The company has maintained steady sales with minor fluctuation. The existing job profile, job description, and job specifications may be reviewed to determine if any adjustments are necessary.

Almost invariably, the company will place an ad in an urban and suburban newspaper. If the position has turned over or changed frequently, the company may choose to go directly to a headhunter or recruiting firm for assistance. The company believes that the recruiting/search firm will help solve the problem for them. It becomes very obvious very quickly that the problem is not just finding qualified candidates.

The End Result

In both cases the initial expenses are very similar. Until we dig a little bit deeper. When we look at the return on investment in the first case, we recognized increased revenues and a growing organization. The cost of hiring new staff members is a small portion of the value of increased sales and has been considered in calculating the compensation for the new position.

Profile

Dian Fossey
(1932–1985)

Upon meeting Dr. Louis Leakey in Africa in 1963, Fossey became interested in studying mountain gorillas. Fossey worked very closely with the gorillas in Africa and eventually they treated her as one of their own. She was the first known person to have physical contact with a mountain gorilla when one touched her hand. When her favorite gorilla, Digit, was killed by poachers, Fossey turned her efforts to campaigning against poaching. In the early 1980s, she headed back to the United States, got her Ph.D., and took a position at Cornell University. Soon after, she started working on her book (now a movie), *Gorillas in the Mist*. In 1985, Fossey returned to Africa and was found murdered in her cabin. To this day, the murder is unsolved. Fossey is credited with the establishment of the Karisoke Research Center and the Dian Fossey Gorilla Fund. Also, thanks in large part to her efforts, mountain gorillas are protected by the government of Africa.

In the second case, the organization is not experiencing any dramatic increase or decrease in growth. The cost of recruiting the new employee increases the basic overhead because it is not linked to added growth. Although the actual dollars expended are the same, the final impact is dramatic.

Accept the Inevitable

No matter what, you will always experience turnover. Turnover is not just a sign of poor management practices. Sometimes turnover is a sign of developmental learning, with people moving on to other job opportunities in other companies. Sometimes employees are looking for more growth and your company cannot offer that growth. In many cases, these same employees will return to your company with greater skills and abilities and will help you move to the next level in company building.

Uncover the Root of the Problem

Before you can address issues regarding retention and recognition, you and your company must identify whether you have a problem and what the problem might be. Use some detective work and conduct research to get to the core of what is eating away at the company.

If few people are leaving, the company is probably doing a good job of recognizing and retaining employees. Employees are feeling respected, valued, involved, and connected to an organization that is fun to work with.

So before you go any further in this chapter, answer these questions:

1. Have you had a large number of terminations for just cause over the past 12 months?
2. Did you exceed your recruiting advertising budget? How much over budget were you?

Words of the Wise

"Had it not been for Dian Fossey, there is no doubt in my mind that the mountain gorilla would by now have joined the list of extinct species."

—*Gilbert M. Grosvenor, chairman of the National Geographic Society*

3. Are employees complaining about constantly having to train new employees?
4. Have you been experiencing excessive quality, accuracy, or customer service problems?

If you found that you answered yes to most of these questions, your company may be experiencing some retention problems. Companies that have employee retention problems generally exhibit similar characteristics:

- Low productivity levels
- High turnover rate
- Low morale
- High incidence of illness
- Lack of enthusiasm
- High degree of cynicism

When investigated, this employee retention problem leads to discovering a lot of critical issues that affect the company negatively. These problems usually fall into one of four categories.

Category 1: An unclear and poorly structured communication system.

This can cause problems because it becomes virtually impossible for members of the organization to know what needs to be achieved. They have no concept of what the vision or the direction of the company should be, and that's because no one bothered to tell them. Without this communication road map, your staff may decide to set its own course and achieve objectives that are not desired by you or the company. The well-designed communication strategy for both internal and external communication will help you to stay on top of your business objectives. These defined strategies will also make your employees, at all levels, better able to accomplish their job duties in the most efficient and effective manner possible.

Profile

Golda Meir
(1898–1978)

Golda Meir served as the first female prime minister of Israel (1969–1974). Prior to her years as prime minister, Golda Meir attended the Zionist Congress in Geneva (1939) to help ensure the protection of European Jews and was part of the People's Council signing the proclamation establishing the State of Israel in 1948. Meir also served as minister of labor from 1949 to 1956 and as the foreign minister for Israel from 1956 to 1965.

Category 2: Unclear and poorly defined policies and procedures.

If this is the issue, it can create opportunities for error and potentially damaging situations. Operational policies and procedures ensure quality product, service, and follow-up. Administrative and personnel policies and procedures ensure a smooth-running business with a higher degree of quality assurance and fewer legal problems. Employees who work with clearly defined policies and procedures are able to manage the day-to-day activities without having to ask you every little question. They become better able to achieve the objectives you want them to achieve.

Category 3: Unclear and poorly defined compensation programs.

Invariably, a lack of definition in this area creates interpersonal resentments and conflicts. New people are paid more than highly functioning senior employees because there is no clear compensation policy. The senior employee finds out and is sincerely hurt by the lack of respect and compensation. The money is important, but more important is the perceived value she has within the organization. The time and energy needed to fix this type of problem are enormous. And, to make it worse, the problem is never really fixed because the senior employee will always resent the fact that she had to speak with you about it in the first place. It was embarrassing and humiliating for this person to demand recognition for the hard work she has done over the years. Watch this senior employee closely. She will soon become part of your turnover rate.

Category 4: Low levels of employee involvement.

This situation creates a sense of unimportance and, in turn, creates low levels of motivation and productivity. Employees want and need to be involved. They spend most of their time at work; they want the work to be interesting and challenging. Treat your employees as partners and as intelligent contributing members of the team. You will see an immediate change in the way they behave, perform, and respond to the challenges they are presented with.

Gathering Information from Exit Interviews

Exit interviews are useful tools that can help pinpoint possible problems in the company. These simple devices offer you a great opportunity to learn why employees are leaving your company and what they plan to do in the future. Frequently, a well-constructed and well-executed exit interview can create a bridge that will encourage an employee to return to your company at a future date with increased skills and knowledge. The benefits of conducting quality exit interviews are enormous.

Exit interviews can be conducted via formal interviews or via direct-mail questionnaires. The purpose of an exit interview is to obtain information that may assist the organization in improving the way in which business is conducted. The exit interview also allows the departing employee to obtain some advice and support as this person moves on to the next career opportunity.

Inform the individual that you will be taking notes and that the information shared during this session will be brought to the attention of the various people who have had an impact on them while employed by your company. Impress on the individual that their honest and detailed comments will be very valuable to the company and to other employees remaining at the company.

If by chance you learn of something negative regarding a manager at the company, don't panic. Reflect on what you have heard or read from the employee who is leaving. Consider the source and the circumstances. Then take more than a few minutes to reconstruct your history of supervision of the manager in question. Once you have done all your research and reflection, have an open conversation with the manager in question regarding issues presented in the exit interview. Use the exit interview information as a steppingstone to an honest, direct, and valuable conversation about the manager's job duties, the value of the employee in question, and how you can work better together to retain more productive employees.

Words of the Wise

"A leader who doesn't hesitate before he sends his nation into battle is not fit to be a leader."

—*Golda Meir (1898–1978), first female prime minister of Israel*

Environment Means Everything

What kind of work environment do you operate in? To obtain a measurement of your company environment, answer the following questions.

- What is the feeling within your organization?
- Are people highly motivated and charged up about doing a good job?
- Do people come to work eager to attack a new problem?
- Do people help each other to solve problems even if they are not directly involved?
- Do people look forward to working with other members of the organization?
- Do people feel comfortable asking questions?
- Are people willing to take chances and possibly make mistakes?
- Are people able to have a well-balanced home life and still give 110 percent to the company?
- How would you describe the morale of the people in your company?

As you think about these questions, you will begin to understand the environment that has been created. It is this environment that will have the greatest impact on the retention of the employees that you worked so hard to recruit and hire.

A strong supportive environment that promotes respect and recognition for all people will help to create a positive workplace environment. An organization that offers support and assistance when people and departments are in need also helps to foster an environment that encourages other people to share and work together. A company that encourages employees to balance home life and work life creates an environment in which everyone understands the need to pitch in when necessary because the company is willing to do the same for the individual when necessary.

Work Can Be Fun!

Creating a fun workplace means more than just blowing up party balloons and serving birthday cake! Today's employees first want to feel respected, to feel that they matter, and to be kept informed. They expect to be treated fairly and consistently, and they expect to be challenged and heard. But a little time out for fun and games—especially celebrations—will help put your company on the path to success.

In general, people want to know what is expected of them in any given situation. In any organization a sense of comfort and trust can be achieved when all members of the company know exactly what to expect regarding their authority and responsibility. To achieve a level of enjoyment and fun at work, some basic expectations, for employees and the company, should be defined.

1. Create a fair and consistent environment. Make sure that everyone you supervise is treated fairly and equally. Supervisors should see to it that employees know where they stand at all times, and how things are going in the company as a whole. It is imperative that each employee knows and believes that he is equal to all other employees in the company. If there is the slightest sense of favoritism or bias toward a group, person, or situation, you and your company are heading for morale issues and possible lawsuits. You know that it is illegal to discriminate against classes of people, but beware of the small issues that might make someone feel discriminated against.

For example: Letting one employee leave early without any obvious explanation and then asking a second employee a series of questions before granting them permission to do the same, can give the appearance of discrimination. It may seem like no big deal to you, but to the second employee it appears that the first one is getting preferential treatment. Your challenge is to be sure everyone believes and feels that you are fair and consistent in dealing with all issues. The development of policies and procedures is generally the way in which companies help to minimize problems with this issue.

2. Challenge people. Whenever possible, try to create jobs that minimize constant repetition with few variations. Be sure to include job responsibilities in which the employee is likely to encounter situations in which she will have to tackle new problems or devise new solutions for her tasks.

When you are designing the job description for various positions, always include an expectation that will direct employees to learn the skills of other positions as part of their job description.

People want to learn and be challenged, but they also want to know what to expect, and it is important not to surprise them with the challenges you set forth. Make it part of the job they agreed to do and you agreed to pay them for. Don't forget to reward them with praise and positive feedback when they do stretch and learn new skills and abilities. As you apply this basic principle, you will discover that existing employees have the capacity to fill key positions within the organization, allowing you to save recruiting dollars and to retain your knowledge base within the company. Remember to keep the challenge positive, and the results will be positive, too!

3. Be attentive to the people in your organization. Listen to each and every member of the company. When people know that you take them seriously, they are more likely to make positive contributions. These contributions may be as basic as simple good work habits or as complex as the development of new products and services.

Taking the time to listen to employees is the greatest strength a manager can possess. Your people have most of the answers to the challenges that face your organization. How many times have you made a decision that has not had the outcome you hoped for? Subsequently you find out that a member of your department made a suggestion that would have worked. This happens all the time in organizations because the people in leadership positions chose not to listen to the people that really know the situation.

4. Communicate success and failure regularly. Be direct and honest in communicating the success of each employee. When it is time to communicate failures and problems, be just as honest and sincere. When presented in a supportive manner, employees will benefit from recognizing how they could have transformed a negative event into an exciting and positive opportunity.

In reality, employees are people and want to know the truth. If you have been fair and consistent, if you have been offering people reasonable challenges, and if you have been really listening, then this step is very simple. When you have created a positive working environment, when you have created a sense of trust, you are able to walk a much broader line in dealing with your employees. You are viewed as a person who respects the people who work with you. You are viewed as a person who has set clear expectations for, and has been attentive to, the needs of the employees. You are perceived as a fair and reasonable boss to work for and with.

When you are at this point, your employees will respond favorably and positively to direct, clear communication of both their successes and their failures. They will look to you for approval and recognition when they succeed, as well as advice and support when they face failure. Be honest, be direct, be sincere, and most importantly, be yourself.

Be Creative

Companies that encourage mistakes are encouraging people to try new ideas and are willing to allow them the fun of stretching their minds, pushing the envelope, and unzipping their brain, all leading to higher levels of personal gratification.

People who work—and that is most of the adult population—spend more than 10,000 days of their lives in the office. This is a very big chunk of one's life. Shouldn't we try to enjoy this time as much as possible?

To enjoy the work we do and the place in which we work, we must have a supportive and safe environment. Fun within the context of the business world means feeling comfortable to be oneself and to interact, even while working and accomplishing tasks, with other individuals you respect.

If a child felt that each new addition to her environment was a potential threat, her degree of enthusiasm and creativity would be greatly reduced. Similarly, an employee exposed to a tumultuous and chaotic environment day after day will also feel threatened and insecure. Companies that create a safe, supportive environment for

Words of the Wise

"Leadership is unlocking people's potential to become better."

—Bill Bradley (1943–),
U.S. senator and
former professional
basketball player

Rosa Parks
(1913–)

Rosa Parks made history by refusing to relinquish her bus seat, instigating the Montgomery bus boycott and creating the spark that ignited the civil rights movement. An active member of the NAACP and the Southern Christian Leadership Conference, Parks founded the Rosa and Raymond Parks Institute for Self-Development, which is geared toward preparing African American youths for leadership and careers. In 1999, she was awarded the Congressional Gold Medal of Honor.

employees have a higher incidence of fun and higher levels of creativity and productivity.

Here are some ideas that can get you thinking in the right direction for your employees and yourself.

1. Organize a company Ping-Pong tournament.
2. Have the whole company spend the day working for a local charity.
3. Create a recipe exchange as part of a monthly bring-a-treat-for-lunch activity.
4. Prepare your favorite food for the entire staff as a surprise.
5. Create a Fabulous Friday program, with each department expected to plan and execute an activity that will create a positive outlook for employees.
6. Institute a Wild Day. Once each month, select an employee's name from a hat and give that person an extra day off. By the next day, the employee must decide the day he will take off, and that day is the Wild Day for the month. When 75 percent of the employees have had a Wild Day, all the names go back into the hat.
7. Plan dress-up or costume days on days other than Halloween.
8. Have community-based contests between departments.
9. Show cartoons or old TV sitcoms during lunch break in the cafeteria or lunchroom. Bring employees back to their childhood.
10. Keep a box of puzzle toys that you can pass out whenever you sense things are getting a bit too tense in the office.
11. Keep some Nerf-type balls and items around to give employees the opportunity to let off a little steam.
12. Set up a few days a year when employees are encouraged to bring their children to work.
13. Organize noontime basketball, softball, tennis, bowling, or miniature golf.

There are many ways in which companies produce safe and supportive environments. Frequently the company will develop outlets that allow employees to feel comfortable and connected to the company while still having fun. These outlets unify employees in a sense of fun and enjoyment and create a general sense of goodwill.

- **Company outings:** These are a great example of expanding the environment and linking it to fun. Regularly scheduled outings as simple as monthly pizza at a local restaurant generate a sense of anticipation and a feeling that "we can get work done and still have fun at the same time." More extravagant family outings on an annual or semiannual basis allow the employees to include the family in a portion of life that oftentimes is all consuming. Interaction among family members helps to create a strong bond between work and home life that subsequently generates a higher degree of productivity and support of the work effort.

  Additionally, the family outing allows all employees to see the managers, supervisors, and other management staff as people who have families very similar to their own. A sense of parity is established when a group of coworkers gets to eat hamburgers and hotdogs at picnic tables with executives of the company.

- **Celebrations are important:** Take advantage of every opportunity to celebrate truly important moments within the organization. You'll want to make these celebrations fun for the right business reason. If you direct the celebration toward birthdays, anniversaries, et cetera, you may not be encouraging improved productivity. If you celebrate project completions, reaching sales goals, new skill mastery, completion of training classes, quarterly profit reports, or anything that measures business performance, you will be creating an environment that equates fun with business success.

  Celebrate these types of victories. After a big sales initiative, after landing a new client, upon the wrap-up of a successful project, or at the end of the exceptionally busy day

that went flawlessly, gather everyone together for a celebration to mark this special event. Serve refreshments and use the opportunity to create an atmosphere of upbeat morale, even if everyone is physically exhausted. You want everyone to go home and tell the family how hard they worked, how much fun it was to complete the task, and how much they enjoyed being recognized for and celebrating the achievement.

- **Keep it interesting:** If your work environment is unattractive, do your best to spruce it up. A can of paint and some Spic and Span can go a long way to perking up any drab space. Borrow artwork from the local library to create a constantly changing gallery in your office. Create situations where the work environment becomes closely aligned with cultural and social endeavors, making work more like fun.

- **Let's get physical:** Whenever possible, support or organize ongoing programs of informal athletic competition. Encourage and support the efforts of employees who want to organize softball, bowling, tennis, or other activities. When these activities are supported by the company, more people will participate, creating another vehicle for work to be equated with fun.

Ultimately you want employees to think and behave in a fashion that always connects work with fun and enjoyment. You want everyone to say, "Wow, what a day. I worked so hard and got so much done. It was great. I actually had fun today!" Fun, physical breaks can help to rejuvenate employees and renew creativity.

Define the Culture

The culture of a company helps to define the level of support an employee will find within the organization. The day-to-day practice of this cultural sensibility is the ultimate driving force for the success of the company. A vivid example of a company that lives and breathes its culture is Harley-Davidson.

This motorcycle manufacturer has a culture defined by five formal values. These values are communicated to all employees as part of the recruiting, hiring, and orientation processes and are promoted, reinforced, and used every day as part of the life of the company.

These values are:

- Tell the truth.
- Be fair.
- Keep your promises.
- Respect the individual.
- Encourage intellectual curiosity.

It almost reads like a list your mom would put together. What this says about an organization is very clear. Harley-Davidson values the basic human values that are part of the Judeo-Christian heritage of Western civilization.

Harley-Davidson goes further and supports these basic values by identifying issues that are always a concern to the organization. All members of the organization are reminded of these concerns via a simple statement that identifies these issues. These continuing concerns are:

- Quality
- Participation
- Productivity
- Flexibility
- Cash Flow

Look again at these two lists. Notice how similar they are to the Golden Rule of times gone by: "Do unto others as you would have them do unto you." It may seem corny, but it still works and is a valuable tool for the successful company of today.

Have you ever heard of a company where many of the employees actually tattoo the company logo on their body? Has Harley-Davidson a secret other companies should learn?

The Role of Employee Recognition

Studies upon studies have shown that employees have very specific needs, as do all people. Most of the time, managers and business owners think that the only thing an employee wants is more money. In reality, this is very far from the truth.

Time and again studies come to the same conclusion: People are more concerned with being recognized for the work they do than any other issue. The next most important concern for employees is knowing that they are part of the "big picture," that they are in on things, and that they are included in the overall process of the business.

The bottom line is that people want to be valued, respected, and recognized for what they contribute to the organization. People are proud and want to experience recognition for whatever they do. At first glance, this seems easy enough to accomplish. But as a leader in the company, you must seriously consider the strategy you will employ to achieve this sensibility of recognition.

In reality, employees are not as concerned with money as people think. In the list of the 10 most important concerns for employees, money was rated right in the middle. First and foremost, employees want recognition, involvement, and honest concern about their welfare from their employer. Interestingly, in the past, most managers and owners have thought employees were not at all concerned about being in on things or knowing what was going on. It is obvious that we have a lot to learn about each other.

Look at the list of the top three issues that motivate employees:

1. Full appreciation for work done.
2. Feeling that they are "in on things."
3. Assistance with personal problems.

When examined, you will realize that you, alone and with no budget, can give employees exactly what they want. It doesn't cost anything to say "thank you for doing such a fine job." It doesn't cost a cent to inform employees that a new product or service will be rolled out on a particular date. It doesn't cost you any money to ask employees about the health of their family or if they have resolved a personal problem that you are aware of.

In reality, the issues most important to employees are the items easiest for a company to provide. But they must be supplied in a fashion that is sincere and consistently applied. You cannot make employee recognition a program that happens at a certain time each year with bells and whistles and fancy awards. The creation of a positive employee recognition strategy demands an ongoing commitment to employees as people and as partners in the company. It must be real, and it must be part of a day-to-day culture of the organization. The annual awards ceremony will be meaningful and have impact only if it is the highlight of an organization that demonstrates recognition and respect for all employees all the time.

Employees will respond with enthusiasm and energy when they know they are valued. They will contribute at higher levels of productivity and creativity when they know they are recognized. They will accept new challenges and will transform problems into opportunities when they know, when they feel, when they experience recognition and respect from their manager.

Many organizations try to create employee recognition programs without first establishing the foundation of valuing and respecting employees. When an employee recognition program is just a program and not a part of the fabric of the company, it fails to achieve its objectives. When the program is an extension of the company culture and sensibility, the program has great impact.

Employee recognition programs can be whatever you want them to be. They should reflect your personal style. If you feel that athletic, outdoor activities are important and valuable, build your employee recognition program around that theme.

Here are some suggestions of programs you can implement:

- Create a vehicle for individual employees to recognize other employees who help them in ways that are frequently overlooked—personal recognition for the person who is always there to help out in a pinch.

- Develop a program to recognize teams that work especially well together to achieve a defined objective. Make the guidelines measurable and linked to the business objective.

- Reinvent and consistently follow the employee-of-the-month program that most companies have had in the past. The key is to keep it going and to make the award meaningful. How are they recognized? How does everyone learn about this? Do all the employees of the month get together at certain times of the year?

- Create employee-of-the-month focus groups where those employees are asked to assist with business problem solving and creative strategic development.

- Periodically surprise everyone with a special award: the "Just Because You Did a Great Job Award." Pretty soon, people will begin doing the kinds of things you appreciate, in the hope they'll receive one of these coveted awards. It's a great way to develop your company culture quickly.

- Rather than having a discipline procedure that only tracks problems and performance issues, have a performance development policy that offers managers the opportunity to praise employees when they reach a new milestone in personal professional development. No longer will people fear the personnel file; they will want to get statements of positive development put into their file.

- Don't forget the tried and true 5-, 10-, 15-year seniority awards, plaques, and events. Again the key is consistent application of these procedures, especially when times are not so good and cash flow is low. This is not the time to skimp on these awards. People need to have some sense of security during the really slow business times.

- It may sound simple, but a friendly note to say "thank you" goes a long way. Consider writing notes to people you catch doing something the way you want it done. Again the key is to make it personal and to consistently follow through.

CHAPTER 14

Express Yourself

Your success with the previous and following concepts is in direct relation to your personality. This is why it is important to take heed of the fourteenth core concept, express yourself. You should use your personality to help others accept and understand your role as leader.

The emergence of leadership occurs when a person is intolerant of the status quo and is committed to making a change. Leaders are creative and quick-witted. People are often sought out for leadership positions because of their intelligence as well as their organizational "common sense." Leaders are also able to present a vision of the future that stimulates, excites, and motivates their followers. They provide an environment where learning is rewarded and the organization becomes self-renewing.

Leaders are motivated by a drive that focuses their actions and interactions on what is right with respect to legal, human, and financial considerations. Leaders are flexible—they take what the prevailing situation offers and run with it. They are not bound by convention just because it is convenient or traditional. Leaders have strength in the face of adversity and demonstrate a sense of reliability and integrity, which they offer and share with their followers, employees, customers, vendors, and colleagues.

It's All about Personality and Self-Confidence

One of the determining factors in what makes a person a leader is personality. A quiet and reserved wallflower type is never going to be able to rally the troops into action. A more charismatic, jovial extrovert will more likely be able to get the job done.

A closer look at Presidential Campaign 2000 illustrates how personality and leadership go hand in hand. From the beginning, the campaign centered on the personality differences between the two candidates. Al Gore was criticized for being "wooden" and "stiff." This image became such a problem for Gore that he did a complete overhaul. Out went the uptight suits and ties; it became more common to

Words of the Wise

"I may have faults, but being wrong ain't one of them."

—*Jimmy Hoffa*
(1913–declared legally dead in 1983),
American labor leader

see him in a polo shirt and khakis when speaking in a public forum. There was also the lip-smacking kiss between Al and his wife, that sent the media into an uproar. Bush, on the other hand, always tried to be a man of the people. More often described as "dimwitted" and "bumbling," Bush had to work hard to make up for flubs made during public speeches. In essence he used his "ignorance" as an asset, claiming the role of any ordinary man who just wants to "get things done."

Whether you agree or disagree with these assessments, it is clear that image and personality are crucial in determining leadership roles. The thing that both candidates shared in common was the desire to become leader of the free world. Each wanted to put their vision into action and lead the United States to continued growth and prosperity.

What you as a leader can take away from this discussion is the importance of being yourself. Know who you are and what you want to accomplish, and you will have no choice but to exude self-confidence (whether you feel that way or not). People will look to you as a leader; as someone who sets an example; makes good decisions and judgments; someone who is not afraid to admit when mistakes are made but is proactive in coming up with a solution to rectify the situation.

Leadership Self-Assessment

As a leader, you should be interested in understanding your leadership style so that you can use this knowledge to become a more effective leader. The following quiz is designed to help gain some insight into your approach.

Overview

This assessment is designed to provide you with a personal profile of your leadership competencies, attitudes, and behaviors. Since leadership only becomes "good" or "bad" in its execution, this assessment should not be considered in that way.

Give yourself 4 points if you answer "Frequently," 2 points if you answer "Sometimes," and 0 points if you choose "Rarely or Never." Total your score when you finish to determine your leadership rating.

Profile

Madonna
(1958–)

Madonna is an American singer, songwriter, and actress who continues to break the mold and reinvent herself. Rebelling against the status quo, Madonna became a cultural icon with her second album, *Like a Virgin,* achieving unprecedented power and control for a woman in the music industry. Madonna was also the first female artist to use music videos to her advantage, emphasizing her charismatic performances with choreographed dance, special effects, and designer clothing. Madonna has been nominated for and won a variety of Grammys and MTV Music Awards for her music, choreography, and videos. As a new bride, new mother, and savvy businesswoman, Madonna is showing women that they truly can have it all.

Employee Assessment Tool

	Frequently	Sometimes	Rarely/Never
SECTION A ACTIVISM/CHANGE			
1. When I sense that something is not right at work or in the community, I find a way to make it better.			✓
2. I understand who in my organization can help me or my employer achieve our goals.		✓	
3. I have little tolerance when inertia overcomes a project or employee.	✓		
4. I respect the past and our company's legacy; however, I do not avoid rethinking "tradition."	✓	✓	
5. I am committed to quality.	✓		
6. I am driven toward high performance.	✓		
SECTION B INTELLIGENCE/LEARNING			
1. I believe that I have the mental capacity to think through most complex situations.	✓		
2. I welcome the challenge of complex issues and problems.	✓		
3. I am committed to creating an environment where mistakes become learning experiences.		✓	
4. I encourage my staff to disagree with me.	✓		
5. I tend to hire people who have talents, knowledge, and skills I don't possess.	✓		
6. I believe I am more intelligent than lucky.	✓	M	
7. I am not intimidated by ingenious people.		✓	
8. I like being around "smart" people.	✓		

(continued on next page)

Employee Assessment Tool

(continued from previous page)

	Frequently	Sometimes	Rarely/Never
SECTION C VISION			
1. I look at things around me and I am able to envision how they can and will be better.		✓	
2. I articulate abstract ideas to others quite easily.			✓
3. I have a picture of the future that I am committed to fulfilling.			✓
4. The vision I have for the company incorporates what is strongest about the firm.			✓
5. I often utilize symbols and images to motivate my employees.			✓
6. I communicate and exemplify high standards of performance.		✓	
SECTION D ALTRUISM/CARING			
1. I generally respect the employees with whom I work.	✓		
2. I hold general conversations with my employees.		✓	
3. I genuinely admire and appreciate the people who work with me.		✓	
4. Knowing about my employees' values is important to me.		✓	
5. Knowing about my employees' hobbies is important to me.		✓	
6. I encourage employees to help each other develop to their full potential.		✓	
7. I communicate often with employees about work.			✓
8. I communicate often with my employees about leisure activities.			✓
9. I provide personal attention to people who may need it.		✓	

(continued on next page)

Employee Assessment Tool

(continued from previous page)

	Frequently	Sometimes	Rarely/Never
SECTION E COMMUNICATION			
1. I am generous in my praise and recognition of my employees who perform quality work.		✓	
2. I seek the opinions of my employees.	✓		
SECTION F FLEXIBILITY			
1. If plans go sour, I recover easily and without searching for a scapegoat.		✓	
2. I have a high tolerance for ambiguity.		✓	
3. When an employee has a "bright idea" I try to find a way to accommodate it.	✓		
SECTION G SPIRIT/SOUL			
1. I have an inner sense of balance that allows me to move through the day with serenity.		✓	
2. I know how to relax.		✓	
3. I take the time to enjoy the nonwork component of my life.		✓	
4. I have an emerging leadership style that is truly my own.		✓	
5. I know how to "play."			✓
6. I allow my employees to see and experience all facets of my personality.		✓	
7. Both in and out of the office, my spiritual foundation guides me.	✓		

(continued on next page)

Employee Assessment Tool

(continued from previous page)

	Frequently	Sometimes	Rarely/Never
SECTION H INTEGRITY/EGO STRENGTH			
1. I do my own "dirty work."		✓	
2. I don't disappear when an employee is in trouble.	✓		
3. I don't ask anyone to do something I would not do.	✓		
4. If I had to choose I would treat employees better than bosses.		✓	
5. I admit or explain when I am wrong.	✓		
6. I can and do take the heat.	✓		
7. I consider myself a symbol of achievement and success.		✓	
8. I am comfortable with who I am.		✓	
SECTION I CREATIVITY/INNOVATION			
1. Ideas come readily to me.		✓	
2. I strive to have employees conceptualize old problems in new ways.		✓	
3. I provide new ways of looking at issues that may seem puzzling to employees.	✓		
SECTION J RELIABILITY			
1. I ensure that my employees have the information and resources necessary to do the job.	✓		
2. If I say it is so, I make it so.	✓		
3. I don't avoid problems or sticky issues.	✓		
4. I make sure that there is congruence between what employees are asked to do and what they can expect from me in support of their efforts.	✓		

(continued on next page)

Scoring

Now, add up your total score.

200+ You are well on your way to being a superior leader. The attributes and behaviors you exhibit tend to motivate, enrich, educate, and inspire others. When those abilities are matched with organizational knowledge and personal drive, they become the mettle for solid leadership.

150–199 You are working well toward the development of leadership savvy. By examining the various factors of the assessment, you can see where you need to focus your attention and possibly even reflect on your assumptions about work, the people who work with you, and why you want to be a leader. You may find from this exercise that you will learn how to stimulate more accountability and independence in others by showing more vulnerability within yourself.

110–149 The reasons for attaining the leadership positions you seek may be more self-centered than organizationally based. Trust is an essential component of leadership, and your score indicates that either you believe that the people you work with are not trustworthy or you doubt your own ability to lead effectively. In either case, you may be holding on too closely or not delegating at all. Consequently, those around you may not be confident of your support. Examine each area of this assessment and reflect on why you are so dedicated to "control" and what you really have to lose by guiding rather than forcing.

0–109 The attitudes, behaviors, and talents you are bringing to a position of leadership are unseasoned. You may be holding on to some archaic notions of "boss/subordinate" relationships, or have been too long under the influence of managers who do not, or a climate that does not value individuals' fundamental objective to do well and to be appreciated. Before you accept or seek a higher position of supervision, management, or leadership, you may want to pursue new mentoring relationships within the organization, take some management courses, read some of the newer writings on management, and consider objectively why you want to lead. The goal of leadership is not out of reach; you are just going to have to do a lot of homework to be effective.

Personality Traits of Leaders

We have already spoken a bit about self-confidence and how it is a necessary trait in leaders. Now, let's dig a little deeper. Here are some more traits that are common to all good leaders.

- **Good Leaders Take a Stand**
  Robert Browning once wrote, "Ah, but a man's reach should exceed his grasp, or what's a heaven for?" Step out and stand for something. People are genuinely attracted to those who move in reasoned, affirmative, innovative, or intrepid directions.

- **Good Leaders Build and Develop Strong Followers**
  One of the hallmarks of exemplary leaders is that they have surrounded themselves with intelligent, action-oriented, dedicated, and ardent followers. The mistake made by so many aspiring leaders is to shy away from or marginalize strong followers. This behavior is grounded in the mistaken notion that the follower may overshadow the leader. But in actuality, by showing confidence in the followers' abilities, providing challenging assignments, and being personally concerned about follower/colleague development, the leader is engendering respect, loyalty, and commitment while also stimulating high-quality performance. The collateral effect is that the leader is also making it easier to delegate and freeing himself to devote more energy to novel and more strategic issues.

- **Good Leaders Communicate Often**
  If you want people to follow you they must know who you are, what you represent, what you can do, and what your vision is. To do that, you must tell them. Disseminate your ideas in meetings as well as in writing. Participate in formal and informal groups that address relevant issues of your firm. Have frequent meetings with your colleagues and coworkers. Inform those around you of what your priorities, dreams, and values are, and let your talents be known. Take advantage of opportunities to feature and utilize your skills.

Words of the Wise

"The difference between the impossible and the possible lies in a man's determination."

—*Tommy Lasorda (1927–), baseball coach*

Cultivate relationships outside of your area, so that when there is a task to be done, you'll be considered for it.

- **Good Leaders Play Up Their Strengths**

  This also means that you should understand and be committed to working on personal weaknesses. As a leader, you must do those things that will make others want to be around you, and you must demonstrate that you are a competent and confident person. For example, if you are not a strong or inspiring public speaker, then do the background research, write the report or the speech, or introduce the subject at the meeting for someone else to present. But also put yourself into situations where new skills and competencies can be developed. Utilize your colleagues', mentors', and followers' expertise to complement and enhance your own. Work with someone—model her behavior, or have that person constructively critique your performance. Take classes, within the company or at a local college.

- **Good Leaders Recognize That Leadership Is Everywhere (Not Just at the Top)**

  Some aspiring leaders wallow in despair because they are not "in charge." They think that just because they don't hold a designated position of leadership, they cannot exercise leadership (or they cannot have models for leadership who are peers). Think of how you can effect change or promote the vision of the designated leader from where you are in the hierarchy. By becoming recognized for making things happen in one context, the opportunities for larger, more significant, more strategic influence will come your way. Search for leadership opportunities; volunteer for tough assignments. Find solutions to problems that your manager doesn't know exist. Then inform him about your findings.

- **Good Leaders *Are* Themselves and *Believe* in Themselves**

  A positive self-image will help you project an aura of confidence that will inspire others. You are human—your leadership style should be a natural extension of who you are. If you find that it isn't, then your leadership venue is inappropriate, you are living out someone else's vision of you, or what you are working for is contrary to your values. While growing and changing, most leaders work very hard at developing skills and competencies. The thing that exemplary leaders do not do is assume a mask that disavows essential anchors of their personalities. It is also important to be natural in your leadership endeavors, because in times of stress, an act or assumed character will disintegrate into your underlying essence, and the people who follow or work with you need to know just who will show up.

- **Good Leaders Understand the "Game"**
  Be politically aware and learn how to effectively and appropriately utilize politics and the political subsystem. No matter what level of expertise you possess, the confidence you exude, or the success you have amassed, if you are politically naive, your leadership acumen will never mature. So much of what leaders do involves negotiating the political environments of organizations. One of the best preparations an aspiring leader can have is to become intimately aware of the power players and political actors in an organization and understand the history and alliances of them. It also doesn't hurt if you are able to observe or work with any of these people.

- **Good Leaders Are Visible**
  There is an old adage that speaks of not hiding your candle under a basket. With leadership, that is especially true. There is nothing arrogant or inappropriate about letting others know what you have done or can do. When you have made a significant accomplishment or received recognition beyond your home base, be sure the word gets back home. Share a complimentary memo, or if the occasion warrants, see that a letter or memo gets back to the supervisor or mentor. Participate in activities that place you in the spotlight, and be well prepared to shine. Don't take on too much, but what you do take on do with quality and panache.

- **Good Leaders Don't Sell Out**
  Always have and keep your integrity. There will never be anything more important than your word in this world, so keep

Profile

Adolph Hitler
(1889–1945)

Master of propaganda oratory techniques, Adolf Hitler served as leader of the National Socialist (Nazi) Party (1920–1921) and dictator of Germany (1933–1945). Under the absolute dictatorship of Hitler, the Nazi Party was responsible for the mass genocide of the Jewish people during WWII.

it. Evaluate situations very carefully and communicate your position clearly. Followers will neither respect nor take risks for leaders who are unreliable. This does not mean that you cannot change your mind. However, that change needs to be conscientiously appraised, and you need to inform those closest to you so they will not be surprised by you and will understand your decision. Be true to your values and what you think is right. Honesty must be your hallmark.

- **Good Leaders Have Genuine Interest, Concern, and Passion for Followers and Colleagues**

  For people to follow, they must believe that you care for them. You must value them, not only for what they can do for you and the organization but also for who they are as individuals. Know who they are and what their strengths and developmental needs are, and design training assignments and offer opportunities for recognition that address each person's profile. Also, become familiar with their personal and vocational interests. In other words, always remember that the people who work with and for you have personalities and lives that go beyond the organization. Knowing them, treating them well, and understanding their needs and values will enhance your leadership.

- **Good Leaders Learn from Mistakes**

  Everyone makes them, so don't agonize over them but find ways to keep the same mistakes from happening again. If a mistake occurs on your watch, quickly debrief and regroup. Assignment of blame is not as important as construction of a recovery strategy. Leadership is about moving forward, not wallowing in the past.

- **Good Leaders Make Sure That Everyone Is Getting the Message**

  Ask people to be sure they are really getting the message you are delivering. At group meetings, ask people what they see as the key components of the company's strategy. At individual meetings or in questionnaires, ask questions like, "Do you feel that the company has a clear future direction?" or "Do you think the company will prosper in the future?"

If it turns out that the people are not comprehending the message, give it again.

- **Good Leaders Extend Leadership to All Parts of the Organization**
  In companywide meetings, or other large meetings, you can show leadership in a broad, visionary way. But you or your managers should have smaller meetings with people in each functional area. People want to feel that their department or function has a clearly defined role and direction within the overall plan.

Presentations and Public Speaking

Okay, so we've established the traits that make a true leader. Among these traits self-confidence will always stand out as the most important and the most useful. Self-confidence not only affects your decision-making process, but it also can be used to your advantage when speaking in public at a meeting or giving a more formal presentation.

What happens in these more formal situations depends largely on you and your ability to "express yourself." You need to be able to sell yourself, your ideas, and your determination to succeed in the public forum. Don't panic. Use your assets to win them over and *wow* them. The easiest way to do that is to be yourself and be prepared!

How to Be an Effective Public Speaker

You will want to get your point across without boring them to death or overwhelming them with one-liners. First, decide the purpose of your presentation. Is it to inform, to persuade, to train, to award and recognize others? Once you have the purpose clear, take a closer look at the audience. Tailor the presentation to the audience. It's essential that you know who they are, why they are there, and what they expect to get out of the presentation. You won't always be able to determine all these factors, but you should try to gather as much background information as possible before your presentation. Of course, if you are delivering the presentation to your staff members, then you already have all the information you need.

Words of the Wise

"I think *Hail to the Chief* has a nice ring to it."

—*John F. Kennedy's response when asked about his favorite song*

Here are some more detailed steps to help you along:

- Decide on your specific topic and focus.
- Gather all the materials you will need and organize your research. This can be done in whatever way will be easiest for you—chronological, pro and con pattern, et cetera.
- Identify problems and explain symptoms. Give appropriate solutions.
- Know your material. Go over it ahead of time. Get comfortable with it and be prepared for any questions that may be asked.
- Give yourself enough time to prepare properly. In most cases, it is better to give yourself extra time than to try and scramble around at the last minute.
- Do an outline of the material (just like you did way back in grammar school).

Tricks of the Trade

Many experts will give the same advice about giving presentations: open by telling the audience what you are going to tell them, use all the information you have collected to tell them, close by telling them what you have told them. You may feel like you are beating them over the head with the information, but in actuality you are just helping to clarify the information.

Another good tip from the experts involves engaging the audience. The easiest way to do this seems to be by using gestures to accentuate your discussion. How you move your arms and hands during a presentation can have a big impact on your success. Think about how you might support a thought or idea with an appropriate gesture. If, on the other hand, you tend to move around too much, try making a speech with your hands clasped behind your back. If this proves too difficult, work on facial expressions and how you project your voice.

Another good addition is humor. This doesn't mean just telling jokes. Introduce amusing, whimsical, comical, or otherwise entertaining elements that make a connection with your audience, to put you and them at ease and to reinforce your message. A little humor at the beginning will loosen everyone up (including you). By using humor throughout the presentation, you are helping your audience to stay alert. Using humor to focus on a key point can help to add emphasis.

Seek out amusing stories from your own life or look to newspapers and magazines for help. Look for quotes by famous people. There are dozens of books and Web sites on quotations. Search for quotes that specifically illustrate the message you are sending.

Another key point is to remember to enunciate. If you mumble or slur words, people are going to have quite a hard time understanding you and will soon lose interest. Few things are more annoying than trying to decipher what a speaker is saying. Poor articulation will also make you appear to be less believable and less authoritative. On the other hand, exaggerated enunciation will make the audience feel that they are being talked down to and patronized. You should strive to avoid falling into either of these categories.

Last but not least, encourage audience participation. Here are some reasons to get the audience in on the act:

- To serve as an icebreaker
- To use up some of the stored energy people have when they are seated for too long
- To wake people up, especially when your presentation is after a meal or the room is too warm
- To help the audience master a task that you are training them to do
- To give the audience hands-on experience with your product
- To emphasize a key point with an activity
- To answer questions

Above all be yourself and try to have a good time.

Profile

Susan B. Anthony
(1820–1906)

In 1866, Susan B. Anthony cofounded the National Women's Suffrage Association, becoming the recognized leader of the suffragist movement. She also helped compile, write, and edit the first four volumes of *The History of Woman Suffrage*. In 1979, she became the first woman to have her image on a U.S. coin in recognition of her contributions to women's suffrage.

CHAPTER 15

Self-Discipline Brings Success

Your self-expression undoubtedly exudes self-confidence. However, you also need a bit of self-discipline thrown into the mix. This fifteenth core concept will teach you how to maximize your time and energy and how to strategize for yourself as well as others.

Chapter 3 was devoted entirely to figuring out ways of keeping employees motivated. Now it's time to talk about keeping yourself in line and moving in the right direction—heading toward success. It's not always easy, but with a little effort, you will be surprised at how much you can achieve.

The *American Heritage Dictionary* definition of self-discipline is "Training and control over oneself for personal improvement." We start learning the concept of discipline at a very early age through our parents. This applies to the basic notion of right and wrong as well as the idea that we do not know everything and there is much to learn. As we grow older, the concept is more often applied to sticking with a diet or workout schedule or even doing housework. In more complex business terms, self-discipline becomes a little harder to distinguish.

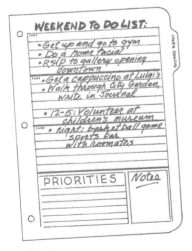

Self-Discipline Involves Motivating Yourself

If you find that all the little tasks have been delegated and you've got some free time on your hands, what do you do? If you answered (a) leave work early and get in 18 holes on the golf course, (b) treat myself to a manicure, or (c) meet friends for a long lunch at the trendy new restaurant everyone is talking about, then you need to work on your level of self-discipline. Sure it's nice *and* necessary to reward yourself every so often for a job well done. However, it isn't necessary to fill your free time with leisure activities while everyone else is slaving away back at the office.

With free time on your hands, take the opportunity to practice what you preach. In other words, use some of the same tools you use to motivate others to motivate yourself.

- Set daily, weekly, and monthly goals that you would like to reach. Perhaps you can look to the future and start developing your vision of the department or organization. By setting specific guidelines for yourself, you will be better able to keep busy and motivated.

  Example: You want to design ad campaigns for products that the company has not promoted very heavily in the past.

Week 1	Arrange to meet with the marketing and sales departments to come up with advertising ideas and promotional suggestions.
Week 2	Meet with the in-house graphic designer to put the ideas in a more visual context.
Week 3	Speak with representatives from magazines and trade journals about pricing and cost of advertising.
Week 4	Think about or develop ideas for integrating these products with the Internet.
Week 5	Write up a proposal and present it to the key people in the company.

- There will also be times when you feel overwhelmed, criticized, and just generally underappreciated. When these times occur, focus on your past successes. Remember the times when you were highly motivated and look for what pushed you and gave you the internal drive. Break down your work into more manageable chunks, and continue to delegate those tasks that do not require your personal attention.

Next, take a closer look at those criticisms that have been aimed at you or your work and see if there is any truth to what has been said. Face your critics head-on and ask for suggestions as to how your work can be more effective. Use your strengths to move forward and seek to improve on those areas where you are weak. Put things into perspective. Take a vacation day and do something you enjoy. (Perhaps you are overworking yourself and could use some time away from the office.) The important thing to

Profile

Harriett Beecher Stowe
(1811–1896)

Harriet Beecher Stowe was an American author, abolitionist, social reformer, and philanthropist. She authored the antislavery book *Uncle Tom's Cabin*, an emotional charge against slavery and one of the most influential texts in American history.

remember is to keep yourself motivated in order to keep those around you motivated.

Some More Self-Motivational Tips

- Avoid procrastination at all costs.
- Do the most unpleasant or most difficult tasks at the beginning of the day and work your way through tasks that get progressively easier or that are more enjoyable.
- Work on one thing at a time.
- If you are really having a hard time, give yourself a short break—get a drink of water or take a quick walk down the hall and back.
- Reward yourself for achieving goals whether large or small.
- Develop a routine that maximizes productivity. Stick to an agenda.
- Set realistic goals for yourself so you don't get too discouraged and so you don't feel overburdened.
- Don't try to be perfect. Perfectionism has been the downfall of many. Accept mistakes and accept failure.

Working Alone, Telecommuting, and the World of the Self-Employed

Here is where self-discipline becomes more important and more difficult. When you work in close contact with others on a team, it is easier to stay on target and focus on the work at hand. After all, other people are depending on you to help them get the job done. In a collaborative work environment, there is more accountability and the other members of the team serve as motivators and help keep you disciplined.

There will be those moments (especially as a leader or manager) when your work day becomes less team oriented and becomes more and more an independent endeavor. These are the times when self-discipline becomes increasingly difficult. Although

Words of the Wise

"Never give up, for that is just the place and time that the tide will turn."

—*Harriet Beecher Stowe (1811–1896), American author and abolitionist* you are working alone, you are still in a leadership position. Now, in these solitary moments, the mettle of leadership is forged. So don't be seduced into thinking that you need a bunch of people behind you to lead. Leadership comes from having the courage, tenacity, foresight, and energy to blaze a trail, investigate a mystery, and take bold action.

You Are Your Own Boss

Although you may be working for yourself in a home-based business, you will still need to feel a sense of accomplishment. Of course, since there is no one else there to support and assess your efforts, you must internalize the sense of accomplishment. You need to feel that you have done a great job.

Establish the criteria that you think encompass a notable achievement or a sizable goal. Then work through the problems or tasks until they are resolved. Recognize your own hard work and give yourself credit where credit is due.

Account for your personality and your personal needs for some level of companionship. Some people have no problem with little to no interaction with the outside world, while others will be chomping at the bit within an hour or two. If you are the latter, arrange with meetings from outside vendors or hire someone to come in on a part-time basis and handle some of the clerical duties.

When contemplating whether self-employment is the right choice for you, take a look at some of the advantages and disadvantages of running a home office. These are some points that should help to promote self-discipline.

Advantages
- You are the one who decides the terms and goals of the business.
- You can build the business in a way that promotes and highlights your specific skills and talents.
- You will see the direct benefit of your own hard work, rather than waiting for praise that has been filtered down through countless other employees.

Leadership Tip

**Private!
Keep Out!**

In just the same way you expect employees to keep personal problems out of the office, you should also keep personal issues out of the workplace. No one likes a boss who uses personal problems as an excuse for not getting his work done properly and on time.

Elizabeth Cady Stanton
(1815–1902)

American abolitionist, author, and suffragist, Elizabeth Cady Stanton helped organize the 1848 women's rights convention and cofounded and served as the president for the National Women's Suffrage Association. She also authored *The Women's Bible* and *Eighty Years and More,* an autobiography.

- You are less vulnerable to the influence of outside forces over which you have no control (i.e., mergers, acquisitions, layoffs, restructuring).
- If you are successful, the monetary rewards will most likely exceed what you might have earned working for someone else.
- You make the rules about benefits and time off.
- You answer to no one but yourself.
- You will gain a broad view of the entire business—you won't spend the majority of your time focused on one specialized area.
- You will gain the status and recognition of an entrepreneur.
- The business will become a reflection of you, not the fulfillment of someone else's vision.

Disadvandages

- It is usually the case that you will need to work longer and harder than you ever thought imaginable.
- If the business is unsuccessful, the financial repercussions could be disastrous.
- You will have to spend countless hours learning about every facet of the business.
- There will be lots of personal sacrifices, and your life will revolve around your work.
- You will be giving up some forms of security that you would gain from a larger company (such as vacations and benefits).
- Your family must be willing to support you through the many strains of the business.

Here are some suggestions that should help get your discipline on track. In a home office, it is easy to get sidetracked, so keep your philosophy simple. Focus on your business. Eliminate the distractions of everyday life such as children, neighbors, and friends. Let friends and family know that you are serious about your work—tell them that they can't just pop into your office whenever they feel like it.

Don't wander into your kitchen for coffee. Don't answer your personal phone line. Don't check on the dog. These diversions will hamper your effectiveness in managing and growing your business. Remember, even though you are in your house, you are really at work.

Also, don't allow yourself to work 24 hours a day, 7 days a week. This will defeat you on many levels. Separate your work from your home. Ideally your office should have its own entrance, and living areas should not be visible from your desk. Try to remove all non-business-related furnishings from the area where you work. Another good idea is to erect internal doors to separate this room from the rest of the house.

Install another phone line that will be used only for the business. Otherwise, you will have to answer any and every call whether or not it is business related. It will cost a little more to install this phone line, but in the long run, you will save time and energy by weeding out needless distractions.

Be sure you have all the necessary equipment you need to run the business properly. This includes computers, phones, fax machines, printers, paper and pens, lighting, filing cabinets, et cetera. You don't want to have to run out in the middle of the day to Kinko's to send a million faxes because you didn't want to make that initial investment.

The Plight of the Telecommuter

Self-discipline can also be a big issue for those persons who telecommute all or part of the time. Here are some basic guidelines to follow:

- Keep to your regular work schedule. If you normally work from nine to five in the office, then do so when you are working from home.
- Know what you need to get done each day.
- Work as if you were in the office. Don't start cleaning or doing laundry while you are trying to get work done.
- Make sure you have the proper technology to get the job done. Technology can include online access,

Profile

Marie Curie
(1867–1934)

Marie Curie was the first woman to win the Nobel Prize. Curie, along with her husband, Pierre, discovered two new elements—radium and polonium—which laid the foundation for breakthroughs associated with radioactivity. It is because of her discovery and trials with radiation that we now have nuclear physics and are able to treat life-threatening cancers. Marie Curie is inspirational to all women in the scientific field.

e-mailing capabilities, a fax machine, or dual phone lines. Whatever you need to keep in contact with the people in your other office is what you should have at home.

Associations for Home Workers

American Telecommuting Association *www.knowledgetree.com/ata.html*
1220 L Street NW, Suite 100
Washington, DC 20005
800/ATA-4YOU
905/521-9888

Association for Work-at-Home Mothers *www.awahm.org*
5515 303rd Street
Toledo, OH 43611
877/643-3788

Home Office Association of America *www.hoaa.com*
133 East 58th Street, Suite 711
New York, NY 10022
800/809-4622

Independent Homeworkers Alliance *www.homeworkers.org*
180 St. James Street South, Suite 300
Hamilton, Ontario Canada L8P 4VI

OutSource2000 *www.outsource2000.com*
675 Gratiot Boulevard, Suite 3
P.O. Box 108
Smiths Creek, MI 48074-0108
810/989-1800

Self-Discipline Means Being Organized

Start with your computer. The computer is the focal point of an organized office. Used properly, it can be a miracle worker for bringing organization to even the most chaotic of work spaces. Make an effort to do and save your work on a computer whenever possible. Even when you are just brainstorming, for example, type up your thoughts on the computer so that they won't be lost, the way they might be if you used a notepad or a piece of paper. Always, always, always back up your computer files. Consider installing a tape backup so that you don't have to back up individual files on disks.

To get truly organized, divide your computer files into related groups and store them in different directories and subdirectories. As a rule of thumb, for quick location and easy access to any given item, you should maintain no more than seven files in any given directory. Use easily recognized names for directories, subdirectories, and individual file names. Don't be stingy about creating new directories when existing ones aren't appropriate.

When you can't store items on your computer, use files, as opposed to stacking papers and documents in desk drawers or in cabinets. Get color-coded files so that related items can be easily filed and retrieved. Clearly label all your files.

To get organized further, you need to ruthlessly eliminate any clutter that begins to accumulate in your office—especially on your desk. Once clutter starts to mount, the common tendency is to think, "It would take too long to even try to organize this mess— why bother? I'll just keep throwing things on top of the heap." Soon, you won't be able to find anything and you'll need a shovel to even find your desk.

Unless you train yourself to keep constantly organized, you are going to be wasting a lot of time looking for things you can't find. All too often, people finally clean up their clutter after they have wasted 10 minutes trying to find a misplaced pen or document. If you spend 10 minutes a day looking for lost items, you

Leadership Tip

Telecommuters by the Numbers

According to the International Telework Association and Council there are currently over 16 million regularly employed telecommuters in this country alone. These telecommuters are defined as those who work at least one day per month and are over the age of 18.

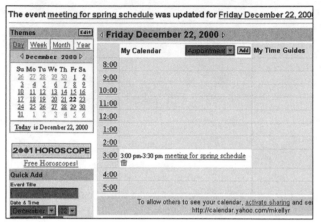

The event meeting for spring schedule was updated for Friday December 22, 200

www.calendar@yahoo.com

will be wasting over 40 hours per year! This doesn't even count the time you spend driving out to the office supply store at the mall to replace that favorite red marker.

When cleaning your office, do not throw out any paperwork you might need to substantiate tax returns, product deliveries, or service performances for which you have yet to be paid; personnel records; information needed to substantiate any current or potential claims; or original software manuals.

Personal Planners Can Help

Take advantage of the technology that is available to help you plan and keep yourself in line. If you are on the Internet for a great portion of the day, consider the personal planner. Most search engines have this feature available either as a planner or a calendar. They work pretty much the same as traditional paper planners, but with a few added bonuses.

Once you have registered with a search engine and personalized a page, it is fairly easy to make use of the planner feature. All you have to do is click on it, and it will take you step-by-step through the process of filling in appointments and recurring activities and even setting up alerts. Most will have the same layout as any other planner. All you have to do is type in the name of the activity and what time it will occur. Once you enter this information, an organized daily schedule will appear on your screen detailing what you need to do at what time.

Additional Features

So far, this personal planner is quite similar to a traditional planner. However, there are options available online that paper just can't seem to make happen. For instance, you can set up an alert feature. This will send an alert to your mailbox within a specified time period, notifying you of an activity's approach. It acts almost like an alarm. Therefore, when you are caught up in work and pay little attention to the clock, you need not worry about missing that important meeting. Your planner will notify you in plenty of time to make it there.

Another handy feature is the ability to mark recurring activities with just a click of the mouse. Think about all the time you spend manually marking the monthly department meeting in your planner. With this planner, you need only set the time and date and mark it as recurring. The activity will pop up automatically on every consecutive occurrence.

Even though these features make keeping an online personal planner a good way to save time, before you set it up consider whether it is worth it for you. If you aren't on the Internet often, you will have to log on to take a look at what is coming up for the day or to take advantage of the alerts feature. Also, keeping a planner on your customized page is not as portable as keeping a paper planner. Take these things into consideration when deciding whether or not to spend your time setting up an online personal planner.

If this type of planner is tempting to you but a paper planner is more accessible, reject the temptation to set up both. You should not have two planners going at once. This makes it easy to miss or overbook appointments. You may write down an activity in one planner, but forget to mark the other. This can create all kinds of time disasters. If you do happen to keep track of activities in both planners, you waste time filling in the same information twice. Choose one planner and stick with it.

Self-Discipline Can Be Learned

Although we are not born with self-discipline, it is a trait that can be developed over time. All you need are the right learning tools and a little hard work.

- Know your purpose and what you want to achieve. This goes for both your work and your personal life.

Leadership Tip

Military Mottos

Army	"Be All You Can Be"
Navy	"Let the Journey Begin"
	"Non sibi sed patriae"
	(Not self but country)
Air Force	"Aim High"
Marines	"Semper Fidelis"
	(Always Faithful)
	"The Few, the Proud, the Marines"

- Have a role model or mentor. Figure out who it is that you would like to emulate and adapt that person's style to your own.
- Visualize situations as you would like them to occur, and visualize yourself reaching the goals you set.
- Believe in yourself and have self-confidence. If you don't believe in yourself, how can you expect anyone else to?
- Be patient. There will be many obstacles and pitfalls along the road to self-discipline; don't give up, work through them.
- Have a plan for yourself, your business, and your future.
- Continue to learn as you go. Don't accept that the knowledge you have is enough. You can always improve yourself. Recognize your weak areas and really work to improve them.
- Last, but not least, make sure you love what you do. A job should suit your interests, talents, skills, and ideals. You should enjoy the work as an extension of yourself and be committed to putting a great deal of personal energy and positive emotions into it.

CHAPTER 16

If at First You Don't Succeed— Learn from Your Mistakes

The sixteenth core concept is learning from your mistakes. Whether you are currently a leader or working toward a leadership position, you are bound to make mistakes along the way. Let's face it, mistakes are an inevitable part of life as well as work. Knowing and accepting this fact, you should be prepared for mistakes, accept mistakes, and, most importantly, learn from mistakes. You will never be able to grow and develop as a leader if you fail to learn lessons from the errors you make along the way.

No one is immune to mistakes, so don't spend countless hours agonizing over them. Instead, channel your energy into making sure that the same mistakes do not occur again in the future. If a mistake occurs on your watch, quickly debrief and regroup. The assignment of blame should never be seen as more important than the construction of a recovery strategy. Leadership is about the ability to move forward, not about wallowing in the past.

If you are in the process of training employees and are worried that they may make mistakes, there are a few things to remember:

- Mistakes are learning experiences.
- Mistakes are okay.
- You cannot prevent every mistake from happening.

Start off with small projects that have a smaller margin for error. This way, there will be minimal negative impact even if something should go wrong. As employees become more comfortable and self-assured, move on to more complex situations with greater potential impact due to mistakes. You will see a definite developmental pattern as your employees become more comfortable with the responsibilities and authority of empowerment.

In any case, don't allow yourself to become so afraid to make a mistake that you render yourself incapable of making decisions on the job. (This is more common in individuals who have been newly assigned to leadership positions.) Whether or not you are a risk taker, it is always best to keep yourself informed and use common sense. Make sure you have all the information you need to make the best decisions possible for you and the organization as a whole. This will cut down on the chance of mistakes due to ignorance or generally being "out of the loop." Make

Leadership Tip

Politically Correct Terminology for a Mistake

1. A teachable moment
2. Opportunity for improvement
3. A moment of truth

assumptions when necessary but be able to back them up with concrete facts that you have gathered. Keep in mind that failure to make a decision can be far more detrimental than making "wrong decisions." Leaders recognize that they have made it to the top by learning from mistakes and some bad judgment calls. Managing to move past these issues is what allows leaders to lead in a meaningful and productive way.

Dealing with Common Leadership Mistakes

Failure 1: Refusal to Ask for Help When Help Is Needed

Just because you are a leader does not mean that you possess super powers. There will be times when you are so swamped with work and interruptions that you will feel overwhelmed and thwarted at every turn. Don't allow yourself to fall into the depths of despair. Instead, take advantage of the resources that are available to you.

To start with, delegate, delegate again, and delegate some more. Pass on to others the tasks that you do not need to be actively involved in. Then, once you delegate a task, sever your ties with it. Trust your coworkers to handle the matter completely and correctly, and *forget about it*. Give them ownership of and responsibility for the work.

Next, close the office door (if you have the luxury of an office door), prioritize your duties, and dig in your heels. Tell other staff members that their cooperation is necessary and that they should not disturb you unless the building is on fire or your car is being towed from its reserved spot.

Last, if you don't know all the answers or you need information from another person or department, ask for assistance. Depending on others should not ever be viewed as a weakness. The workplace is a cooperative effort and functions best when people support each other. Make sure that each person is responsible for her own work. Don't take on the responsibilities of others because it seems easier; you have enough to worry about as it is. You shouldn't have to sort through someone else's file cabinet to find a copy of the report he was supposed to send you last week.

Gloria Steinem
(1934–)

American feminist, author, and political activist, Gloria Steinem is a leading voice for modern feminist politics and activism. Steinem cofounded *Ms.* magazine in 1972. *Ms.* provided the first open forum for the feminist movement and continues to be dedicated to women's issues today. Gloria Steinem remains an active participant in the feminist community and continues to author articles and books on the issues that face modern women. In 2000, Steinem proved that the feminist perspective is ever changing when she chose to get married at the age of 66. Steinem was quoted as saying, "Feminism is about the ability to choose what is right."

Failure 2: Refusing to Be Flexible

As a leader, you must be ready, willing, and able to keep up with changes as they occur. A leader who cannot accept change and refuses to try anything new will remain stagnant within the body of the company. In drastic cases, this type of leader may even bring the entire company down with her.

By being flexible, good leaders allow themselves to change with the times. They take on new responsibilities with enthusiasm and work them into already tight schedules with minimal effort. These leaders know that flexibility leads to personal and professional growth.

Flexibility becomes a major factor when:

- Duties and responsibilities change
- Technology advances
- Staff members come and go
- The competition or industry changes
- Budgets are cut
- New strategies are developed
- Deadlines are rescheduled
- Things just don't work out the way you planned

Flexibility is crucial because leaders have to be able to guide themselves as well as their team through whatever challenges and obstacles are set before them.

Failure 3: Inability or Unwillingness to Recognize Where You Came From

Great leaders are not born, they are created. Leadership is acquired and developed over time through learning valuable skills, excelling in performance, and training with supervisors and mentors.

Take the time to retrace and reflect on the path you have taken to achieve success. Instead of snubbing those who taught you along the way, keep in touch with them on a regular basis. Go to lunch together, have coffee, send an e-mail. Keep these people informed of your successes and failures. Chances are that they will continue to have valuable pieces of advice and wisdom that can help you polish up your leadership skills. You didn't make it to the top alone, and you surely cannot stay on top without the help of seasoned professionals.

Failure 4: Assuming That Leadership Is the Same as Dictatorship

Many a leader has met an untimely end by exercising harsh and stern tactics. The key point to remember here is that you will catch more flies with honey than with vinegar. Treat people with the kindness and respect that they deserve, and you will be rewarded with kindness and respect in return. It is a simple concept and it works.

You always want to express to staff members that their work is valuable and important and that you are approachable and open to suggestions. Acting like a tyrant and barking out orders will only serve to anger, frustrate, and humiliate the team you need to depend on when the chips are down.

Failure 5: Talking *At* Employees Rather Than *To* Them

If this continues to be a problem for you, perhaps you should reread Chapter 2, which deals with the art of communication. The process of communicating with others is a give-and-take. Each side should be giving input as well as receiving messages from the other party.

Failure 6: Taking a Self-Centered Approach to Leadership

Thinking of yourself first is always a bad idea. Take the "I" out of your thought process. Focus on doing what is best for your team, and then look to see how that can be applied to the company. Being selfish may help you be happy in the short term, but the long-term effects could be insurmountable.

Consider the fact that by spending so much time thinking about your own wants and needs you will lose touch with everyone else. Soon they will begin to resent you. The work will get sloppy; some employees may become so frustrated that they will pursue other job

---

Leadership Tip

Leadership Goal
Your goal as a leader is to be respected, not feared.

In 1907, Irish-born Antarctic explorer Ernest Shackleton led an expedition which made it to within 97 miles of the South Pole, closer than any previous explorer. In 1914, Shackleton returned to the Antarctic, leading an ill-fated transantarctic expedition. When his ship was crushed in the ice, Shackleton led his men on a five-month journey across ice floes to reach Elephant Island. From there, Shackleton and five of his men set out in a small boat, battling over 500 miles of wild seas to reach a whaling station. He then returned with a rescue party for the rest of his men. Despite the harsh conditions, Shackleton managed to save all the men he left behind.

opportunities. If the situation advances to this point, you may find yourself short-handed and doing your own work as well as the work of the long-gone staffer. Quickly, the department will begin to break down and other departments will become frustrated because you are holding them up. In a matter of weeks or even days, you may be on the verge of a breakdown yourself.

Do yourself a favor and don't let the situation deteriorate to that point. Lobby for the needs and wants of your team. Keeping them satisfied will make for a happier work environment and a happier you.

Also, share the perks you receive with others. If your number one client supplies you with season tickets for your hometown's baseball team, share them with the office rather than family members and friends. Don't keep that huge box of Godiva chocolates for yourself at Christmastime—be sweet and leave them in the break room for everyone to enjoy!

Failure 7: Believing That as a Leader You Are Immortal

We have already established the fact that leaders do not posses super powers. Along those same lines, it is important to recognize that as a leader you are not immortal. Leaders come and leaders go. You may not be in charge forever. Your effectiveness could diminish in the blink of an eye.

Strike while the iron is hot. Continually implement new strategies and goals. Present your vision in all that you do and say. Be prepared for the time when you will need to step back or even step down from your role as leader.

Failure 8: Keeping Everything to Yourself

In order for any company to survive, employees must grow. In order for that to happen, you need to pass the knowledge you have on to others. Don't leave your team in the dark. The team is only as strong as its weakest member. However, if all members are encouraged to learn new skills, take on additional responsibilities, and tackle additional problems/projects, your group will start to edge out and gain momentum on competing groups.

In the event that you are asked to transfer to a different office or department, you will want to have at least one person who is prepared to take on your current role. In order to ensure departmental survival, always have someone in training for a higher position.

Failure 9: Making the Same Mistakes Someone Else Already Made

True or false: History always repeats itself. False—what was considered a mistake or bad decision five years ago may not necessarily hold true today. Here is an example. In 1995, the Internet was just starting to reach its potential. It didn't make sense for your company to set up an online retail outlet when print catalog sales were reaching their peak. Today, online retailing is the norm and a large percentage of sales can be tapped from online shoppers. Just take a look at Amazon.com and how it has single-handedly redefined a consumer's shopping experience.

Just because you believe that you can do something better than your predecessors or upper management, doesn't mean that is the case. It is always a good idea to closely examine the successes and failures of those that went before you. The lessons that can be learned will be immeasurable. What worked and what failed from the get-go? What can you do differently? Turn another person's work misfortunes into your good fortune.

Major Blunders from Corporate America

Mistakes can benefit both individuals and businesses. At the core of mistakes are lessons that can have great learning value. If you think that well-known corporations are successful because they never make mistakes—think again! There are two prime cases that come to mind over the past century, and we can examine them as examples of learning from mistakes and errors in judgment.

The Infamous Edsel

Ford Motor Company has been at the forefront of the automotive industry since Henry Ford started it all in 1903. With an initial invest-

ment of $28,000 in cash, Ford Motor Company has grown into one of world's largest producers of cars and trucks, with operations in more than 30 countries.

The one great blunder that stands out in Ford's history can be summed up in one word . . . "Edsel." Designed in 1952, the Edsel was meant to be a "full-size car with a more daring design." Ford wanted to overtake the market share of General Motors. The strategy was to market and advertise the Edsel to the "new executive." As such, Henry Ford and his management team decided to have this new car be the product of a whole new division. So, the company was restructured into more distinct divisions. This proved to be the first mistake for the company.

The second mistake made by the company was in the decision to name the new automobile the Edsel. This was the name of Henry Ford I's only son. The name was significant to the Ford family, but it had no appeal for the average consumer. Research polls even indicated that the name Edsel conjured images of pretzels and weasels. Nonetheless, the name was decided upon and never changed.

The third mistake was in the car's design. Ford wanted to achieve a higher brand recognition factor and initially decided to go with a vertical theme to set it apart from other cars. However, changes needed to be made to account for cooling, ventilation, and to cut back on production costs. In the end, the only recognition that Ford received was negative.

The fourth mistake Ford made was cutting off sales to the Edsel by introducing the more popular and lower-priced Ford Fairlane to the market, at approximately the same time. Many consumers saw the Fairlane as a better value for their money and the fact that it was less expensive (and more visually appealing) also helped. Thrown into the mix is the fact that all this was going on during a recession period in the American economy; people had to be tight with their money.

What Is the Moral of This Story?

Overall, the Edsel was a huge flop and production ceased in 1960. However, the Ford Motor Company was able to learn some very valuable lessons from the experience and, in doing so, did not repeat the same mistake.

Ford learned that it needed to pay close attention to consumer input and suggestions. For example, when consumers said repeatedly

Henry Ford on Failure

Henry Ford was a great businessman, but he didn't get as far as he did without making some mistakes along the way. The difference between Ford and many others is that he recognized the value in the mistakes he made, learned from them, and then capitalized on them. Here are some of his thoughts on the subject.

- "Even a mistake may turn out to be the one thing necessary to a worthwhile achievement."

- "There are no dead ends. There is always a way out. What you learn in one failure, you utilize in your next success."

- "All that I personally own of any value is my experience, and that cannot be taken away. One should not complain of having one's fund of experience added to."

- "The best pay I ever got was experience, which I think is still the most valuable thing in the world. That's what we're put in the world for, to get experience and to help others get it. It's the one thing no one can take away from us."

- "Life is a series of experiences, each one of which makes us bigger, even though it is hard to realize this. For the world was built to develop character, and we must learn that the setbacks and grieves which we endure help us in our marching onward."

that they did not like the name "Edsel," the decision-making executives should have listened to their opinions. Ford also learned that advertising hype has limits in terms of influence on consumers. The average person will not buy a car simply because you tell them it is great. They want the most value for their dollar. What it all boils down to is this—consumers make or break a product. Ford was able to rebound from the Edsel disaster, and it continues to thrive and be a leader in the automotive industry.

The New Coke Fiasco

Another American icon is Coca-Cola, concocted in 1886 by Dr. John S. Pemberton in Atlanta, Georgia. Finding themselves in much the same position as Ford did with General Motors, Coca-Cola was concerned about a continued loss in market share to Pepsi. In 1985, Pepsi was gaining ground quickly through a more effective advertising campaign, and Coke was slipping as America's favorite soft drink.

Coca-Cola's marketing team was hard at work developing a solution. They considered the possibility that consumer tastes were changing and, if that were true, maybe they should change the taste of Coke. All the market research was telling them that Coke drinkers loved Coke the way it was and didn't want a change. But Coke pressed on and in 1984, had developed a formula that beat Pepsi in taste tests 75 percent of the time. Thus came the release in 1985 of the so-called New Coke.

Much to the chagrin of marketing executives at Coca-Cola, the new formula was widely unpopular. Coke drinkers felt loyalty toward the original formula and began hoarding it; cases were even sold on the black market for staggering prices. Overall, New Coke was a disaster.

What Is the Moral of This Story?

Regardless of the sales figures, Coca-Cola is a sentimental favorite with American cola drinkers. In an attempt to sweeten the flavor of the product and appeal to a younger generation of consumers, the company failed to listen to what the public was telling it. Consumers didn't want anyone changing their favorite drink. They liked it in its original form. A better decision would have been to simply change its marketing and advertising to target a younger audience.

They were able to recover from this mistake by thinking quickly on their feet. Instead of changing what people had grown to know and love, they chose to develop new product categories within the brand. Not only was original Coke brought back to supermarkets everywhere (New Coke disappeared from shelves), but Diet Coke and Cherry Coke were introduced within that same year.

Coca-Cola realized that with Coke drinkers, there is an emotional attachment to the brand. Coke has been with the American public through two wars, the Depression, and the assassination of John F. Kennedy. It realized the tremendous importance of brand loyalty, and it is not likely to forget it.

Amazingly, no one was fired or reprimanded, and Coke did not lose money as a result of this fiasco. In fact, the stock price even jumped. There remains some question as to whether Coke ever actually intended to sell New Coke or if it was just a brilliant marketing strategy to boost the sales of America's "favorite drink." It is likely that we will never know the whole story.

What-If Syndrome

There may be times when you find yourself saying, "What if I had done that differently?" or "If I could do that over again, I would do it differently." As a leader you will make some good decisions and some bad decisions. No one can be right or perfect 100 percent of the time. There will be ups and downs, and they will probably occur daily.

Decision making comes on a situation-by-situation basis. Therefore, it is unlikely that you will be given a second chance with anything. You can only do your best. Try to make the best decisions you can at the time you are presented with them. If you falter a little, so be it. Think about what you could have done better or how you could have been more informed, and next time take those factors into consideration.

Famous Takes on Failure

Just for fun, see how successful you can be at matching up these famous people with their famous quotes about mistakes and failure.

Profile

Julius Caesar
(100?–44 B.C.)

A Roman general and statesman, Julius Caesar was a great military leader, credited with conquering Gaul and renowned as the victor of the Civil War (49–46 B.C.). Prior to his assassination in 44 B.C., Julius Caesar instituted several policies in the Roman Empire, including the reformation of the Roman calendar; a standard pattern of self-government in Roman territories; an increase in the size of the Roman Senate, with representation for all Roman citizens; and a policy for granting Roman citizenship to those who settled there from other areas. The life, times, and government of Julius Caesar remain alive today through Shakespeare's tragedy *Julius Caesar*.

Famous Takes on Failure

1. "Failure is only opportunity to more intelligently begin again."
2. "You always pass failure on the way to success."
3. "It is better to fail in originality than to succeed in imitation."
4. "Best men are often molded out of faults."
5. "Show me a thoroughly satisfied man, and I'll show you a failure."
6. "I don't know the key to success, but the key to failure is to try to please everyone."
7. "Failure is an event, never a person."
8. "I have learned throughout my life as a composer chiefly through my mistakes and pursuits of false assumptions, not by my exposure to founts of wisdom and knowledge."
9. "While one person hesitates because he feels inferior, another is busy making mistakes and becoming superior."
10. "Don't be afraid to fail. Don't waste energy trying to cover up failure. Learn from your failures and go on to the next challenge. It is OK to fail. If you are not failing, you are not growing."
11. "There are mistakes—and mistakes. There are true, copper-bottom mistakes like spelling the word 'rabbit' with three Ms; wearing a black bra under a white shirt; or, to take a more masculine example, starting a land war in Asia. These are the kind of mistakes described by Mr. David Letterman as Brushes With Stupidity, because they have no reasonable chance of success."
12. "Mistakes are the portals of discovery."
13. "Sometimes we may learn more from a man's errors, than from his virtues."
14. "Experience is the name everyone gives to their mistakes."
15. "Mistakes are part of the dues one pays for a full life."
16. "Reflect upon your present blessings, of which every man has plenty; not on your past misfortunes, of which all men have some."
17. "Victory goes to the player who makes the next-to-last mistake."
18. "Freedom is not worth having if it does not include the freedom to make mistakes."
19. "After making a mistake or suffering a misfortune, the man of genius always gets back on his feet."
20. "Only two things are infinite, the universe and human stupidity, and I'm not sure about the former."

a.   Mahatma Gandhi
b.   John Cleese
c.   James Joyce
d.   Henry C. Link
e.   Henry Ford
f.   Bill Cosby
g.   Napoleon Bonaparte
h.   Herman Melville
i.   Albert Einstein
j.   Oscar Wilde
k.   Mickey Rooney
l.   Shakespeare
m.   Thomas Edison
n.   H. Stanley Judd
o.   William D. Brown
p.   Igor Stravinsky
q.   Henry Wadsworth Longfellow
r.   Sophia Loren
s.   Chessmaster Savielly Grigorievitch Tartakower
t.   Charles Dickens

1. e, 2. k, 3. h, 4. l, 5. m, 6. f, 7. o, 8. p, 9. d, 10. n, 11. b, 12. c, 13. q, 14. j, 15. r, 16. t, 17. s, 18. a, 19. g, 20. i

CHAPTER 17

Take the Lead as a Volunteer

Following through with your leadership position requires you to set yourself as a good role model. The previous core concepts will get you to this point, but now you need to take your initiative a step further. The seventeenth core concept, volunteering, will help you to sharpen your leadership skills while at the same time setting yourself as a good example.

One great way to build your leadership presence both in and out of the office is to become a volunteer. This is the perfect opportunity to sharpen the skills that you need as a leader and to gain new skills or learn more about your community. All types of leadership traits may be utilized when you take part in any charitable or volunteer organization. It can be to your benefit to make the most of these types of opportunities. You can help people and learn something at the same time.

Reasons for Volunteering

- To demonstrate commitment to a cause or belief
- To exercise and gain leadership skills that can be applied to the workplace
- To learn a new skill or set of skills
- To explore new career opportunities
- To network and make professional contacts
- To spruce up an otherwise bland resume
- To fulfill religious duties or obligations
- To feel more a part of the community and world around you
- To gain status in the community or in your industry
- To be an agent of change and to influence the lives of others
- To learn more about something that has affected your life (i.e., illness, disease, addiction)
- To increase physical activity (and maybe even lose weight)
- To work as part of a team and brush up on coaching skills
- To help others who are less fortunate or in need of assistance
- To gain a higher level of self-esteem
- To do something you enjoy
- To improve the environment
- To fight or prevent crime

Every individual is likely to have her own reasons and motivations for volunteering. Keep in mind that your initial motivations for joining might not be the same incentives that keep you in the organization. Once you are involved in any volunteer or community organization, the benefits you reap from helping others and reaching a common goal may be the reason you keep on keeping on.

Making the Right Choice

When you are shopping around for an organization you might like to join, it is important to make sure it is the right fit for you. Take the time to explore all avenues. Don't be quick to jump at the first thing you hear about. You want to find a group that you can be happy with for a while. There are thousands upon thousands of opportunities lying before you. Consider coaching a team, taking part in a charity event, starting a new club or group, leading a choir, teaching a class, working with children, being a mentor, running for local office, or joining a trade organization. Ask yourself reflective questions such as:

1. What causes or issues matter the most to you? Are you willing to found a new effort toward that cause?
2. Do you want to volunteer for something that relates to your work skills, or would you rather volunteer to do something you simply take enjoyment in?
3. What skills or talents do you want to put to use?
4. What do you want to gain from the experience of volunteering? Would it be fun to tackle something new? Do you want to gain new skills?
5. What are the things that you definitely do not want to do?
6. How much time do you want to devote to the organization? One day? One month? One year? Every spare moment?
7. Would you consider joining with a friend or family member?
8. Are you willing to participate in training sessions or would you prefer to dive right in?

Leadership Tip

Doing Their Part

Each year more than 90 million Americans give some of their free time and support to help others in need.

Initiative and Commitment

The first step is to take the initiative and get involved in something—anything. Be sure that whatever activity you choose is something that suits your skills, talents, and interests. Don't volunteer to work with children if you can't stand the sight of them. Also, don't consider the local cat hospital if the mention of the furry creature sends you into a violent sneezing episode. As a volunteer, you should be informed, involved, and dependable. Look for a place where you can be these things.

If you are managing a volunteer organization or taking on a supervisory role, the same leadership principles apply to activities outside the workplace as in the workplace. Above all, you have to be committed. Commitment is the willingness and desire to do something. The best type of commitment is the type that starts from within. Consider the example of losing weight. It is better to make the decision to lose weight in order to be healthy rather than to do it because someone at work told you your outfit makes you look heavy around the midsection. You have to volunteer because you want to and because you feel that there is value and satisfaction in the task or activity.

- Remember that the environment where the organization meets or the activity occurs must be one in which the people involved feel good about performing. A flooded playing field with craters at every step will not inspire feats of grandeur; instead, no one will want to play. You need to also make sure that each member of the team or group feels challenged. What's the point of a book discussion group if you don't give anyone the chance to speak his mind and ask questions? The more challenged the group feels, the more eager it will be to participate and help out.
- It is also important that the *group* be committed in the sense that it wants to win, be successful, reach a goal, or see an event through to the finish. Your group members need to have the desire and the drive to achieve the goals you as a leader have set.

Leadership Tip

No Time?

If you feel that time away from loved ones may be too much, consider volunteering with family members. It is a good way to spend quality time together.

- You need to inspire a commitment to the task at hand no matter how minimal the task may be. Example: If you simply ask Shannon to sell raffle tickets at the church entrance and she goes off to check on booth setup and to make sure the kitchen staff knows where the knives are, she is not committed to the task. Shannon must understand that the raffle brings in the most profit at the fair. She needs to see why a task she views as boring and menial is really vital to the success of the event as a whole. It is your job to make sure she sees and understands the big picture.
- Make sure that people are given positive feedback and recognition for their work. Everyone has chosen to join the group of her own free will and therefore should be recognized and thanked for her participation and contributions. Recognize and reward people often and consistently.

If you follow these rules, all the people involved will likely volunteer to help the next time an event approaches. Strive for full performance commitment and 100 percent involvement.

100 Volunteer Organizations

The following is a list comprising nationwide volunteer and charity organizations. Use this list as a guide to researching the activity that is the best fit for you. Locally, there will be hundreds more opportunities available. Check online or in the Yellow Pages for more ideas.

ABC Quilts Project
www.mv.com/ipusers/abcquilts

AIDS Action Committee
www.aac.org

America's Promise
www.americaspromise.org

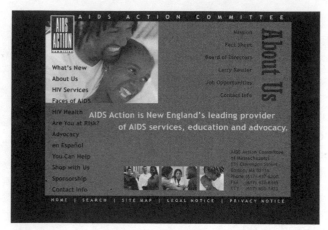

www.aac.org

www.cancer.org

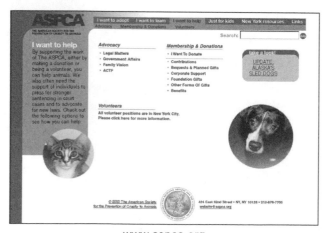

www.aspca.org

America's Second Harvest
www.secondharvest.org

American Cancer Society
www.cancer.org

American Heart Association
www.americanheart.org

American Hospice Foundation
www.americanhospice.org

American Red Cross
www.redcross.org

American Social Health Association (ASHA)
www.ashastd.org

The American Society for the Prevention of
Cruelty to Animals (ASPCA)
www.aspca.org

Amnesty International USA
www.amnesty-usa.org

Arthritis Foundation
www.arthritis.org

Association for the Advancement of Retired
Persons (AARP)
www.aarp.org

The Association of Junior Leagues International
www.ajli.org

Best Buddies
www.bestbuddies.org

Big Brothers Big Sisters of America
www.bbbsa.org

Boy Scouts of America
www.bsa.scouting.org

Camp Fire Boys and Girls
www.campfire.org

CARE USA
www.care.org

Catholic Charities USA
www.catholiccharitiesusa.org

Childhelp USA
www.childhelpusa.org

Christmas in April
www.christmasinapril.org

Compeer
www.compeer.org

Corporation for National Service
www.cns.gov

Cystic Fibrosis Foundation
www.cff.org

The Danny Foundation
www.dannyfoundation.org

Department of Veterans Affairs
www.va.gov

www.bbbsa.org

www.childhelpusa.org

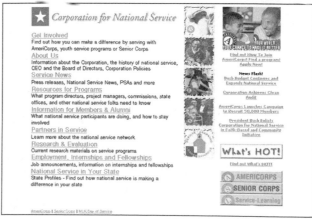

www.cns.gov

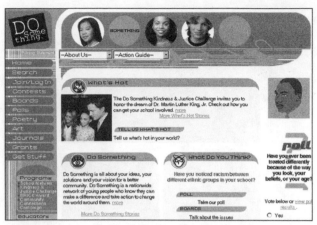

www.dosomething.org

www.gfwc.org

www.habitat.org

Disaster News Network
www.disasternews.net

Do Something!
www.dosomething.org

Feed the Children (FTC)
www.christianity.com/feedthechildren

General Federation of Women's Clubs
www.gfwc.org

Girl Scouts of the United States of America
www.gsusa.org

Great Books Foundation
www.greatbooks.org

Greenpeace
www.greenpeace.org

Habitat for Humanity International
www.habitat.org

Heart of America Foundation
www.heartofamerica.org

The Holiday Project
www.holiday-project.org

Kiwanis International
www.kiwanis.org

Laubach Literacy
www.laubach.org

Literacy Volunteers of America
www.literacyvolunteers.org

Little Brothers—Friends of the Elderly
www.littlebrothers.org

Make-A-Wish Foundation
www.wish.org

March of Dimes
www.modimes.org

Meals On Wheels
www.projectmeal.org

Mothers Against Drunk Driving (MADD)
www.madd.org

Muscular Dystrophy Association
www.mdausa.org

National Assistance League
www.nal.org

National Associations for Community Mediation
www.nafcm.org

National Center for Missing and
Exploited Children
www.missingkids.org

National Coalition Against Domestic Violence
www.ncadv.org

National Coalition for the Homeless
http://nch.ari.net

www.wish.org

www.mdausa.org

www.missingkids.org

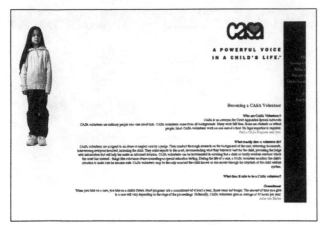

www.nationalcasa.org

www.nesc.org

www.nmss.org

National Council of Jewish Women
www.ncjw.org

National Court Appointed Special
Advocate Program
www.nationalcasa.org

National Easter Seals Society
www.easter-seals.org

National Exchange Club
www.nationalexchangeclub.com

National Executive Service Corps *www.nesc.org*

National 4-H Council
www.fourhcouncil.edu

National Hospice Foundation
www.hospiceinfo.org

National Industries for the Blind
www.nib.org

National Marrow Donor Program
www.marrow.org

National Multiple Sclerosis Society
www.nmss.org

The National PTA
www.pta.org

The National Park Service
www.nps.gov

National Trust for Historic Preservation
www.nthp.org

National Urban League
www.nul.org

National Voluntary Organizations Active in Disaster (NVOAD)
www.reactintl.org/nvoad.htm

National Volunteer Fire Council
www.nvfc.org

National Wildlife Federation
www.nwf.org

OASIS
www.oasisnet.org

The Orphan Foundation of America
www.orphan.org

Oxfam America
www.oxfamamerica.org

People for the Ethical Treatment of Animals (PETA)
www.peta-online.org

Points of Light Foundation
www.pointsoflight.org

Project America
www.project.org

Project Linus
www.projectlinus.org

www.nvfc.org

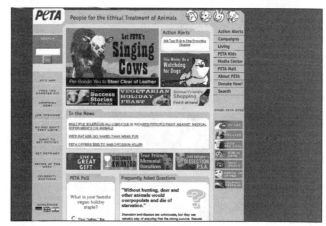

www.peta-online.org

www.project.org

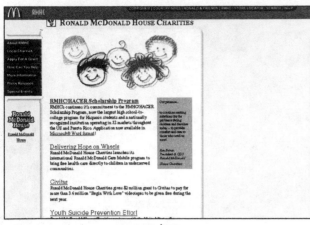
www.rmhc.com

www.savethechildren.org

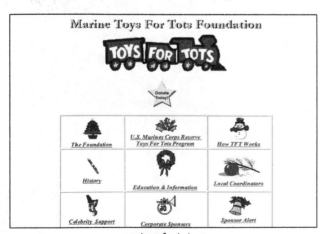
www.toysfortots.org

Recording for the Blind
www.rfbd.org

Ronald McDonald House Charities
www.rmhc.com

Rotary International
www.rotary.org

The Salvation Army
www.salvationarmy.org

Save the Children
www.savethechildren.org

Service Leader
www.serviceleader.org

Share Our Strength (SOS)
www.strength.org

Sierra Club
www.sierraclub.org

Special Olympics
www.specialolympics.org

Toys for Tots
www.toysfortots.org

21st Century Teachers
www.21ct.org

U.S. Funds for UNICEF
www.unicefusa.org

United States Army Reserves
www.paed.army.mil/acrc

United Way of America
www.unitedway.org

Volunteer America
www.volunteeramerica.com

Volunteer for Our Children
www.child.net/volunteer.htm

Volunteers in Service to America (VISTA)
www.friendsofvista.org

Volunteers of America
www.voa.org

Wilderness Volunteers
www.wildernessvolunteers.org

Women in Community Service (WICS)
www.wics.org

WorkingForChange
www.workingforchange.com

World Wildlife Fund
www.worldwildlife.org

YMCA of the USA
www.ymca.net

YWCA of the USA
www.ywca.org

Youth Crime Watch
www.ycwa.org

www.friendsofvista.org

www.ymca.net

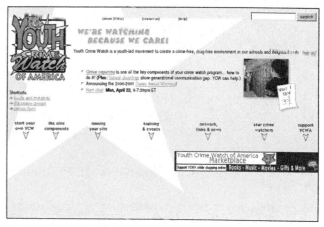

www.ycwa.org

Recruiting and Training Volunteers

If you are in charge of a specific organization or event, there will come a point when you will have to recruit volunteers. At times, this may prove to be a difficult task. Remember that volunteers come in all shapes and sizes, and you may find recruits in the most unlikely of places. Keep your mind open to taking on students and seniors alike. These two diverse groups may surprise you with the amount of energy and enthusiasm they bring to the organization.

Here is your chance to let creativity run wild. The idea behind the flyer is to give as much information and promote as much excitement as possible within the limitations of an 8½" × 11" piece of paper.

Give Stuff Away

Who doesn't love free stuff? From T-shirts to hats to yo-yos to keychains, no one can pass up a freebie. Have items with your organization's logo emblazoned on them. People will see them, want them, and come over to ask questions.

Set Up a Booth

Location is everything. Arrange to set up booths or tables at local colleges, senior centers, libraries, supermarkets, and community centers. Bring the flyers and promotional items you have created. Man the booth with current volunteers who want to share their enthusiasm for the cause. Be sure that there is always someone at the booth or have cards and a drop-off box so potential volunteers can fill

---

Get In On

The Ground Floor

What is it?

A community-based group that builds homes for victims of house fires. Hundreds of people fall prey to the tragedy of fire each year and you can help them rebuild their lives.

Join Us

Volunteers are needed.
Individuals of all ages are urged
to attend the sign-up meeting.
Saturday, December 5th
12:00 P.M.–1:00 P.M.
Bank Street Armory

Call 555-HOME
for more details.

YOU CAN MAKE A DIFFERENCE!

out name and address information to be contacted later on. Be sure to make the table or booth as fun and appealing as possible. Target the appropriate audience with decorations, balloons, signs, and whatever else you can come up with.

Word of Mouth

Never underestimate the power of talking it up! Tell everyone you know about your group and tell them to tell everyone they know. Soon the whole town will be abuzz with the latest news on the great things your organization is doing for the community. Give presentations wherever and whenever you can. Contact the local media (newspapers, radio, cable access network) when you are hosting an event and arrange to have a photographer there to capture the moment on film. The more ways you find to spread the word, the more accessible your organization becomes to others.

Volunteer Fairs

These work much in the same way as a career fair. Once again, set up shop at colleges where a day is devoted to getting new recruits. The difference between setting up a booth in general and attending a fair is twofold. One, the students who attend are already interested in joining some type of group. Maybe yours will be the one that matches their interests perfectly. Two, this is an event organized by the college. More people will be involved and there will be more competition for those recruits. The tough part is finding a way to outshine those other organizations.

Newspaper Advertising

If you really want the word to reach a larger audience, consider placing an ad in local newspapers. Use the same strategy as you would with the creation of a flyer. Inform, excite, and entice readers to join in the fun and vision of your organization.

How to Retain Volunteers

One of the most difficult parts of taking on a leadership position in a volunteer organization is finding a way to keep volunteers. After all, these people are giving up their free time to work hard and expect to receive nothing in return. The novelty may wear off quickly for some, while others will devote their lives to the cause with little thought of compensation. What can you do to make them happy enough to keep coming back?

- Your top priority should be to make sure that all volunteers are involved and challenged. From the moment an individual steps in the door, they should have a task and a purpose. Each person needs to know that his individual contribution works toward the success of the organization as a whole.
- Explain each person's role, task, and the importance of each. People need to understand the "why" behind "what" they are doing.
- Be very clear about the vision of the organization. Goals and expectations should be spelled out at the outset. Each time a new member joins the group, these ideas should be stated to them. No one should be left in the dark; you want everyone to be on the same page, moving in the same direction, toward a common goal.
- Allow for flexibility in scheduling. Don't arrange to have every event occur on a weekday during prime work hours. Instead, allow people to have the chance to help by having events in the evenings and on weekends. You want to make sure the majority of the volunteers can participate a majority of the time.
- Provide motivators at meetings and get-togethers. Arrange to have snacks and refreshments. If a meeting is scheduled close to dinnertime, have it catered or have pizza delivered. Whatever you do, don't expect the volunteers to bring the incentives. For example, one too many potluck dinners may discourage those who barely have time for the meeting in

the first place (never mind having to cook Swedish meat-balls or potato salad for 35 people).

- Recognize volunteers in meetings and presentations. Honor them for their assistance, their commitment, and their role in the organization. A kind word goes a long way to making someone feel appreciated.

- Give people titles and create a hierarchy. "Volunteer" is pretty vague; instead try "project coordinator," "team leader," "event planner," et cetera. This will instill a sense of empowerment in the group members. It also helps to clarify the roles within the group. It tells others who is making decisions and who they can go to with questions or concerns.

- Keep communication lines open. Communication allows for open discussions and new ideas and ensures that everyone is up to speed. This is important to the future growth and development of the organization.

Corporate Volunteerism

In many cases your company may already be involved in some sort of corporate volunteer service. If that is the case, get involved. Many businesses feel that volunteering helps build stronger relationships in the community, which in turn builds stronger relationships in business. For many years, volunteerism was viewed as being outside the corporate structure. If you wanted to participate, great; if not, no big deal. Nowadays, there seems to be a shifting attitude toward the importance of volunteering on both corporate and individual levels. It has become increasingly more common for employees to be allowed to leave during the day to participate in volunteer or service activities. Traditionally, businesses would donate money rather than services. Now, there tends to be more personal involvement rather than check writing.

Over time, employees have come to see the value of volunteer work. Time spent on these activities can help to establish new contacts, develop strategic planning skills, and gain a better understanding of what is going on in the community and the world.

Words of the Wise

"Service to one's community is an integral part of what it means to be an American."

—*William Jefferson Clinton, president of the U.S. from 1993–2001*

Volunteer Facts

Recent studies on volunteering have revealed the following results:

- Close to 50 percent of top companies have volunteer projects in place. GE and Texaco are among these companies.
- Although the number and percentage of adult volunteers has increased over the last decade, the amount of time spent doing the volunteer work has decreased slightly.
- On average, women participate more often in volunteer activities than their male counterparts. However, men who volunteer typically give more *time* than female participants.
- Senior citizens and minority groups are volunteering in larger numbers these days.
- Of those surveyed, 86 percent said they volunteered because they felt compassion for those in need. Seventy-two percent volunteered because they had a genuine interest in the activity or service.
- Nine out of ten individuals volunteered when asked.
- Survey respondents came to the unanimous decision that corporate volunteering helps create healthier communities and improves a company's corporate image. Most felt that the activity also sparked improved employee teamwork.
- For 41 percent of volunteers, volunteering is a one-time or sporadic activity.

CHAPTER 18

Being a Leader Without Being in Charge

Being a leader without being in charge is the eighteenth core concept. The focus of leadership is shifting away from position and title and moving more toward knowledge. You've heard it before: knowledge is power, and that point is well illustrated in a corporate environment. In today's culture, a leader is less often defined as "the boss" and more commonly defined as anyone who can point people in the direction they need to go.

That said, you no longer have to be the CEO or a manager to be a leader. Heck, you don't have to have any authority at all. There are ways to lead no matter what position you hold within a company. Everyone has the potential to be a leader. It doesn't matter where you went to school or how smart you are—it has everything to do with whether or not you want to accept the role and what you do in the role once you take it on.

Take Initiative

In order to lead as a follower, you will have to take initiative often. This means taking on jobs that no one else wants to handle. It also means working beyond your job description. If you normally handle only new accounts and the boss asks for someone to develop new marketing copy for a print ad, offer your services.

- Initiative also involves helping others whenever possible. If Sharon is still having trouble operating the new database and you mastered it last week, give her some assistance. Don't wait for the manager to get back. If you have the knowledge that can help alleviate a problem, by all means use it. Chances are good that it will not go unnoticed.
- Initiative involves taking risks. If you have an off-the-wall idea that you think may work for your company, pitch it to management.
- Initiative involves seeing projects through to completion. Don't dump a half-finished project off on someone else. If you started it, you should finish it as well.

The Leader of the Pack Will Rise to the Occasion

In a group setting, often one person is singled out as a leader, whether or not they have any real power. Typically, the leader is decided on the basis of charisma, vision, or just plain motivation. Most studies of "teams" or groups show that even among peers, different people naturally and nonverbally assume different roles. One will lead; others will follow.

In a team setting, you can be the person who takes the lead and gets the group organized. If you take hold of the reigns, there will be less of a chance for others to shy away from doing their fair share of the work. Each person will be assigned tasks and be held accountable for them. Embrace the opportunity to take on additional responsibilities, get team members to cooperate, and achieve a common goal. Leading in this capacity, you are exercising no real power or authority. However, you are acting as a catalyst for the group and facilitating the work process.

Your role can be that of facilitator. Bring people together and help them to achieve their common goals. Be aware and informed. Create momentum and pay attention to the dynamic the group is creating.

Above All, Be Committed

Whether you actively seek out a protégé or vice versa, the relationship will not work unless you are both committed. Before starting to develop such a relationship, make sure that you have the time and energy to make it happen. If you can be available only from 9:00 A.M.–9:20 A.M. on the first Monday of every odd month, it is likely that the mentor/protégé thing isn't an option for you right now.

Ideally, you should be available to the protégé at regular intervals. It would be nice if you could manage to interact with the person on a daily basis in one manner or another. The protégé should find you easily accessible and willing to help or give advice whenever it is necessary, not just when it fits into your schedule.

Words of the Wise

"For many generations, more than we can count, we bowed our heads and submitted to blindness and beggary. This blind and deaf woman [Helen Keller] lifts her head high and teaches us to win our way by work and laughter. She brings light and hope to the heart."

—*Anonymous*

The best idea would be to build time into your schedule for regular meetings. Perhaps you can have lunch on Mondays and meet for more formalized meetings on Wednesdays and Fridays. Find out what will work best for both of you.

Lead Through the Simple and the Mundane

Although you may feel that you have limited control in the work environment, nothing could be further from the truth. Sure, you cannot develop company policy or hire the new vice president of marketing, but you can control yourself and the work you do. You can also build leadership by improving even the most mundane of tasks.

- If your office space is dingy or just disorderly, rally a small group together and fix things up. It's amazing what some Spic and Span and a few new filing cabinets can do for the area.
- If there is no system in place for the distribution of monthly reports, offer your services and a plan to make things move along more smoothly and effectively.
- If the holidays are getting close, organize a food drive to get everyone in the office in the spirit.

Don't be afraid to ask for change and make suggestions where you feel improvements can be made. It doesn't really matter whether your ideas are utilized; it matters more that those in authority know that you are involved and aware of what is going on within the company.

Think Outside the Box

Great leaders are able to look at problems and ideas from a variety of perspectives. They are able to see the big picture. Train yourself to think along those lines. Have a collective knowledge of how projects and issues were handled in the past, and then bring that wisdom to new situations.

Find the right incentive to change people's behavior.

Words of the Wise

"The future belongs to those who believe in the beauty of their dreams."

—*Eleanor Roosevelt (1884–1962), former First Lady and human rights activist*

Step Right Up and Ask for New Responsibilities

Whenever you feel that you can handle more, ask for additional responsibilities. There are numerous benefits that come from speaking up. First, it shows others that you can and will handle a heavier workload. Second, it shows that you have an active interest in cultivating your role within the company and department. Third, it shows that you are enthusiastic about the work you do and you want to work harder to help the company accomplish its goals. Fourth, and most important, it sets an example for your coworkers. Actions speak louder than words. Who knows, you being a more active participant in the office may inspire someone else to do the same. The people you work with on a daily basis will start to perceive you as a leader because you have become more involved and you have more information about what is going on. They may even begin to depend on you as the problem solver as they will begin to come to you more frequently for solutions. (This also means they will spend less time bothering the manager, and she will definitely appreciate that!)

Be a Spokesperson for the Group

Once again, it will be important to take the "I" out of your thought process here. Specifically, if you are working in a team dependent environment, you will need to pay attention to the group's input. Take it upon yourself to listen to all that each person in the group has to offer. Listen to complaints, suggestions, and new ideas, and then communicate those ideas to the people who institute change.

Perhaps the group is upset because it has had continued successes with a marketing campaign, yet it has been given no recognition or rewards for all its effort and hard work. You can be the person who speaks to the department head about the situation. Of course, you will want to do so diplomatically and respectfully. In this way, you will be nurturing important relationships on different levels. Your team members will see you as someone they can rely on and who listens to them. Supervisors will see you as the voice

Profile

Anna Eleanor Roosevelt
(1884–1962)

Eleanor Roosevelt was one of the most active and involved First Ladies (1933–1945). She was committed to working toward the resolution of racial equality and human rights issues. Eleanor was a member of the Women's Trade Union League and an active participant in the Democratic Party. After the death of President Franklin D. Roosevelt, Eleanor served as an American delegate to the United Nations General Assembly and as the chairperson for the United Nations Commission on Human Rights. Eleanor Roosevelt has been credited with showing the world that compassion can be a part of the political world.

of the people and the person who can help motivate the team through both easy and difficult periods.

Networking Is Not a Dirty Word

Networking can have a negative connotation for some people, but there is nothing wrong with networking. In the simplest terms, networking refers to making useful contacts. The process is successful when it allows you to learn more about what is going on in the company and lets others know that you want to be involved. Essentially, networking puts you "in the loop."

First, you should establish who the key players are. Who can help you get ahead? Who has the information or knowledge that is of the most value to you in your current position? Second, understand that the key to effective networking is to make it a give-and-take relationship. You should always start out by giving far more than you take. Of course, it will work only if you have knowledge or expertise in an area where someone else is lacking.

Once you have developed the giving part of the relationship, then you can begin to get something in return. There is nothing backhanded about networking. It is an essential part of developing relationships in the business world. In certain company cultures, networking may be the only way to ever move beyond your current role.

Office Politics

Be aware of the politics within your organization by paying attention to what goes on around you and listening to everyone from the receptionist to your supervisor. You will be amazed what you can learn about the company from the person who strikes up a conversation with you at the water cooler.

Know whom you can deal with and who is to be avoided at all cost. Know who does what and the best way to approach each person. Above all, remember that the ultimate goal is to gain respect from others, not make them resent you. Always maintain a sense of professionalism and don't let fruitful conversations turn into idle office gossip.

Manage Your Projects as Well as Your Time

An earlier chapter went into a lengthy explanation of time management and why it is important. In the case of leading as a follower, it will be imperative for you to manage your workload just as efficiently as you manage your time. This means getting things done on time or ahead of schedule, doing them well, and getting along with other staff members every step along the way.

But wait, it's not that easy! Further apply these skills to your career. Figure out where you would like to be in 2 years, 5 years, 10 years, and then plan a strategy for getting there. Put yourself on a clearly defined career path. Start yourself moving in an upward direction and continue to chart your course with each new project and promotion. Make sure, however, that you are always able to contribute to the core path of the company. Figure out how your skills and talents can best be put to use, and then get to work!

Take Them Under Your Wing— Be a Mentor

Once upon a time in Greek mythology, Odysseus, King of Ithaca, sailed off to the Trojan War. Unfortunately, he was forced to leave his wife, Penelope, and their young son, Telemachus, behind. Days turned into weeks, weeks turned into months, and months turned into 20 years. Before leaving, Odysseus asked his faithful and trusted servant Mentor to take on the role of counselor to Telemachus. When the Trojan War ended and his father had not returned, Telemachus set out to find him. The goddess Athena assumed the form of Mentor on several occasions to give Telemachus advice and support.

Profile

Famous Mentors and Their Protégés

Sigmund Freud to C.J. Jung

Anne Sullivan to Helen Keller

Martin Luther King Jr. to Jesse Jackson

Socrates to Plato

Plato to Aristotle

Ralph Waldo Emerson to Henry David Thoreau

Reuben "Hurricane" Carter to Lesra Martin

Qui-Gon Jinn to Obi-Wan Kenobi

Today a mentor is someone who acts as a trusted counselor and teacher to a protégé (French for "protected"). Many companies already have mentorship programs in place. Often they are not successful because participants have been forced to join. In your case, you will be participating because you genuinely want to help others as well as establish your leadership abilities. Your goal as a mentor will be to help someone with less professional experience gain the skills and confidence she will need to succeed in her job.

In most cases a mentor holds a higher position in the company than the protégé, and often the mentor is a great deal older. However, that may not be the case in your situation. In this day and age, individuals who are managers and hold leadership positions are younger than ever before. With the booming dot.com industry and young entrepreneurs taking charge, this model is likely to continue for years to come. As long as you possess the knowledge and experience necessary to help someone along, that is all the qualification you need to be a successful mentor.

So Now That I'm a Mentor, What Do I Do?

Your ultimate goal as a mentor is to help your protégé to further his career. This can be accomplished in a variety of ways. You need to decide what options are available to you, and then decide on the right balance for you and your protégé.

- If you have the power to give input on promotions, be a champion for your protégé. Put in a good word or two every now and again. Showcase the strengths of your protégé by pointing out all the successes he has had in the past. Express 100 percent confidence in your protégé's abilities to move up to the next level. After all, he is a reflection of your hard work and coaching.
- Encourage your protégé to tackle projects of increasing importance and difficulty. If you happen to be the person's direct supervisor, assign her to projects that are challenging and

Profile

An excerpt from "The Odyssey" by Homer

Then Telemachus went all alone by the sea side, washed his hands in the gray waves and prayed to Athena. "Hear me," he cried, "you god who visited me yesterday, and bade me sail the seas in search of my father who has long been missing. I would obey you, but the Achaeans, and more particularly the wicked suitors, are hindering me that I may not do so."

And thus he prayed, Athena came close up to him in the likeness and with the voice of Mentor. "Telemachus," said she, "if you are made of the same stuff as your father you will neither be fool nor coward henceforward, for Odysseus never broke his word nor left his work half done. If, then, you take after him, your voyage will not be fruitless, but unless you have the blood of Odysseus and of Penelope in your veins, I see no likelihood of your succeeding. Sons are seldom as good men as their fathers; they are generally worse, not better; still, as you are not going to be either fool or coward, henceforward, and you are not entirely without some share of your father's wide discernment, I look with hope upon your undertaking. But mind you never make common cause with any of those foolish suitors, for they have neither sense nor virtue, and give no thought to death and to the doom that will shortly fall on one and all of them, so that they shall perish on the same day. As for your voyage, it shall not be long delayed; your father was such an old friend of mine that I will find you a ship and come with you myself. Now, however, return home, and go about among the suitors; begin getting provisions ready for your voyage; see everything well stowed, the wine in jars, and the barley meal, which is the staff of life, in leather bags, while I go round the town and beat up volunteers at once. There are many ships in Ithaca both old and new; I will run my eye over them for you and will choose the best; we will get her ready and will put out to sea without delay."

provide the opportunity for both personal and professional growth. Work that allows the person to learn a new job skill would be ideal. For example, have her work closely with the marketing department to develop a flyer for the new software product your team has been working on. Not only will your protégé gain exposure to the sales and marketing side of the business, but she may even have a chance to learn some basic graphic design tools.

- Do not attempt to solve problems for your protégé. Encourage him to find solutions on his own. Have him come to you when he has developed a solution, and at that point, provide him with feedback and constructive criticism. If a problem comes up that involves more technical skills, then by all means step in and lend a hand. Go through the solution process step-by-step and encourage your protégé to take notes for later reference. Make sure that you will not have to get involved should the problem occur again.

- Explain in detail the inner workings of the company. How do things really get done? Take your protégé on a "behind the scenes" tour and introduce her to key members of the organization. When giving instruction, explain the who, what, when, where, why, and how of it.

  - Who is the targeted market?
  - What is the main product or service you are promoting?
  - When are the deadlines for each step?
  - Where will meetings be held?
  - Why have you assigned the protégé to this particular project?
  - How will the outcome of the project help save the company money in the long run?

  By arming your protégé with all of this information, you will help her develop a better sense of the big picture. She will also be more motivated because she has a greater understanding of your vision for the project.

- On a more personal level, a mentor can offer moral support and friendship to the protégé. When work gets a little rough, a mentor can offer words of encouragement or just a sympathetic

Leadership Tip

Yoda is the Ultimate Mentor

Consider some of the advice Yoda gave to Luke Skywalker.

"Try not. Do, or do not. There is no try."

"You must unlearn what you have learned."

"Always in motion is the future."

ear. A mentor can be important in helping to reduce the stress levels of the protégé by referring him to others who can help and preventing him from getting in over his head.

Five Myths about Mentorship

The times are changing and so is the idea of mentorship. Here are some myths about mentorship that are slowly being diffused.

- **Myth 1:** Only men are mentors. This is absolutely, positively not true. With more women in the workforce than ever before, women are becoming increasingly more involved in organized mentorship programs.
- **Myth 2:** A mentor is someone who is old and holds a higher position than her protégé. It is becoming more common to have mentors who are coworkers and peers rather than vice presidents or CEOs. People are finding that the best advice often comes from those who experience the same sorts of issues and problems as they do. Anyone who can provide guidance, whether inside or outside the company, will make a great mentor.
- **Myth 3:** Mentors should share similar interests and philosophies. Once again, not true. Sometimes the best matches are those that seem the most unlikely. More ideas can be generated when people have opposing views and opinions. The creative spark is more easily ignited in such a dynamic, and new thought processes are developed.
- **Myth 4:** A mentor always chooses the protégé. It is acceptable and even preferable for a protégé to actively seek out a mentor.
- **Myth 5:** Mentoring begins at the top and works its way down. Some companies have reversed this model and have younger members of the organization provide insight and direction to the top-level executives. This model is beneficial because often younger executives are susceptible to false assumptions that can be discussed and challenged in the mentor/protégé forum. Higher-level executives can learn from new ideas introduced by the lower-level executives who are closer to the inner workings of the company.

CHAPTER 19

The New Workforce

Understanding the new workforce, the nineteenth core concept, is essential for a leader. This concept will require a thorough execution of the first 18 concepts. The rules of the game are constantly being altered. A good leader will learn to change with the times and successfully incorporate everything from communication to expressing himself in relation to the changes that are taking place.

The twenty-first-century workforce constitutes a new breed of worker. The days of subordination are over, and as a twenty-first-century leader, you need to change with the times. Today's workers are more independent, self-reliant, and creative than any generation before them. They have different standards for the workplace and require different characteristics in their leaders. The smart leader is one who embraces the changing workplace. Use the newest trends to your advantage; find innovative ways to keep your staff both interested and productive. The new worker is expecting more from you. She requires more focus on quality-of-life issues, more autonomy in her work, and more recognition that she is an integral part of your organization. For you to succeed as a leader, it is necessary to make an extraordinary effort toward both capturing your staff's attention and keeping it.

Before you can implement an updated plan for leading the new workforce, you need a little background information on what the "new" workplace is all about. Well guess what, we're going to give you a few helpful hints. First of all, it's vitally important to take all of your preconceived notions about the workplace and throw them out. That's right. Throw all of that useless information away. You see, everything you once knew about being a leader doesn't apply anymore. Big business no longer calls the shots. Employees have more power now than ever before, and you are responsible for harnessing their energy and directing it so that it's productive for your organization.

A Little Bit of History

Once upon a time, the modern economic world was categorized by high-volume, mass-produced, standardized products and services. Unfortunately, this type of production was carried over into the management and created autocratic management practices that have been the norm until just recently. The "old school" management system had clear, albeit unwritten, rules. As long as an individual stayed with a company for a number of years and performed his job well, there was an implied contract that motivated him. At his retirement, he was pretty much guaranteed a party, decent retirement benefits, and well wishes from his company.

Incorporated into all of this was an understanding that when the company did well, the employees would benefit. Special awards, bonuses, and incentives were used to motivate employees. Keeping the masses happy little bits at a time, that's how big business worked. Not unlike a parent/child relationship, if the employee worked well for the company, it would take care of him. The whole theme of business remained paternalistic in nature. Leading into recent years, this has been the basic management message that has driven the modern economy. Then came a decade of reengineering, downsizing, and right-sizing. The world has changed, and the people that drive the economy have changed along with it. The new workforce has different priorities and different needs, which you, as a leader, need to recognize. In the past, leaders directed and controlled their employees. Now, leaders need to empower their employees to direct themselves.

What They Have in Common

The new worker is no longer content to sit at her desk from nine to five, waiting for a few words of praise from the company bosses. Most new workers don't fit neatly into the description of the post–World War II worker or the me-generation children of those workers. No, the new workforce is operating from a whole different agenda. The employees of the successful company of the twenty-first century share some very distinctive characteristics.

The workforce that you've been asked to lead is very distrustful of institutions. And that includes your organization. Today's workforce has experienced some of the most traumatic periods of modern history, creating a belief that traditional institutions don't care about its needs. From the economic crisis in Germany to the downsizing and reengineering of the American workforce, the modern worker has witnessed the results of blind faith in an institution. Change is now the norm, and

Words of the Wise

"The younger generation doesn't want equality and regimentation, but opportunity to shape their world while showing compassion to those in real need."

—*Margaret Thatcher (1925–), Europe's first female prime minister*

as a leader you need to stay on top of it. You need to embrace the new opportunities that change presents, and use these opportunities to develop new, innovative solutions to old problems.

The modern workforce is also highly independent. Workers today won't ask you to hold their hand throughout the work day, and they don't expect you to, either. Today's workers are self-reliant and highly skilled at the daily task of solving problems. The majority of the modern workforce was raised in either a single-parent or dual-income family. This emerging group is quite capable of working independently and solving problems with available resources by stretching the boundaries of creativity and existing guidelines.

Technological knowledge is another integral part of the modern workforce. The twenty-first-century worker is expected to be computer literate. She understands the enormous potential that comes from available technology, and she realizes that there's much more to come. Today's workers have grown up with computers as a normal part of their daily lives. To them, bytes and chips are like interest rates and credit lines were to their parents. Beware, you may find yourself in the uncomfortable position of having your staff know a lot more about your company technology than you do.

Oh, if you aren't nervous enough, there is one more thing. This generation of workers is stereotyped as the MTV generation. It is independent and operates with a one-track mind toward instant gratification. These workers really just don't have the time for you to make decisions for them. They know what they want, and they want it *now*. A definite realization among businesses today is that the new workforce will change jobs as quickly as it switches the channels on the television. The days of corporate loyalty are long gone.

Each of the characteristics addressed so far is powerful and daunting enough in its own right. When they're all wrapped together in the mantle of an enormous need for feedback and gratification, the prospect of leading this workforce presents some exciting and difficult challenges.

What They Want

A high quality of life is the battle cry emerging from the new workforce. Job seekers are well aware of the options made available to employees by the various companies with which they interview. Smart companies use this knowledge to create benefits packages that potential employees just can't pass up. They incorporate quality-of-life programs and benefits into the original job offer. In order to attract skilled employees, companies have begun to pay closer attention to many of the details that make the lives of their employees more enjoyable. Remember, keeping your staff happy is sure to create a feeling of satisfaction and productivity.

The new worker expects more from his employer than ever before—and he can get it. Companies that recognize the dilemma of a family in which both spouses work or the demands of a single-parent household are way ahead in the game. This is the key to retaining your employees. Companies that have assistance programs to support and help employees have an added advantage. In their efforts to keep employees happy, some companies have even gone to enormous expense and trouble to add perks such as high-quality restaurants and coffee shops to the workplace. Some companies encourage and frequently subsidize special vacation packages for their employees and their families.

What You Need to Do

By now you are bound to be feeling apprehensive or a little bit nervous. But let's face it, today's leaders have several challenges ahead of them. The daunting task of leading this new workforce can make even the most confident leader a little queasy. Twenty-first-century leaders will achieve success only when they're able to communicate throughout an entire organization in a fashion that captures and holds the attention of the new workforce. You need to map out a plan of action that will create an environment that is interactive, engaging employees whenever and wherever possible.

You need to make work exciting. Your staff should be interested in the product, service, or commodity that your organization markets. The successful company must be perceived as both "hot" and "cool" and be able to grab the attention of the new workforce. Change is a constant factor in any modern organization. It generates excitement, excitement generates interest, interest generates creativity, creativity generates innovative ideas, and innovative ideas generate new concepts. These

new concepts are what make the world go round. They create new products, services, and commodities that reach to every corner of the world. The exciting news: You are the leader of this emerging workforce. The power to harness energy and intellect and put it to work in your organization is an exciting challenge.

Values Are Consistent

Put your mind at ease. The challenge is great, but it doesn't change the core values of our economy and way of life. As a matter of fact, quite the opposite is true. Recent surveys indicate that the new generation of workers agrees on the fact that hard work is a major factor in getting ahead in life. These workers realize that, in order to get ahead and stay ahead, they have to work for it.

It is important to note, that although the modern workforce realizes the value of hard work, there's still a huge difference between it and the existing workforce. The twenty-first-century workforce will work hard but it will *not* wait quietly by the wayside while management decides to take action. The demand for workers is much higher than the supply. It isn't just getting skilled employees, it's retaining them that's the problem. Take charge and make sure that you create an office environment that attracts employees and keeps them. The modern workforce realizes that the old adage "the early bird catches the worm" still applies in today's workforce. It wants to know exactly what's going on, as well as how it can be involved in it.

The traditional values of security, loyalty, and playing by the rules are being replaced by new values of challenge, fun, independence, and opportunity. But fear not. That does not diminish the fundamental core values that hold both the traditional and the new values together. Trust, harmony, and honesty are still an intrinsic part of what drives our world. In fact, a company built on these fundamental core values will achieve higher levels of success than a company that chooses to ignore them. The company, or leader for that matter, that does not promote these basic values sends a message of exclusion and distrust to its employees. In fact, it's the leader's responsibility to create a relationship with workers that incorporates the sensibilities of partnership and shared values. The successful new workplace is comprised of employees that are responsible for making their companies profitable, as well as companies that are responsible for making their employees valuable.

Pay Attention to Retention

As you recall, an entire chapter has already been devoted to the topic of employee recognition and retention. However, it is an important issue and merits attention once again in this chapter. Assuming that your company has succeeded in hiring the best and brightest, as a leader it's your responsibility to ensure that you retain those very same employees. Today's recruits, being talented and ambitious, are deciding not to stick around very long at any one place of employment. In fact, the more that leave, the more that need to be wooed all over again with bigger perks and better benefits. Unfortunately for you, the new economy is making the young and gifted worker lunge at higher-paying jobs offering an options package with a future. The key lies not only in getting the employees but keeping them as well.

It's important to remember that retention doesn't mean you need to hang on to every employee you hire. Rather, it means recognizing that key people can't, and won't, be taken for granted. For some reason, there remains in the business world a failure to understand that knowledge is a tangible asset. Every time employees leave an organization, they take with them all of their knowledge. This can range from something as insignificant as a familiarity with company policy, to something very significant such as customer preferences, database expertise, or product knowledge. At the very least, the cost of replacing a valuable employee can be over double the departing person's salary.

In the olden days, the company ran the show. Not anymore. Instead, the message that companies preached over the past decade—down with lifetime employment, up with self-taught skills—is the same one that's causing them so many problems. When big business went through a general trend of downsizing and reengineering, the common theme was—"It's good for the business." The new workforce has now taken that theme and turned it right back around. They're more self-confident and mobile.

If they have an offer somewhere else—"It's not personal, it's business." The employees are more empowered than ever before.

What can you do to combat this? Companies today are finding it very difficult to provide what workers want. Things like job satisfaction, the ability to balance life and work, and opportunities for growth are difficult to guarantee. It's even more difficult to pinpoint what each employee needs and how you are supposed to cater to his individual desires. However, this responsibility comes with the territory. As a leader, the best thing you can do for your staff is to help your new recruits. Educate them not only about their jobs, but about the company as well. Help them assimilate into your workplace without losing their creative drive. New hires are going to look to you for leadership and support. In order to retain them, you need to make sure that you deliver.

Why You Could Feel Lost

Confronting the new workforce as a leader is a challenge. You see, your staff is going to scrutinize your every move and see if you have what it takes to make it in the new, technological economy. The best thing you can do is put aside all of your preconceived notions of leadership and get down to the basics. You've already learned about the integral "basics" of being a leader. All sorts of helpful hints have been provided to help you along the way. However, the self-confidence needed to lead the new workforce can only be supplied by you. The times are changing. If you stand up in a suit and tie and confront your staff members with charts and economic trends and statistics, they may laugh you right out of the building.

What employees once found awe inspiring doesn't appear to mean as much anymore. Translation: If you drive a fancy car, belong to an exclusive country club, make a million bucks, or even have a string of management awards, your employees aren't going to be impressed. No, you have to impress your staff through your knowledge. If you're an interloper in the new economy, they're savvy enough to realize it and let you know. When it comes to leading the new workforce, books and numbers aren't the only kind of education you need. You need to be aware of the latest technology and industry trends, even if they aren't in your area of expertise

The New Trend to Teamwork

With the demand for specialized skills steadily increasing, employers are finding it more difficult to retain the staff they need in-house. In fact, many specialized workers have found that they can make more money on their own terms by joining consulting firms or striking out on their own. Therein lies the dilemma. Melding contract and permanent staff into an effective team is bound to be a challenge for any leader. There are sure to be conflicting personal dynamics, and possibly work ethics, between in-house and third-party employees. Your responsibility is to apply your knowledge of teams to this new and integrated work group.

There are a few things you can do to attempt to smooth out any wrinkles that may develop between the different groups. Communication is still the name of the game. Make sure you're accessible to both in-house and third-party employees. To be an effective leader of this type of team, you need to be aware of all sides of the issues and mediate positive resolutions to any problems that may crop up. Be careful. Favoritism breeds jealousy, and jealousy breeds internal disaster. Make sure that you listen to both groups equally, understand their different points of view, and guide them to a solution.

There are a couple of different leadership techniques that you can use to create cohesiveness within a blended workforce of contract and permanent employees. Utilize each group's skills to benefit the other. For example, your contract employees will most likely come highly specialized in a single area, very independent and self-sufficient, and familiar with working autonomously. Your permanent staff can benefit from their expertise. Promote intergroup training and knowledge sharing. Your in-house staff will be excited about the possibilities of learning new things, and the contract staff will be more inclined to feel like part of the group. On that note, be sure to include your contract staff in department events and reward programs. One of the first steps to making a diverse team work is creating cohesiveness. This, you can do.

The word "teamwork" is taking on a whole new meaning in today's new economy. It's becoming much more difficult to hire and retain qualified, full-time staff members, thus creating a need for contract groups. Leaders who are unable to lead a melded team of permanent,

Profile

Napoleon Bonaparte (1769–1821)

Wielding powerful leadership skills, Napoleon Bonaparte worked his way through the ranks to become Napoleon I, Emperor of France. Best known for his military organization, Napoleon sought to expand the French Empire to encompass most of Western Europe. Although he was unable to institute complete French domination as Emperor, Napoleon still had a major impact on the Western world. During his rule, he restructured military organization and training, introduced civil-law codes, abolished feudalism, and emphasized the importance of education, science, literature, and the arts.

temporary, and contract staff members won't remain in a leadership position for long. In order to effectively lead such a diverse group of individuals, you need to be sure to understand the different motivations for each group, and create incentives that will benefit all facets of your team. As a leader, you need to create an inclusive culture, melding together a variety of individuals, skills, and personalities to create a team that works effectively and successfully.

Balancing Your Company's Wants and Your Employees' Needs

A well-oiled machine is a good description for the successful business of the twenty-first century. Companies are going to have to obtain the greatest productivity from the least amount of employees if they want to remain at the top of their industry. This is where you come in. The only way that your organization will become successful using this strategy is by taking great pains to ensure that employees don't get burnt out. As a leader in your organization, you must find a balance between work and well-being and make sure you know where to draw the line between a company's wants and your employees' needs.

Leadership in the new economy means being equally concerned about both the employee's productivity and the employee's personal well-being. You need to maintain a balance between achieving task accomplishments and nurturing relationships that support the organization both internally and externally.

In the past, employees did exactly what they were instructed to do. If they didn't receive clear directions, then nothing got done. In fact, if they received instructions that they knew would produce a low-quality product, they carried them out anyway. That was how the management/employee relationship worked. The new workforce presents the polar opposite viewpoint. Today, employees are expected to make minute-by-minute decisions related to their work tasks. They are more independent. The company no longer expects to have to give specific instructions for each task or problem. Instead, employees are asked to direct their own workflow and to keep productivity up even when required resources are limited or not available.

A quick look into the future shows an emphasis on increased independent actions and decision making by individual employees. Businesses will expect more from their employees. Increased pressure to perform and deliver flawless products and services will place employees under even greater stress. Your ability to reduce this pressure and translate it into developmental and exciting opportunities is what will set you apart as a successful and capable leader.

Promoting Self-Improvement

One thing is for certain, as the economy surges ahead and the new workforce becomes more empowered, every successful business will incorporate some type of continuous improvement philosophy into their corporate strategy. Today's modern workforce is obsessed with constant self-improvement. That's what your employees want.

Our economy is driven by people who want to improve their looks, their wardrobe, their investments, and their status. They want their children to go to prestigious schools and want to own name-brand products. These are the people that you are leading. They want to know that the organization they work for is the best. They want to know that they're affiliated with the top dog in the market. In parallel, businesses have realized that continuous improvement is the way of the future. It is the lifeblood that prevents businesses from cycling back to older, less intelligent, and less efficient forms of management.

Guess what, you are the leader that needs to find the balance. Twenty-first-century leaders must carefully balance factors such as production, profits, and employee needs. No one issue can overtake the importance of the others. The new workforce, in the midst of this constantly changing environment, knows when the scales are tipping against it. And it'll tip them right back. Leaders able to maintain a steady balance will be the long-term success stories of the twenty-first century.

Respecting Your Elders

Did you ever get scolded as a child for not respecting your elders? Along with several other inherent values, most children are brought up

to believe that their elders are wiser and more experienced and deserve respect because of it. The new workforce is challenging these beliefs as leadership positions are being swallowed up by twenty-somethings on a fast track to success. How do you deal with employees that are older than you? Very carefully, that's for sure.

Young bosses are now managing employees old enough to be their parents, and there is definitely a very thin line between assertiveness and arrogance as far as the older workers are concerned. Older workers are concerned that young leaders have patronizing attitudes and a tendency to micromanage. Listen to your employees, but above all, respect them. Whether you're older or younger than your staff, respect is still an integral part of being a leader. On the other hand, don't be intimidated by your staff's age. After all, you are still the leader. You're in a position that commands respect, and don't ever forget that. While you certainly don't want to come off as condescending or arrogant, you still have to maintain your leadership status. Have confidence in your position. Just as you were raised to respect your elders, older workers were raised to respect authority.

Diversity in the Workplace

The changing workforce of the twenty-first century requires company leaders to change the ways that they relate to their employees. In fact, the realization that diversity is an integral part of organizational success is the key to company growth. It is vital that leaders understand that the talent pool includes all types of workers, including minorities, women, older workers, and persons from various cultural and religious backgrounds.

The leading companies and organizations in the new millennium will need to place emphasis on multicultural inclusiveness. A number of studies show that multicultural inclusiveness in the workplace breeds higher productivity, better camaraderie, and a more positive attitude amongst employees. Any way you look at it, the benefits that can be gained through a diversity of thought, gender, political affiliation, religion, race, sexual orientation, and other characteristics can have a profound impact on both the workplace and the global marketplace.

CHAPTER 20

Teaching the Old Dog Some New Tricks

he final—though no less important—core concept is keeping yourself educated. Amidst all the reconstruction taking place, it is imperative that you, as a leader, keep yourself well informed.

The business world is constantly changing, and you want to make sure that you and your organization change with it. As new ideas and opportunities continue to pop up throughout the business community, the only way to guarantee that your organization remains on the cutting edge is through education. Education can always be achieved through the traditional methods—seminars, conferences, and continued schooling. Those will be covered in more detail shortly. However, education and learning don't have to always center around the traditional. If you know where to look, you may find that some of your best resources are sitting down the hall or right next to you. Either way you look at it, learning is critical to any business or organization that wants to keep up. Leaders are responsible for making sure this happens.

Staying in School

When you think of education, what's the first word that pops into your head? "School," of course. In today's society, continuing your education is imperative to staying in the game. And, education is easier than ever to pursue. Through grants, loans, and tuition assistance or reimbursement, people are finding that going back to school is not the financial crisis that it once was. Then again, school isn't your only option. Trade shows, seminars, and conferences are other great avenues for continuing your education. However, furthering your education isn't restricted to outside sources. There are endless possibilities available to you right in your own office. Even if you aren't in a leadership position right now, pursuing an education will give you an extra edge next time a promotion comes up.

Taking the Classes

As a leader, you want to make sure that you are aware of the newest developments in the business. This can be done by taking the time to do a little extracurricular work. Most colleges and universities offer a variety of specialized classes. Take the time to grab a course schedule from nearby schools or even surf the Internet to find out what different schools have to offer. Monetarily, school can always set you back, but if you do your research, you may be pleasantly surprised to find that your business is willing to pay for your classes. Take the initiative to find out what is offered and what you can learn that will improve your company. Then break down the costs and find out if it would be a beneficial investment for your company. Many companies offer a tuition reimbursement plan. If a program or class relates to your job, your company may give you some, if not all, of the money needed to complete the course.

If your company or organization can't afford the added investment of continued education, look to your state government. Several states offer some form of vocational or adult-education training funds for company employees. It could be something as simple as getting funds to help your staff get a high school education, or as complex as securing grants for graduate classes.

As a leader, staff members will come looking to you for answers, and you want to make sure that you have them to give. Educating yourself is only the first step, however. You also need to make sure that you use that knowledge to the best of your ability and pass it on to the rest of your organization. While you're asking for company funds or reimbursement, suggest that it would also be beneficial to have one or two staff members come with you. That way, less time and energy will be wasted on additional training.

Incorporating New Technology

Technology is what everyone is talking about these days, and it isn't just changing your workplace. It's changing your education opportunities as well. Education is made even easier by the availability of online classes and degrees. If you're really motivated about continuing your education, but feel as if you don't have the time due to your commute or difficult schedule, you may find that online classes are just what you need.

Profile

Marian Wright Edelman
(1939–)

American author, lawyer, and social reformer, Marian Wright Edelman founded the Children's Defense Fund in 1973. She has also published a number of works addressing civil inequality and children's welfare. Marian Wright Edelman has been the recipient of several humanitarian awards as well as a MacArthur Foundation Fellowship (1985).

Degrees achieved online are exactly the same as those received by more traditional methods. A transcript won't indicate whether a class was taken online or in person. According to most colleges offering them, online classes and traditional classes are equally challenging. The same materials are used for both classes, and a professor is almost always available for questions via e-mail or discussion boards. Use the Internet to find what schools have the classes you want available online. You might even find yourself with an additional degree from across the country.

Just like introducing new learning processes in your organization, an online education will take some adjustment. You need to have the necessary computer hardware and software available to you. You also have to feel comfortable and motivated enough to ensure that you keep up with your coursework without "encouragement" from a professor. In the end, however, online classes give you the opportunity to improve your education on your own time. After all, isn't the whole purpose to improve your skills and become a better leader?

Other Resources

Seminars, trade shows, and conferences are another way to keep learning. Associations that specialize in your area of business are bound to have suggestions or links about how you can find out about any upcoming seminars. They may even offer some themselves. Seminars and conferences offer a little more leeway than a strict school schedule. Chances are, you'll have more intensive sessions over a shorter period of time. This type of learning is also conducive to getting your whole department involved. You can either split the group between a couple of different conferences and swap lessons, or send everyone together. Remember, it gives your staff members a sense of self-worth and motivation if they are constantly challenged.

When you're researching the various seminars, look for ones where the keynote speakers are experts in their fields. Preferably, seminars will be geared toward professionals in a particular industry. Experts aren't trying to sell you anything and therefore

have nothing to gain by providing faulty or questionable information. You also have a great chance to network with other professionals and an opportunity to learn from others involved in the same business. You may find some suggestions for a current problem your department or business is struggling with, or even provide some help that will be reciprocated down the line. Either way you look at it, you're getting a chance to go out and learn new things that will help educate both you and your organization.

One more thing: Don't just focus on seminars pertaining to your business. Keep an eye out for leadership and management seminars as well. While this book is helpful in getting you started, you'll find that interaction with other leaders is also beneficial. Again, you may find that you learn more from the other attendees than the keynote speaker. Leadership requires work, and building knowledge requires some extra effort. However, the ends certainly justify the means.

Formulate Your Plan

Deciding to continue your education is a specific choice that you need to make, and once you make that decision, you need to be sure that you follow through. Learning is both an active and interactive process. As a leader, you need to value education as an important tool for improving your business. Take a hard look at your organization and see what needs improvement. Only then can you create a plan and embrace education as a strategic activity.

Education and Vision

Organizing a plan for continued education can be a lot like creating your vision. You still need to sell it to your organization. Education is just one of the steppingstones needed to achieve your vision, and you need to make that clear. When you outline your vision, explain how additional education will help you reach your goal faster and more efficiently. Describe what new skills are needed and how you plan to help your employees acquire those skills. You'll be surprised to find out that your staff may be just as

Words of the Wise

"Education is a precondition to survival in America today."

—Marian Wright Edelman (1939–), American author and social reformer

excited about the whole prospect as you are. Continued training and education will create more motivated employees and cultivate company loyalty.

Stay in Line

While you are delving into your leadership responsibilities and planning for all sorts of improvements, it's important to remember that you're a leader; not a control freak. As a leader, realizing that control and learning don't mix very well is one of the first steps toward implementing your reforms. You need to make sure that you provide the venue, but then you must relinquish total control and let your employees learn for themselves. Also, beware of the "old-school" employees. Those are the people stuck in a rut, confident that you'll always be around to tell them what to do and uncomfortable with interactive education. It may take them a while to get used to the fact that you expect them to take some initiative in their learning experience.

Internal Education

As you search out ways to improve the learning process in your organization, be aware of overlooking a solution that may be available right next door. Improving your education doesn't always mean you have to take classes or acquire a formal education. You'll find this also means taking the time to listen to the person next to you. Opening your eyes and ears in the workplace can help you to learn more about your organization than you may think.

Introduce Yourself and the Organization

Implementing learning inside your organization isn't only about acquiring new skills. It's also about utilizing the ones you already have. Give your staff members an opportunity to share and gain new knowledge from each other. There are all kinds of creative ways to promote internal learning, but starting with the basics would help. For example, does your organization have a high turnover rate? Do you find that your staff doesn't know what goes on in other areas of the organization? How about whether it knows or at least recognizes different people in the company and what department they work for? Does your staff know what its contribution to the organization is?

Although it may sound like a bad cliché, it can all start with an introduction. Being a leader means that it's your responsibility to make sure that your staff members know each other as well as the organization, what it does, and how it all comes together. You have to start any learning process with information. Encourage departmental and interdepartmental meetings or lunches. Take the time to introduce your staff around. You can even assign specific duties that will promote interaction with other areas of the business. Rotate these assignments every month to create a change of scenery as well as an opportunity for everyone to meet new people. Simple introductions go a long way toward creating a comfortable office atmosphere, as well as opening the lines of communication. When people feel at ease, they are more likely to share their knowledge and experience with coworkers. You are the leader. Set an example and encourage your staff members to get to know one another and other company employees.

Learning the Ropes

Simply opening the lines of communication will contribute to the flow of information in the office, but you need to ensure that there's some actual learning going on as well. Take the time to educate your employees about the organization itself. You know that knowing your own job isn't enough to impact an organization. You also realize that you need to know where your job fits into the big picture, and how improvements in your position will have an impact on the organization as a whole. Well, your employees need to realize this, too.

Educating your staff about the organization is an easy thing to do; you just need to make the time to do it. Utilize your preexisting contacts to help out your department. Contact your public relations department and arrange for a copy of current press releases to be

---

Profile

Frederick Douglass
(1817–1895)

Frederick Douglass escaped slavery to become an influential leader in the human rights movement, an avid abolitionist, and a renowned literary figure. In 1841, Frederick Douglass addressed an antislavery convention in Massachusetts and was recruited as an agent for the Massachusetts Anti-Slavery Society. Douglass was forced to go abroad after the publication of his autobiography in 1845 and managed to gather the funds to officially purchase his freedom. Upon his return to the United States, Douglass started his own antislavery newspaper, *North Star;* served as a consultant to President Abraham Lincoln during the Civil War; and fought for full civil rights and women's rights during Reconstruction. Douglass became the first African American to hold high rank in the U.S. government, serving as the assistant secretary of the Santo Domingo Commission (1871) and U.S. minister and consul general to Haiti (1889–1891).

sent to your staff. Find out if your company has a brochure that provides the organization's history and pass it out to your staff. Also, take the minutes from managerial meetings and create a memo updating your staff on current news and events. The more your staff knows about the organization, the easier it will be for it to define its own role in the company, as well as recognize problems and suggest solutions as the need arises.

Utilizing Your Space

Office space isn't there just to create a pleasant atmosphere, it's there to create camaraderie among coworkers. You're the leader. Think of innovative ways to utilize the space available to make an interactive and learning-conducive atmosphere. Some people may assume that visual aids are useful only in children's education, but such devices can also be helpful in an organizational situation. Take some tips from your preschool teacher. Bulletin boards, games, and interactive communication are helpful when educating all ages.

Tear Down the Wall

Do you have wall space in your office just crying out for the perfect picture? Perhaps you have the picture, but it just isn't right for that space. Any fixture that's wasting space needs to go. You're in charge; take it down. Use the space wisely and create an effective learning tool. Erect a department information center. Bulletin boards, for example, are great for reminder notes and scheduling. Use them for educating as well. Set a new standard in your organization by keeping your staff aware of all developments. Whether someone new is hired or someone old quit, don't make your staff rely on the grapevine for information. If you're free with information output, you'll soon see that people will speak to you more freely, too.

There are millions of things that bulletin boards can be used for. Posting memos, company news, birthdays, and holiday decorations are great ways to not only keep people informed but to encourage camaraderie as well. Unfortunately, e-mail, like regular mail, is full of junk these days. On the same note, everyone's inbox is overflowing. Take a load off your staff for once. Make things easy for employees by posting information once, instead of putting 100 different memos in their in-boxes. Allow them to have a little space of their own on the department bulletin board. Create an outlet where people can post random news they receive. Whether it be company- or industry-related, or even something simple like a new e-mail virus warning, allow your staff to feel like it is actively participating in the education process.

Games for All Ages

Games are played for several reasons, the number one being that they're fun. People enjoy participating as well as observing a variety of sports and other types of games. Think of the general atmosphere at a baseball game. It's fun, relaxing, and exciting. Now, transfer some of those same sentiments to your workplace and watch out. Your employees will not only begin to take a more active interest in their work, but they will enjoy it more as well.

Use some of your extra space to set up interactive office trivia games using company facts, industry-related trivia, or even cost assessments. Tweak your staff's knowledge (and interest) by setting up a point system or rewarding the weekly winner for his achievements. Take suggestions from your staff for good questions. You may even learn a thing or two. All too often, a company's employees are an untapped resource in the education process. Don't let it happen in your department. Encourage the learning process by making it fun and interactive.

Scope Out the Competition

As you seek to implement a learning process within your organization, it's important to remember that your organization is not the entire business. Think about it: No matter what organization or business you are in, there have to be competitors out there somewhere. Whether it be competition for buyers, business, fundraising, or advertising, it's important to realize where the threat is coming from and take steps to educate yourself. Being a leader doesn't only

mean that you call the shots, it also means that you take charge of a situation and guide your troops. This sometimes means a little extra work on your part, and while researching quarterly reports of other companies doesn't sound like a whole lot of fun, you'll be surprised at what you can learn.

Using the Reports

In today's business world more and more companies are going public. This means that there's a wealth of information at your fingertips, providing you with additional knowledge if you know where to look. Every time a company makes the decision to go public, they've opened themselves up to the scrutiny of not only their customers, but their competition as well. Being a savvy leader means that you'll take advantage of this added bonus. Buy a few shares of stock in the competition. Stockholder reports from rival companies are sure to include information about the state of the industry, the cost of their products, and who their suppliers are. You can also pick up a little extra "scoop" such as their major marketing approaches, any litigation they're facing, and how much they pay their executives.

Some people may say that you're cheating if you get ideas from rival businesses, but they're there for the taking. It just makes you a little wiser. You may find, hidden away in another company's report, that your marketing department has made a mistake or that there was a change among consumer buying trends that you missed. Take everything you learn with a grain of salt, but use it to your advantage by finding opposing approaches to business. Learn not only from industry successes, but from failures, too. Being a good leader means that you have the ability to seek out available knowledge and use it to your advantage. Make sure your company is remaining competitive, not just with your products or services, but with your employee compensation packages as well.

When seeking out market information or research, you don't always need to look only at your competition or industry. You may find that another organization in a completely different area of service found great marketing success with a certain technique. Capitalize on that information and find out if you can use similar techniques to your advantage. Even without buying stock in another company, prospectuses are available just by calling the investor relations department. Look over all the information you can acquire and see if you can use it to improve your organization.

Create an Intelligence Team

We all know that, as a leader, you don't have a ton of time on your hands. So delegate. Create a team whose responsibilities include gathering intelligence both internally and externally. Not only will your staff learn more about your organization and its competition, but you're opening up one more line of communication. Let's be honest, being in a power position means that much of the information you receive has been carefully filtered. There are gatekeepers scattered throughout any organization who pick and choose what they feel is important information, and by the time it reaches you, a vital source of knowledge may have been lost along the way. Your intelligence team is there to make sure that you remain informed and educated about your staff, the competition, and your organization.

Creating a special team to help you gather information is not only beneficial to you, but to the team as well. You're adding another educational facet to the team members' job, granting them the opportunity to learn new things. At the same time, your staff will feel as if you trust them. Just remember, you're asking for all the information that you get. Make it very clear to your team that they won't be held responsible for passing on any news that you don't like. All too often a leader is the last one to know when there are problems. In the business world, ignorance is not bliss, and you want to make sure that you're constantly on top of things in your organization.

Profile

Hillary Rodham Clinton (1947–)

A former lawyer and First Lady who served as the chairperson of the Task Force on National Health Care Reform, Hillary Clinton founded Arkansas Advocates for Children and Families and authored a book entitled *It Takes a Village* (Touchstone Books, 1996). Clinton is also the first woman to be named senator for the state of New York.

Finding Additional Business Tips

As a leader, it's important to realize what resources are available to help improve both your staff's knowledge and your own. There are a number of places you can look to keep on top of recent trends, marketing strategies, and business successes and failures. The most common place to get information to help you out is from magazines and newspapers. These are published frequently enough to provide current events and information, and they're also considered reliable resources. Books and computer software can provide information on specific topics or new technologies. Self-help books are geared toward building your knowledge base. As we mentioned before, associations and organizations related to your area of business are helpful in providing not only current news, but also links and suggestions for other available resources.

Above and beyond all else, don't forget about the Internet. Technology is the key to getting ahead, and the Internet can be your window to the outside world. Information that could take you hours to research is now available at your fingertips. You, as a leader, are supposed to be a source of information for your staff; therefore, build your knowledge pool daily.

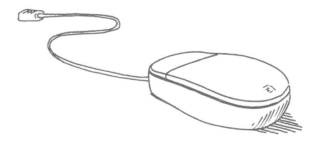

Leadership
Q & A Session

Q:How would you characterize a person's leadership style?

A:Leadership is no longer being the "Lone Ranger," and followers won't be led by the nose on pure faith. You have to offer people something of value (intangible, such as a preferred vision, or tangible, such as improved profitability) for them to muster the energy and dedication to support your leadership. The self-fulfilling prophecy is real; if you don't think much of others, you won't get much from them. Attitude has a lot to do with the level of accomplishment.

Q:What attributes distinguish me from others?

A:Think of the people in leadership positions whom you admire. What draws you to them? Make a list of those qualities, and then make a list of your own "leadership magnets." Do you have a winning attitude and a track record to back it up? Have you taken an unpopular or novel approach that reaped unforeseen benefits? Do you create a working environment that encourages and supports others? How much do you need to be "the star"?

Q:What behaviors can I exhibit that will draw out my employees' commitment and that will stimulate their carrying the message of my vision?

A:While you cannot be expected to always put on a happy face, you should also not assume the role of poster child for the end of the earth. Energy, confidence, competence, and a refuse-to-fail attitude will affect and infect others. And if you have taken the time to carefully draw up your vision and have presented it for all to see and examine and contribute to, you will have

sown the seeds for a bumper crop of commitment and loyalty.

Q:What should I be willing to do or endure to achieve my vision?

A:Leadership is not easy. It becomes easier after achievements accumulate, but the road is often not paved (or the path may not even be clear). As the leader, you are the "point." People up and down the hierarchy will be looking to you for answers, strategies, reasons, and positive outcomes.

Q:How do I get an employee to take responsibility for his or her own performance?

A:Managers create the environments that foster motivation and responsibility. In such an environment, communication is open and safe, employees know the work they do is meaningful; they know why it is critical for them to produce quality work. Also in this environment, risk taking is encouraged, goal setting is ongoing, and both managers and employees are involved in problem solving and decision making. In addition, managers provide feedback, resources, and growth opportunities; communicate encouragement and acknowledgment; and provide recognition, rewards, increased levels of responsibility, and job advancement. Employees experience the benefits of taking responsibility for their performance.

Q:How do I motivate employees to take initiative rather than rely on me for continuous direction?

A:Taking initiative is a risk. If you want your employees to make decisions and not rely on you for continuous direction, you have to create a work atmosphere that encourages risk taking.

That means when an employee makes a mistake, she is guided, not chided! When you, as the manager, allow and encourage initiative without backlash, it will happen.

Q: What do I have to change as a manager to use the coaching process?

A: As a manager, your first step is to recognize that coaching is different from what may be your traditional management style. You must recognize that to receive the benefits of coaching, you must be willing to give up some of your control, because coaching is based on leading and influencing rather than directing. You achieve results through questions rather than directives and through listening and supporting rather than controlling. The new method may feel uncomfortable at first, but you'll get the hang of it soon enough.

Q: How do I help employees develop the ability to evaluate their own ideas and suggestions?

A: One very good way is to use open-ended questions to help them think through the implications of their suggestions. This method of questioning helps develop a "mental balance" scale that employees use to evaluate the pluses and minuses of their ideas.

Another way is to suggest that they evaluate their ideas from the perspective of another person involved, such as a customer, supplier, or fellow worker, and determine how they might respond to the suggested approach.

Q: What will be the biggest challenge I'll face in developing a team approach?

A: The biggest challenge will be the temptation to change the rules and expectations for

performance once the team starts working. You cannot change the rules and still have a productive, efficient team. Only the team can change the rules. Don't interfere unnecessarily.

Q: Why should I develop self-directed teams?

A: Self-directed teams are a powerful management tool you can use to strengthen your company. These teams have the potential to improve the speed and accuracy of resolving problems within your organization. Ultimately, they have the potential to make your company more profitable.

Q: What if there is conflict within the team?

A: Some conflict within the team is a good sign. It indicates that the creative process of problem solving is taking place and that members are challenging each other. A well-developed team will have a communication strategy in place to resolve conflict. This strategy will serve as a model for the organization. Encourage positive, respectful disagreements.

Q: My company does nothing to empower me. Can I use empowerment only within my department?

A: You can try, but you may be rowing upstream. For empowerment to really have an impact, it must have the support of senior management and the policy makers. You will be able to increase the self-confidence of your employees and you will be able to have them assume more responsibilities and authority within your department, but it will be within an isolated environment. Be prepared for your employees who have gained self-confidence to be more resentful and negative about the circumstances that exist in the company once you have given them a taste of empowerment.

Q: Do hourly workers really care what direction the company is headed in?

A: Some lower-level employees may have little or no interest in what the company's plans for the future are, but they will want to know that they belong to a winning team. They want to be able to tell their families and friends that they work for a great company. If they feel that they are working for a company that is going to succeed, they will feel more involved and thereby work harder and smarter.

Q: What kinds of things should I communicate?

A: You should communicate anything and everything that has a direct impact on employees. Give them information. Information is knowledge, and knowledge is power. A powerful workforce is a critical tool in making your company successful.

Q: How do I ensure that I am getting good communication from my staff?

A: The best way for you to be sure that you are getting complete and accurate communication from your staff members is to listen to them and let them tell you everything they intend to tell you. Then you should ask for clarification, and if necessary, ask as many questions as possible to fill in any gaps in information.

Q: Do I need to be a public speaker to be a good communicator?

A: Not at all. What you need is a clear, consistent strategy for communicating what you want people to know. You should be able to communicate very effectively and only infrequently need to stand in front of a large group of people. Use other vehicles such as memos and e-mail, use other people whom you know understand your philosophy, but be sure that the meaning and content you are transmitting are yours. Also be sure you are always confirming and clarifying what is being communicated through this strategy.

Q: I think I am saying and doing all the correct things, but I don't feel that it is working. What could be wrong?

A: Maybe you are communicating more messages than you think. People are not just hearing and listening to your words, they are also perceiving your body language. Sometimes body language can be so strong that people don't hear the words. Think about how you present yourself and the settings in which you tend to talk to people.

Q: Why is change necessary?

A: The concept of staying in place or standing still in business is little more than an illusion. You're either moving forward or falling behind. It may be slow, and you may not notice it on a daily basis, but it's happening. Change is the catalyst for moving ahead. Think what life would be like without change!

Q: What can I do to accelerate the acceptance of change?

A: Very often your attitude, motivation, and behavior toward change are vital in setting the tone for others. If people understand that you also share their unknowns but approach them in a positive and trusting manner, they will find it easier to follow your way. No one wants to feel alone when a change that will alter his professional existence is about to take place.

Q: When is the optimal time to confront and resolve a conflict?

A: Take into account energy levels based on factors such as the time of day and fatigue, the amount of time available to devote to the process based on workloads and meetings scheduled, and emotional readiness.

Q: If I am the third party who is helping others resolve a conflict, what should I do?

A: As long as the parties involved are cooperative, explain the 10-step process and emphasize that your role is to facilitate their going through each step as they concentrate on listening to each other. Then you can help develop a solution that meets everyone's needs.

Q: What legal issues must I consider when conducting a review?

A: Protect yourself and the company by evaluating performance as objectively as possible and by not evaluating the employee on a personal level. Be honest in your appraisal, and always use examples as supporting evidence.

Q: How do I get an employee to want to achieve goals?

A: It's imperative that goals be set with the employee and preferably by the employee. You can accomplish this by explaining the problem to the employee, then working with her to develop a solution. This process helps her to "own" the goals and want to achieve them.

Q: What is the best way to get an employee to agree to what I request?

A: Get the employee involved in the process. Ask him what he is willing to do to solve the problem or what kind of milestones or checkpoints he would like to establish.

Q: Why do I need a plan to hire a good person?

A: Without a plan you are not able to make midstream decisions quickly and with full information. Without a plan you will not be able to delegate portions of the interview and hiring process to others without being concerned about errors and inconsistency. A defined plan will allow you to have consistent hiring practices for all employees.

Q: How do I attract a diverse group of candidates that includes minorities to become part of the candidate pool?

A: It is always good to advertise in a wide range of media. The range of media should include minority newspapers, radio, television, and community groups. Be sure your advertisements include a statement about your corporate philosophy regarding diversity. It also helps to develop relationships with organizations that represent various minorities.

Q: Do I need to have a big, elaborate orientation program for new employees? Can't I just have the new person assigned to another employee for the first day?

A: You don't need an elaborate program, but you do need a clear and consistent program that will operate all the time and in the same way for all employees. If you want to incorporate a buddy system into the orientation program, do so. Be sure everyone involved knows what she is to do.

It would be wise for you to train the people who are going to be the buddies. The important part is to ensure that you communicate the new job duties.

Q: Can I delegate the process to others?

A: Yes. But you will need to stay involved and to maintain veto power over final decisions. You will want to get other people involved so you can slowly but surely have them represent the mission and the culture of the organization as well. Someone else may coordinate the program, but you will still be an integral component of the program.

Q: I already have an orientation program in place. How can I make it better?

A: Congratulations! The best way to make your program better is to ask the people who have gone through the program for suggestions, criticisms, and ideas. Invite the most recent hires to a meeting with an agenda to get their feedback regarding the orientation program. You will be surprised at the amount of quality feedback you will receive. If you implement any of their suggestions, the next time you do the feedback session you will get even more information.

Q: What if I don't have a budget to implement a recognition program for my department?

A: Even with a limited or nonexistent budget, supervisors and managers can make a difference. Consider walking up to an employee when you see her doing a task correctly and letting her know that you appreciate her effort. Write that same employee a note that will get copied to your boss, so that the employee knows other people have been informed. At staff meetings use the good work of employees as examples for others in the work group to follow. None of these costs anything except your time and determination.

Q: How can I learn to say "no"?

A: First, realize that what you really want is to say yes to yourself. Sometimes managers are so busy being caretakers and martyrs that they let their own needs get shelved. This is draining and ineffective. Learn to be emotionally honest. In other words, don't lie to yourself. Don't say or do something you don't mean. This is a particular challenge for new supervisors who are managing former peers and don't want to appear authoritative.

Q: How much money should I budget for fun activities?

A: In many cases, you can create dynamite fun activities for very little cost. A genuine smile doesn't cost a cent, and it goes farther than anything else to create a positive and fun environment.

Pull a group of your employees together and ask them for some no-cost ideas to make the work environment more fun. Within a few minutes this group will come up with a dozen or more free or inexpensive ideas.

APPENDIX B

Leadership Web Sites

One of the easiest and fastest ways to acquire information is over the Internet. To get a little help on your personal quest toward successful leadership, you may want to review the following list. Below you will find a number of Web sites that carry a variety of information on basic leadership skills as well as leadership conferences, forums, links, magazines, publications, resources, and seminars.

Advanced Leadership Book
www.adv-leadership-grp.com
Offers several articles, evaluations, presentations, training programs, and other resources.

American Management Association
www.amanet.org
This member-based organization offers assessment and customized learning solutions; books and online resources; as well as conferences and seminars.

Association for Leadership Educators
www.aces.uiuc.edu/~ALE
A membership organization that hosts an annual conference and offers various presentations, a quarterly newsletter, a membership directory, and the ALE Listserv that provides a forum for sharing information.

Association for Quality and Participation
www.aqp.org
A nonprofit membership organization that hosts a variety of educational events including anannual conference, on-site training, and numerous publications. The organization is also the cofounder of The School for Managing, a series of courses and workshops about leadership.

Business Training Media
www.businesstrainingmedia.com

Provides videos, CD-ROMs, and online courses in the areas of teamwork, harassment in the workplace, motivation, and other leadership concepts.

Center for Creative Leadership
www.ccl.org
Offers several leadership conferences, seminars, and workshops through its affiliates nationwide. The Center for Creative Leadership also operates four main campuses in California, Colorado, North Carolina, and Belgium.

Center for Innovative Leadership
www.cfil.com
A good resource for leaders in the new economy, offering videos, books, leadership forum postings, and articles.

Community Leadership Association
www.communityleadership.org
A membership organization that sponsors annual leadership conferences, offers several publications, and provides links to other leadership resources.

Covey Leadership Institute
www.covey.com
Offers leadership workshops and training courses nationwide.

Dynamics of Leadership, Inc.

www.dynamicleadership.com

A for-profit organization that offers leadership training, seminars, and workshops. The organization's Web site also provides a list of resources, articles, and links pertaining to leadership and management.

EmergingLeader.com

www.emergingleader.com

A user-driven Web site that provides leadership forums, articles, links, and related resources. This site promotes the sharing of information between new and experienced leaders.

Enlightened Leadership International

www.enleadership.com

A for-profit education, consulting, and resource company offering a wide variety of leadership conferences, programs, seminars, workshops, and resources.

KaplanCollege.com

www.kaplancollege.com

Offers online professional development courses and certificate programs including accredited associate and bachelor degrees in business management.

Leaders and Leadership

www.leadersandleadership.com

Offers access to a quarterly leadership e-magazine, *Leadership in Practice*, leadership resources, and leadership programs.

Leadership Knowledge Base

www.sonic.net/~mfreeman

Operates as a hub of information and links related to leadership information, conferences, programs, seminars, workshops, and resources.

Linkage Incorporated

www.linkageinc.com

Offers links to conferences, workshops, and training programs. Linkage also publishes a newsletter and calendar that lists national and international leadership conferences and related events.

Linkage Incorporated

www.linkageinc.com

Offers links to conferences, workshops, and training programs. Linkage also publishes a newsletter and calendar that lists national and international leadership conferences and related events.

McGraw-Hill Online Learning

www.mhonlinelearning.com

Offers online interactive business and management courses in areas including marketing, business strategy, managing people, presentation skills, and communication.

National Management Association

www.nma1.org

A nonprofit, membership organization that offers forums, conferences, coaching, and other resources. The organization has chapters and sponsors events nationwide.

Ravenwerks Information Center

www.ravenwerks.com

Offers a wide range of information, articles, and resources about leadership, marketing, technology, and teamwork. Ravenwerks also publishes a free bimonthly newsletter.

Refresher Publications

www.refresher.com

Provides access to the monthly newsletter, *The CEO Refresher.* The newsletter offers information and articles on resources pertaining to creative leadership, competitive strategy, and performance improvement.

SmartLeadership.com

www.smartleadership.com

Provides a variety of leadership information including a Mag-Ezine, links to related sites, articles, resources, and forums. SmartLeadership.com also sponsors live events all across the country.

Strategic Leadership Forum International

www.slf-boston.org

A Web site that encourages sharing of ideas among business leaders. The site also includes links to strategic planning Web sites, financial news coverage, and an abundance of information on other leadership resources.

World Wide Learn

www.worldwidelearn.com

Provides online courses in a wide range of disciplines including career development, business, legal issues, e-commerce, and even MBA programs.

APPENDIX C

Glossary of Leadership Theories and Concepts

Active listening: A leader's ability to hear not only what an employee is saying, but also what the employee is feeling. This type of listening can be learned and allows leaders to "hear" what is not being said.

Appreciator: A type of listener who is pleased to hear all the information the speaker has to offer. The Appreciator identifies all components of the conversation that will allow him to hook on to or continue the dialogue.

Behavior descriptions: Interview questions that tell you how a candidate behaved in situations in previous instances.

Body language: Nonverbal gestures that can reveal your attitude about a given situation or another person.

Brainstorming: A problem-solving technique whereby a group tries to obtain as many wild and crazy ideas as possible to help formulate the few ideas that will ultimately emerge as possible solutions.

Coaching: Meeting with employees to go over problems and/or progress, providing support and resources to employees, and providing guidance and encouragement.

Comfort zone: That safe place where everything is familiar and risk free.

Comprehender: A type of listener who tries to capture as much information as possible. The Comprehender tries to understand all the facts in the message that is being sent.

Corporate volunteerism: A trend in business today operating under the belief that volunteering helps build stronger relationships in the community, which in turn builds stronger relationships in business.

Delegation: Allowing others to do some of the work that you did in the past. The most common concern with delegation is that the work will not get done the way the leader or manager wants it to.

Dictatorship: A style of management in which the manager or leader has absolute power and control. Adolf Hitler is a perfect example of a dictator.

Discerner: A type of listener who takes messages in very carefully in order to get very clear and accurate information. The Discerner gets the main message and then sifts out what she considers to be the most important details.

Downsizing: See *Layoff*.

Eighty-Twenty Rule: In order to achieve a highly functional and productive workforce, a leader should do only 20 percent of the talking and let the other person do the talking 80 percent of the time.

Empathizer: A type of listener who directs all his energy toward identifying how the message being sent is similar to situations he has experienced.

Empathy: Identifying with and understanding the feelings of another person.

Employee orientation: Whatever happens to a new employee when she arrives on the job. Investing time and energy into the orientation of a new employee can only benefit managers in the future.

Empowerment: The transmittal (by leadership) of the idea that employees are valuable contributors to the success of an organization. Through empowerment, leaders should involve employees in the process of running the business at all levels.

Evaluator: A type of listener who is motivated by a desire to figure out how this communication fits into the bigger picture.

Extrinsic motivators: Outside influences such as money, titles, benefits, and recognition. These types of motivators fail in the long run because they don't satisfy all of the basic human needs.

Halo effect: Giving an undeserving employee a favorable evaluation based solely on the performance of the previous month or so.

Hot button: A leader's threshold for tolerating difficult behavior patterns.

Intrinsic motivators: The inner drives that compel employees to do their best. Employees are motivated to complete a task because they perceive the outcome will satisfy one or more of their basic human needs such as security, acceptance, respect, fun, power, fulfillment, choice, or self-esteem.

Layoff: Suspension or dismissal of employees, especially for lack of work. Layoffs can be temporary or permanent.

Leader-directed team: A team run by a specified leader who sets the agenda, runs meetings, and delegates tasks to the other members of the team.

Management by directive: Also known as the traditional approach model. In this system, it is generally accepted that the manager possesses the knowledge, information, and decision-making rights. Employees exist only to carry out the orders of management. This was a popular management style for many years but has recently undergone some changes.

Measurable criteria: The methods you use to judge whether the employee has accomplished what you asked. The criteria can be expressed either as an objective that can be concretely measured—such as increase sales volume by 20 percent—or by desired behavior—such as maintain a friendly demeanor when answering phone or follow up orders without complaining.

Mentor: A person who acts as a trusted friend, counselor, and teacher to a protégé. The word "mentor" has its origins in Greek mythology.

Mission statement: A description of a company usually written by a respected and senior member of the organization. A mission statement points out the core values of the company and what it is working to achieve.

Morale: Refers to the level of satisfaction workers feel with the company and their own jobs.

Multitasking: Taking on more than one task at the same time. An example would be talking on the phone while responding to e-mail.

Networking: Making and maintaining a "network" of business contacts both inside and outside of an organization.

New workforce: Workers of the 21st century who are more independent, self-reliant, and creative than any previous generation.

Pass-the-Buck syndrome: A situation that occurs when an employee refuses to accept responsibility for an error or mistake he has made; instead, he blames someone else.

Positive reinforcement: Rewarding someone for achieving the desired outcome. Through the use of positive reinforcement, leaders express clear expectations, instructions, information, and time frames, instilling within employees a sense of security, respect, power, and control in their jobs.

Protégé: A person who is taught and counseled by a mentor.

Resolvable conflict: Conflict that occurs when two individuals' viewpoints on an issue are initially seen as opposing fixed positions but are actually based on different needs, goals, values, or interests that first need to be understood and then worked out to their mutual satisfaction.

Self-directed team: A team that is composed of members from multiple areas of the organization. Self-directed teams are built on the premise that the team will be driven by internal leadership and won't require senior management supervision on daily or even weekly intervals.

Self-discipline: Training and control over oneself for personal improvement.

Self-evaluation questions: Questions asked of a candidate on a job interview that encourage the candidate to make comments or statements about herself.

Self-talk: The things we say in the privacy of our own minds. Positive self-talk increases an individual's potential for success.

Severance pay: Remuneration given to a terminated employee for any unused vacation or personal time, all regular overtime hours worked, and previously unpaid, earned bonuses and any other earned pay.

Suggestion box: A communication tool that (when used properly) allows for exciting, creative exchanges and the discussion of ideas on a regular basis.

Synergy: Cooperative interactions among groups. The combined effect is greater than the sum of individual contributions.

Thinking outside the box: Refers to learning to think outside of traditional norms. This type of thinking involves the incorporation of creativity and imagination.

Turnover: Calculated as the number of employees who have left in the course of a year divided by the number of staff budgeted multiplied by one hundred. *Example: 6 employees left/10 on the budget = 0.6 x 100 = 60 percent.*

Undefined contribution: Those skills or knowledge an employee has gained over a period of time. An undefined contribution is what makes an employee so valuable. Often the value is not realized until the employee leaves the organization.

Unnecessary conflict: Conflict that occurs when individuals have differing perceptions, lack of information, or hostile feelings that can appear unexpectedly, cause disagreements, and build up into full-blown conflict if signs are not noticed early enough.

Vision: A leader's picture of the future that he is committed to fulfilling. A leader's challenge is to stimulate enthusiasm, dedication, and perspective of the vision to others.

What-If syndrome: Thinking about past mistakes and wondering "What if I had done that differently?" or "If only I had . . ." Typically, this line of thinking is unproductive and does not help to rectify past errors.

Work ethic: Measures an employee's level of hard work and diligence to get ahead. Someone with an exceptional work ethic is willing to pay dues, contributes 100 percent, and reaches goals she has set for herself.

INDEX

A

advocacy, for team, 69
Anderson, Marian, 14
Anthony, Susan B., 111, 211
appreciator, 17
assertiveness, 158
attitude, time management and, 79

B

Barton, Clara, 93, 268
behavior problems, 162–164,
   165–166, 168
Berlin Wall, 114, 115
Bhutto, Benazir, 161
body language, 155–156, 157
books, in work space, 83
Bosch, Robert, 179
Boulanger, Nadia, 168
Bradley, Bill, 189
brainstorming, 24, 102
breaks, at work, 86
Brown, Helen Gurley, 36
Browning, Robert, 205
bulletin boards, 286–287

C

Caller ID, 96
Carnegie, Andrew, 58
Catherine the Great, 167
celebrations, 191–192
challenges, 32–33, 188
Chamberlain, Joshua Lawrence,
   33, 107
change, 7–8, 110
   acceptance of, 119–120
   awareness of, 111–112
   examples of, 114–119
   resistance to, 112–114
   understanding of, 110–111

workforce and, 269–270
cheerleader role, 72
Churchill, Winston S., 141
Clinton, Hillary Rodham, 289
Clinton, William Jefferson, 253
close-ended questions, 131
coaching, 4–5, 36–37, 42, 52
   basics of, 44–45
   benefits of, 44
   contrasted to managing, 42–43
   of nonemployees, 51
   process of, 45
   sample sessions of, 47–51
   time management and, 92
Coca-Cola, 234–235
Comaneci, Nadia, 145
commitment
   of team members, 69
   to volunteer activity, 240–241
communication, 2–3, 16
   consistency and, 26
   creative interaction and, 20–21
   with customers, 19
   with difficult employees, 155–159
   dos and don'ts of, 25
   with employees, 18–19, 120, 183,
     188–189, 229
   with key players, 19
   as leadership trait, 205–206
   listening's importance to, 16–18
   at meetings, 21–22
   with new workforce, 275
   within team, 71
   tips for promoting good, 23–25
   of vision, 19
   worksheet for, 168–172
commuting
   by car, 88–89
   by public transportation, 86–88
company outings, 191
compensation, retention and, 184
competition, 287–289

comprehender, 17
computers
   multitasking with, 85–86
   organization and, 221–223
conflict
   prevention of, 108
   resolvable, 101–103
   signs of, 107–108
   within team, 76
   unnecessary, 100–101
conflict resolution, 7, 100
   benefits derived from, 7
   dos and don'ts of, 103
   problem-solving approach to, 7, 104
   sample resolutions, 104–107
continuous training, 36
convenience, in work space, 82–83
corporate volunteerism, 253–254
counselor role, 72
creative problem solving, 33–34
cross-functional team, 73
Curie, Marie, 219
customers
   coaching of, 51
   communicating with, 19

D

daydreaming, 94
delegation
   as empowerment, 5, 56–58
   of information gathering, 289
   time management and, 92
Devils advocate role, 72
difficult employees, 9
   basics of managing, 154–159
   examples of specific, 159–165
   firing of, 172–175
   simple solutions for, 165–168
   worksheets for handling, 168–172
disarmer, 17–18
discipline. *see* self-discipline

discrimination, 187
Disney, Walt, 133
distractions, 92–93
    controlling of, 93–94
    costs of, 94–95
    interruptions as, 95–98
    scheduling time for, 98
diversity, 278
documentation, of evaluation,
    142–143, 150
Dorsett, Tony, 32
Douglass, Frederick, 285
downsizing, 61–63
driving time, 88–89

E

e-mail, 23
Earhart, Amelia, 158
Edelman, Marion Wright, 281, 283
Edsel automobile, 231–232, 234
education, 14, 280, 289–290
    about competition, 287–289
    among co-workers, 284–286
    personal plan for, 283–284
    traditional, 280–283
    using work space for, 286–287
80/20 rule, 63–64
Eisenhower, Dwight D., 24, 30, 31, 51
Elizabeth I, 113
empathizer, 17
employees
    assessment tool for, 36–39
coaching of, 4–5, 36–37, 42–52
    communicating with, 18–19, 120,
        183, 188–189, 229
    dealing with difficult, 9, 154–175
    empowerment of, 5, 54–66
    evaluation of, 8–9, 140–152
    hiring of, 8, 122–136
    orientation of, 136–137
    retention of, 9–10, 178–196
empowerment, 54–56, 66

    adjusting to, 65–66
    delegation and, 5, 56–58
    downsizing and, 61–63
    80/20 rule and, 63–64
    life skills and, 58
    responsibility and, 45
    trust and, 58–60
evaluation, of employees, 8–9
    formal process of, 140–145
    legal issues of, 148, 149
    questions and answers about,
        149–152
    review writing for, 145–147
    successful vs. not-so-successful,
        148–149
evaluator, 18
exit interview, 185
extrinsic motivation, 31

F

facilitator role, 72
failure
    Henry Ford on, 233
    quotes about, 236
family outings, 191
faxes, 85
fear
    of change, 35
    as motivator, 30
feedback, to coaching, 45
films, list of, 13
firing, of employee, 172–175
follower, leading as a, 12, 256
    commitment, 257–258
    initiative, 256–257
    mentoring, 261–265
    networking, 260–261
    responsibility, 259–260
Ford, Henry, 69, 233
Ford Motor Company, 231–232, 234
Fossey, Dian, 181, 182
Franklin, Aretha, 129

Freud, Sigmund, 265
Friedan, Betty, 105
fun, in workplace, 186–192

G

games, 287
Gates, William H., 55, 57
Geronimo, 155
Glenn, John, 62
goals
    coaching and, 45
    employee evaluation and, 143–145,
        150
    for pace of work, 160–161
    personal, 215
    time management and, 79–80, 91–92
Gorbachev, Mikhail, 150, 151
gossip, 117, 165–166
Grant, Ulysses S., 107
grapevine. see gossip
Greenspan, Alan, 195
Grosvenor, Gilbert M., 182

H

Harley-Davidson, 192–193
hiring, of employees, 8
    interviewing, 128–135
    making offer, 135–136
    needs assessment before, 122–124,
        125–126
    resume sorting, 124, 127
Hitler, Adolph, 208
Hoffa, Jimmy, 59, 198
Homer, 263
humor, 211

I

"I" statements, 157
Iacocca, Lee, 17

illegal interview questions, 134
independence, of workforce, 270
information resources, 290
initiative, 256–257
integrity, 207–208
intelligence team, 289
interaction, of employees, 20–21
Internet
    business information on, 290
    education on, 281–282
    leadership websites on, 298–300
    personal planners on, 222–223
interruptions, 95
    social, 97–98
    telephone and, 95–97
interview process, 128
    follow-up to, 132
    sample questions for, 133–135
    steps in, 129–131
intrinsic motivation, 31
involvement, fostering, 57–58, 184

J

jealousy, 75
Jefferson, Thomas, 83, 84
Joan of Arc, 9
Johnson, Lyndon B., 46
Julius Caesar, 235

K

Kennedy, John F., 47, 64, 65, 209
Kennedy, Robert Francis, 124
key players, communicating with, 19
Kimbell, Ward, 135
King, Dr. Martin Luther Jr., 21, 100
Kissinger, Henry, 18
knowledge, 59, 256

L

Lao-Tzu, 76

Lasorda, Tommy, 25, 26, 205
Lauder, Estee, 207
layoffs, 61–63
Lazarus, Emma, 11
leader-directed teams, 70–71
leadership, 2
    likened to parenting, 60–61
    qualities of good, 39
    questions and answers about,
        292–296
    traits of, 205–209
Lee, Robert E., 43
legal issues
    of employee evaluation, 148, 149
    of interviews, 134
life skills, 58
Lincoln, Abraham, 116
listeners, types of, 16–18
listening
    coaching and, 45, 46
    conflict resolution and, 102
    creative interaction and, 20–21
    to difficult employees, 156–157
    80/20 rule and, 63–64
    to employees, 188
logs
    of interruptions, 98
    of telephone calls, 95–96
    of time, 82
Lombardi, Vince, 23, 44
Lombardi, Vince Jr., 45
lunches
    multitasking and, 85
    time management and, 92

M

Machiavelli, Niccolo, 146
Madonna, 199
mail, management of, 90–91
Malcolm, 61
managing, contrasted to coaching,
    42–43

meetings, 21–22
Meir, Golda, 183, 185
membership, of team, 69, 70
memos, 23
mentors, 257, 261–262
    myths about, 265
    role of, 262, 264–265
military mottoes, 223
mistakes
    common, 227–231
    examples of corporate, 231–232,
        234–235
    learning from, 11, 208, 226–227
    "what-if" syndrome and, 235
Mothers Against Drug Driving
    (MADD), 72
motivation, 3–5, 30, 40
    employee assessment tool and,
        36–39
    fear and, 30
    intrinsic vs. extrinsic, 30–31
    "recipe" for successful, 31–36
    recognition and, 194–196
    of self, 4, 39–40
    self-discipline and, 214–216
multitasking, 85–86
Murdoch, Rupert, 34
muse role, 72

N

Napoleon Bonaparte, 275
networking, 260–261
new workforce. see workforce, new
Nightingale, Florence, 89

O

objective, of team, 69, 70
Odyssey (Homer), 263
offer of employment, 135–136
online education, 281–282
open-ended questions, 130

organization. *see* time management
orientation, of employees, 136–137

P

paper, tips for handling, 81–82, 90
Parks, Rosa, 190
pass-the-buck syndrome, 34
Pemberton, John S., 234
performance review. *see* evaluation, of
    employees
Perón, Eva, 60
personal issues, 217
personal planners, 222–223
personality traits, of leaders, 205–209
politics
    of office, 260–261
    of organization, 207
positive reinforcement, 31–32
potential, utilizing employee's, 55–56
power. *see* empowerment
presentations, 209–211
Presley, Elvis, 241
priorities
    inventory of, 79
    in work space, 91
problem-solving approach, to conflict
    resolution, 7, 104
protégés. *see* mentors
public speaking, 209–211
public transportation, 86–88

R

radio
    in car, 89
    in work space, 86
Ramos, Andreas, 115
recognition, of employees, 194–196
recruitment, of employees, 122–124,
    action plan for, 125–126
    cost of, 180–182

recruitment, of volunteers, 250–251
resolvable conflict, 101–103
responsibility
    assuming of, 259–260
    coaching and, 45
    for performance, 34
    see also empowerment
resumes, 124, 125
retention, of employees, 9–10, 178
    identifying problems with, 182–195
    importance of, 178–182
    new workforce and, 272–274
    recognition and, 194–196
    work culture and, 192–193
    work environment and, 186–192
retention, of volunteers, 252–253
review, of employee's of performance,
    145–147
Rohn, Jim, 3
Roosevelt, Anna Eleanor, 258, 259
Roosevelt, Franklin Delano, 4, 102, 103

S

Salk, Dr. Jonas, 147
Saturn automobiles, 64–65
Schwarzkopf, Norman, 74
self-appraisal, 143, 149, 199–204
self-confidence, 198–199, 209
self-directed teams, 71–72
    roles within, 72–73
    sample workings of, 73–75
self-discipline, 11, 214
    learning of, 223–224
    motivation and, 214–216
    organization and, 221–223
    self-employment and, 216–220
self-employment, 216–220
self-expression, 10–11, 198
    confidence and, 198–199
    leadership self-assessment, 199–204
    personality and, 198–199, 205–209

public speaking and, 209–211
self-image, 206–207
self-improvement, 277
self-knowledge, 157
self-motivation, 4, 39–40
self-talk, 120
seminars, 282–283
severance pay, 174, 175
Shackleton, Ernest, 230
skills
    employee's lack of, 159–160, 166–167
    of team members, 69, 71
sloppiness, 159, 160–162
slow work pace, 160–161
socializing, time management and,
    97–98
Stanton, Elizabeth Cady, 218
Steinem, Gloria, 227
stockholder reports, 288
Stowe, Harriet Beecher, 215, 216
strengths, of leaders, 206
stress
    management of, 78, 79
    physical effects of, 80
    psychological/emotional
        effects of, 81
suggestion boxes, 24–25
supplies, for work space, 83–84
support, for team, 69, 71

T

tape recorder, 85
tardiness, 164–165, 167
teamwork, 5–6, 68–69
    leader-directed vs. self-directed,
        72–75
    new workforce and, 275–276
    problems of, 75–76
    qualities of successful, 69
    recognizing success of, 76
technology, 270

telecommuting, 219–220, 221
telephone calls
    as interruption, 95–97
    multitasking and, 85
    while driving, 89
Thatcher, Margaret, 269
time log, 82
time management, 6–7, 78–79
    basic steps of, 79–80
    commuting and, 86–89
    distractions and, 92–98
    maintaining of good, 90–92
    multitasking and, 85–86
    self-discipline and, 221–223
    teamwork and, 69, 70–71
    work space organization and, 80–84
Truman, Harry S., 175
trust, of employees, 58–60
turnover, of employees, 179–182

U

unnecessary conflict, 100–101
update meetings, 22

V

values
    of company, 192–193
    of new workforce, 272–273
vendors, coaching of, 51
visibility, 207
vision, communication of, 19
volunteers/volunteerism, 12, 238–239
    commitments to, 240–241
    corporate, 253–254
    lists of organizations needing,
      241–249
    recruitment for, 250–251
    retaining of, 252–253

W

walking, communication and, 24
Walton, Samuel, 137
Washington, George, 164, 165
"what-if" syndrome, 235
Whitehead, Alfred North, 119
women, list of powerful, 7
work environment, 186–192
work space
    communication/education in,
      286–287
    organizing for convenience, 82–83
    paper-handling in, 81–82
    supplies for, 83–84
workforce, new, 12, 14, 268
    characteristics of, 269–270
    company's needs and, 276–277
    contrasted to "old," 268–269
    diversity of, 278
    leadership of, 271–274
    older employees and, 277–278
    retention of, 272–274
    self-improvement and, 277
    teamwork and, 275–276
    wants of, 270–271
workload, managing, 261
World Wide Web. *see* Internet

Y

Yoda, 264

We Have EVERYTHING!

Everything® **After College Book**
$12.95, 1-55850-847-3

Everything® **Angels Book**
$12.95, 1-58062-398-0

Everything® **Astrology Book**
$12.95, 1-58062-062-0

Everything® **Baby Names Book**
$12.95, 1-55850-655-1

Everything® **Baby Shower Book**
$12.95, 1-58062-305-0

Everything® **Baby's First Food Book**
$12.95, 1-58062-512-6

Everything® **Barbeque Cookbook**
$12.95, 1-58062-316-6

Everything® **Bartender's Book**
$9.95, 1-55850-536-9

Everything® **Bedtime Story Book**
$12.95, 1-58062-147-3

Everything® **Bicycle Book**
$12.00, 1-55850-706-X

Everything® **Build Your Own Home Page**
$12.95, 1-58062-339-5

Everything® **Business Planning Book**
$12.95, 1-58062-491-X

Everything® **Casino Gambling Book**
$12.95, 1-55850-762-0

Everything® **Cat Book**
$12.95, 1-55850-710-8

Everything® **Chocolate Cookbook**
$12.95, 1-58062-405-7

Everything® **Christmas Book**
$15.00, 1-55850-697-7

Everything® **Civil War Book**
$12.95, 1-58062-366-2

Everything® **College Survival Book**
$12.95, 1-55850-720-5

Everything® **Computer Book**
$12.95, 1-58062-401-4

Everything® **Cookbook**
$14.95, 1-58062-400-6

Everything® **Cover Letter Book**
$12.95, 1-58062-312-3

Everything® **Crossword and Puzzle Book**
$12.95, 1-55850-764-7

Everything® **Dating Book**
$12.95, 1-58062-185-6

Everything® **Dessert Book**
$12.95, 1-55850-717-5

Everything® **Dog Book**
$12.95, 1-58062-144-9

Everything® **Dreams Book**
$12.95, 1-55850-806-6

Everything® **Etiquette Book**
$12.95, 1-55850-807-4

Everything® **Family Tree Book**
$12.95, 1-55850-763-9

Everything® **Fly-Fishing Book**
$12.95, 1-58062-148-1

Everything® **Games Book**
$12.95, 1-55850-643-8

Everything® **Get-A-Job Book**
$12.95, 1-58062-223-2

Everything® **Get Published Book**
$12.95, 1-58062-315-8

Everything® **Get Ready for Baby Book**
$12.95, 1-55850-844-9

Everything® **Golf Book**
$12.95, 1-55850-814-7

Everything® **Guide to Las Vegas**
$12.95, 1-58062-438-3

Everything® **Guide to New York City**
$12.95, 1-58062-314-X

Everything® **Guide to Walt Disney World®, Universal Studios®, and Greater Orlando, 2nd Edition**
$12.95, 1-58062-404-9

Everything® **Guide to Washington D.C.**
$12.95, 1-58062-313-1

Everything® **Herbal Remedies Book**
$12.95, 1-58062-331-X

Everything® **Home-Based Business Book**
$12.95, 1-58062-364-6

Everything® **Homebuying Book**
$12.95, 1-58062-074-4

Everything® **Homeselling Book**
$12.95, 1-58062-304-2

Everything® **Home Improvement Book**
$12.95, 1-55850-718-3

Everything® **Hot Careers Book**
$12.95, 1-58062-486-3

Everything® **Internet Book**
$12.95, 1-58062-073-6

Everything® **Investing Book**
$12.95, 1-58062-149-X

Everything® **Jewish Wedding Book**
$12.95, 1-55850-801-5

Everything® **Job Interviews Book**
$12.95, 1-58062-493-6

Everything® **Lawn Care Book**
$12.95, 1-58062-487-1

Everything® **Leadership Book**
$12.95, 1-58062-513-4

Everything® **Low-Fat High-Flavor Cookbook**
$12.95, 1-55850-802-3

Everything® **Magic Book**
$12.95, 1-58062-418-9

Everything® **Microsoft® Word 2000 Book**
$12.95, 1-58062-306-9

**For more information, or to order, call 800-872-5627
or visit everything.com**
Adams Media Corporation, 260 Center Street, Holbrook, MA 02343

Available wherever books are sold!

Everything® **Money Book**
$12.95, 1-58062-145-7

Everything® **Mother Goose Book**
$12.95, 1-58062-490-1

Everything® **Mutual Funds Book**
$12.95, 1-58062-419-7

Everything® **One-Pot Cookbook**
$12.95, 1-58062-186-4

Everything® **Online Business Book**
$12.95, 1-58062-320-4

Everything® **Online Genealogy Book**
$12.95, 1-58062-402-2

Everything® **Online Investing Book**
$12.95, 1-58062-338-7

Everything® **Online Job Search Book**
$12.95, 1-58062-365-4

Everything® **Pasta Book**
$12.95, 1-55850-719-1

Everything® **Pregnancy Book**
$12.95, 1-58062-146-5

Everything® **Pregnancy Organizer**
$15.00, 1-58062-336-0

Everything® **Quick Meals Cookbook**
$12.95, 1-58062-488-X

Everything® **Resume Book**
$12.95, 1-58062-311-5

Everything® **Sailing Book**
$12.95, 1-58062-187-2

Everything® **Selling Book**
$12.95, 1-58062-319-0

Everything® **Study Book**
$12.95, 1-55850-615-2

Everything® **Tall Tales, Legends, and Outrageous Lies Book**
$12.95, 1-58062-514-2

Everything® **Tarot Book**
$12.95, 1-58062-191-0

Everything® **Time Management Book**
$12.95, 1-58062-492-8

Everything® **Toasts Book**
$12.95, 1-58062-189-9

Everything® **Total Fitness Book**
$12.95, 1-58062-318-2

Everything® **Trivia Book**
$12.95, 1-58062-143-0

Everything® **Tropical Fish Book**
$12.95, 1-58062-343-3

Everything® **Vitamins, Minerals, and Nutritional Supplements Book**
$12.95, 1-58062-496-0

Everything® **Wedding Book, 2nd Edition**
$12.95, 1-58062-190-2

Everything® **Wedding Checklist**
$7.95, 1-58062-456-1

Everything® **Wedding Etiquette Book**
$7.95, 1-58062-454-5

Everything® **Wedding Organizer**
$15.00, 1-55850-828-7

Everything® **Wedding Shower Book**
$7.95, 1-58062-188-0

Everything® **Wedding Vows Book**
$7.95, 1-58062-455-3

Everything® **Wine Book**
$12.95, 1-55850-808-2

Everything® **Angels Mini Book**
$4.95, 1-58062-387-5

Everything® **Astrology Mini Book**
$4.95, 1-58062-385-9

Everything® **Baby Names Mini Book**
$4.95, 1-58062-391-3

Everything® **Bedtime Story Mini Book**
$4.95, 1-58062-390-5

Everything® **Dreams Mini Book**
$4.95, 1-58062-386-7

Everything® **Etiquette Mini Book**
$4.95, 1-58062-499-5

Everything® **Get Ready for Baby Mini Book**
$4.95, 1-58062-389-1

Everything® **Golf Mini Book**
$4.95, 1-58062-500-2

Everything® **Love Spells Mini Book**
$4.95, 1-58062-388-3

Everything® **Pregnancy Mini Book**
$4.95, 1-58062-392-1

Everything® **TV & Movie Trivia Mini Book**
$4.95, 1-58062-497-9

Everything® **Wine Mini Book**
$4.95, 1-58062-498-7

Everything® **Kids' Baseball Book**
$9.95, 1-58062-489-8

Everything® **Kids' Joke Book**
$9.95, 1-58062-495-2

Everything® **Kids' Money Book**
$9.95, 1-58062-322-0

Everything® **Kids' Nature Book**
$9.95, 1-58062-321-2

Everything® **Kids' Online Book**
$9.95, 1-58062-394-8

Everything® **Kids' Puzzle Book**
$9.95, 1-58062-323-9

Everything® **Kids' Space Book**
$9.95, 1-58062-395-6

Everything® **Kids' Witches and Wizards Book**
$9.95, 1-58062-396-4

Everything® is a registered trademark of Adams Media Corporation.

For more information, or to order, call 800-872-5627 or visit everything.com

Adams Media Corporation, 260 Center Street, Holbrook, MA 02343